A *leap* INTO THE FUTURE

A Vision for Kenya's Socio-political and Economic Transformation

ANYANG' NYONG'O

AFRICAN RESEARCH AND
RESOURCE FORUM (ARRF)

Published 2007 by
African Research and Resource Forum (ARRF)
P.O. Box 57103-00200
Nairobi, Kenya

www.arrforum.org

ISBN - 10: 9966 7062 6 7
ISBN9 - 13: 978 9966 7062 6 3

Publishing consultants: WordAlive Publishers Limited
Printed in Kenya by English Press Limited

Foreword

Academic terms come and go. Then they resurrect. In the volatile 1960s, the term "praxis" entered the social science literature in a particularly forceful manner, starting particularly from the critical left, before finding widespread acceptance elsewhere in the political spectrum. At its most elemental, the terms signified the combination of political activism that was symptomatic of that age with intellectual fire power; indeed the word "praxis" was invented by fusing different syllables from "practice" and "analysis". It was also intended to convey the existence of both practical action and analysis in one and the same event, or in one and the same person. As so often happens in the social sciences, the term fell into disuse as populist concepts like "bonding", and "participatory decision-making" (involving everyone and led by "civil society") were adopted in order to confront globalization and economic liberalization in the 1990s and the opening years of the twenty-first century. Worthwhile as some of these efforts have been, it was a pity that serious intellectual analysis was drained from practice in deference of what "the people" had really said they wanted; an approach that praxis had seriously questioned.

Yet all is not lost. The essays you are going to read in this book represent the best tradition of praxis, spanning the last decade. It is the product of analytical work by Professor Anyang' Nyong'o on contemporary events in Kenya and the rest of Africa, combined with personal experience drawn from his own political involvement in the quest for social and political reforms in the region. For that reason it is a rare and welcome publication.

In the exhilarating phase of Africa's history immediately after independence, African political leaders wrote much about their personal involvement in the struggle for African independence, laid bare their analysis of what was wrong with colonialism and how they expected our newly-won sovereignty to correct that in the interest of African peoples. Those books by Leopold Sedar Senghor[1], Kwame Nkrumah[2], Eduardo Mondlane[3], Tom

---

1   See, for example, I.L. Markovitz, Leopold S. Senghor and the Politics of Negritude (New York: Athenum, 1969).

2   Kwame Nkrumah, Ghana: the Autobiography of Kwame Nkrumah (London: Thomas Nelson, 1957).

3   Eduardo Mondlane, Struggle for Mozambique (Harmondsworth: Penguin Books, 1969).

J.Mboya[4], Julius Nyerere[5], Jomo Kenyatta[6], Jaramogi Oginga Odinga[7], Patrice Lumumba[8], Dunduzu Chisiza[9], Kenneth Kaunda[10] and dozens of others were read and re-read as much for their historical value as for their analyses of African social and political problems and the best ways to solve them. Very sadly, this tradition had disappeared by the 1970s as what this book calls "presidential authoritarianism" and military governments placed an iron grip on most African states stifling both freedom of expression and freedom of political action within the law, which in essence is what the struggle for independence was about.

That situation changed dramatically in the 1990s. Africans are a resilient people and two decades of authoritarian rule, decaying economies, corruption and human rights abuses — sometimes done with the support of external powers — was more than they could bear. Popular demonstrators toppled the authoritarian and financially bankrupt government of Benin in early 1990 and installed a "sovereign national conference" to manage the transition to an uncorrupt, popularly-elected democracy. In doing so, Benin set an example for the rest of Franco-phone Africa as national conferences attempted to repeat this feat, with varying successes in Mali, Cameroon, Gabon, Togo, Niger, Madagascar and the then Zaire.

The tumult did not spare Anglophone Africa either, as popular demands for multiparty democracy instead of autocratic one-party and one-leader rule spread from one country to another. It shook authoritarian governments in Kenya, Malawi, Zambia, Ghana, Nigeria, Tanzania, Uganda, and Sudan (in 1985 till the military came back in 1989). For good measure, apartheid finally gave way after years of struggle to majority rule in South Africa in 1994. True enough, there were unprecedented great human tragedies in the process as some putative transitions gave way to horrific bloodshed — in Liberia, Rwanda, Burundi, Democratic Republic of Congo, Central African Republic, Sierra Leone, Somalia and now Darfur. But for the most part all popular demands transformed the political and economic face of Africa, mostly for the better.

---

4   T.J. Mboya, Freedom and After (London: Andre Deutsch, 1963).
5   Julius Nyerere Freedom and Unity (London: Oxford University Press, 1967)
6   Jomo Kenyatta, Suffering without Bitterness (London: Heinemann, 1968).
7   Jaramogi Oginga Odinga, Not Yet Uhuru (London: Heinemann, 1966).
8   Patrice Lumumba, Congo My Country (New York: Praeger, 1962).
9   Dunduzu Chisiza, Africa: What Lies Ahead (New York: African American Institute, 1962).
10   Kenneth Kaunda, Zambia Shall Be Free (New York: Praeger, 1963).

Professor Anyang' Nyong'o was both a participant in many of these changes —
as a political leader in opposition during the darkest days of the KANU
dictatorship in Kenya, as an independent international observer in Zambia's
inaugural multiparty election in 1991, and as a frequent traveller representing
his political party and the Kenya opposition generally to Senegal, Uganda,
Tanzania, Zimbabwe, Mozambique, Ethiopia, South Africa and many other
African countries. He played a central role in crafting the National Rainbow
Coalition (NARC) which put an end to four decades of authoritarian rule
in Kenya, and also served as Kenya's Minister for Planning and National
Development between 2003 and 2005, in which role he distinguished himself as
the leading exponent of the Government's economic development strategy. But
as he practiced, he also analyzed and continued to write about his observations in
the broader perspective of Africa's post-independence heritage and unfulfilled
aspirations mentioned earlier.

The essays presented in this volume largely reflect the combined outcome
of that practical experience and the author's analysis of it. It opens with an
introduction on the author's observations on Kenya's experience in making
the historic transition from authoritarian rule to democracy in December 2002
and the problems encountered in the coalition government that was set up in
2003. Other essays on Kenya deal with the need for political and constitutional
reform in the country, and the most appropriate strategies for reversing Kenya's
economic decay in the 1990s. But the scope is wider than that. Some of the
essays deal with Africa's attempts to live to the expectation of the 1960s as spelt
out by the founding fathers of African nationalism; indeed one of the most
remarkable chapters is a tribute to the work of Tom Mboya who was himself
the country's second Minister of Planning in the 1960s. Kenya's first President,
Jomo Kenyatta, held this portfolio while he was the Prime Minister during the
self-governing period just prior to independence in December 1963.

This book provides some useful insights on continental initiatives,
notably the New Partnership for Africa's Development (NEPAD) which was
intended to be Africa's own blue-print for its economic and political renewal.
As Minister for Planning and National Development, Professor Nyong'o
played a key political and diplomatic role in getting Kenya to be among the first
four African countries to subject themselves to "peer review" under NEPAD's
African Peer Review Mechanism (APRM). As conducted in Kenya, APRM has
won the country much praise, critical as the report was of specific aspects of
Kenya's political and economic governance. From that experience came out the

profound analysis of the APRM in one of the chapters in this book which deals with how APRM was expected to function; no reader who is interested in the subject should miss it. There is a variety of essays on other Kenyan and Africa-wide topics of interest as well.

From his student days to the present, the author never lacked the courage to follow his convictions. I know that for a fact. But as problems arise so too the author's instinct to weigh in. For that reason, some of the readers may find the book too wide-ranging and diverse in its interests, but such is the nature of praxis — it confronts problems wherever they are. It does not choose what terrain to fight in. In any event, Kenya's historiography could use more books of this nature. A nation grows mainly by learning from its mistakes, and the more these are recorded the better. For that reason alone this book should be welcome even with the full diversity of topics it covers. One also hopes that other Kenyan and African political leaders who have actively pursued respectable social ideals, and who can commit their thoughts to paper, will also do the same.

The book is arranged in five parts. Part One deals with Planning for "leap-frogging" Development. These essays deal with planning, issues of economic growth and opportunities for rapid economic take-off as the author saw them when NARC took over government. Part Two deals with the Challenges of Development such as corruption, technology and culture. Part Three focuses on The Political Context of Development given problems of transition from authoritarian rule to democracy or something else. It also examines the issue of political practice that social scientist face in such contexts. Part Four focuses on Development in the context of Pan-African and Global Partnerships, looking at proposals coming out of the New Partnership for Africa's Development (NEPAD), the Blair Commission and how the African Peer Review Mechanism (APRM) can enhance both democratization and development. Part Five is dedicated to those who have had visions for Africa's future: those who built for the future. If Africa is to leap into the future, men and women of vision such as Tom Mboya, Father Keiser, Thomas Odhiambo and Alexander Kipsang Muge will be needed. Those who can join with others to build teams for change such as Michael Wamalwa did, will equally be of service to the African revolution.

Professor Michael Chege
Board Chairman, ARRF
Nairobi, June 2007

Contents

Acknowledgments

I would like to thank all the staff at the Ministry of Planning and National Development with whom I worked very closely from January 2003 to December 2005. I want to specifically acknowledge my Permanent Secretaries: Joseph Kinyua from January to June 2003; David Nalo from June 2003 to June 2005 and Dr. Ng'eno thereafter. My advisors: Professor Michael Chege, Dr. George Outa and Sam Mwale were always at hand to discuss many issues with me and to give wise counsel. I would like to thank Prof. Chege for the many ideas he has helped me think carefully about ever since we taught together at the University of Nairobi's Department of Government from 1977 to 1981.

At the African Resource and Research Centre (ARRF) Michael Chege, George Omondi and Caleb Opon have given me invaluable help in preparing this book for publication. My wife Dorothy Nyong'o, herself a professional editor, gave useful editorial comments before the manuscript was handed over to David Waweru of WordAlive Publishers. David's persistent encouragement made me finish the preparation of the manuscript for publication in record time.

Finally my sincere thanks to my family which has endured my long incidences of absence as I attended to national duty, conferences and lectures in Kenya and abroad, at times when my presence was really needed.

List of Abbreviations and Acronyms

AAPAM   - African Association of Public Administration and Management

AAS   - African Academy of Sciences

ACEG   - African Centre for Economic Growth

ACP   - African, Caribbean and Pacific

AGOA   - African Growth and Opportunity Act

ANC   - African National Congress

APDF   - Africa Project Development Finance

APRM   - African Peer Review Mechanism

ARRF   - African Research and Resource Forum

ASALs   - arid and aemi arid lands

ASEAN   - Association of South East Asian Nations

BOT   - build operate transfer

CBS   - Central Bureau of Statistics

CDF   - Constituency Development Fund

CODESRIA - Council for the Development of Social Research in Africa

COMESA   - Common Market for Eastern and Southern Africa

COSATU   - Congress of South African Trade Unions

COTU   - Central Organisation of Trade Unions

CPP   - Convention People's Party

CPTM   - Commonwealth Partnership for Technology Management and Technology

DDC   - District Development Committee

DP   - Democratic Party (of Kenya)

DRF   - Duty Remission Facility

EAC   - East African Community

ECA   - Economic Commission for Africa (UN)

ECK	-	Electoral Commission of Kenya
EEC	-	European Economic Community
EPZs	-	Export Processing Zones
ERS	-	Economic Recovery Strategy (for Wealth and Employment Creation)
ESAF	-	Enhanced Structural Adjustment Facility
FSAP	-	Financial Sector Assessment Programme
EU	-	European Union
FAO	-	Food and Agricultural Organisation
FBI	-	Federal Bureau of Investigations
FKE	-	Federation of Kenya Employers
FLN	-	Front de Liberation Nationale (Algeria)
FORD	-	Forum for the Restoration of Democracy
GAP	-	Government Action Plan
GDP	-	Gross Domestic Product
GNU	-	Government of National Unity
GSP	-	Generalised System of Preferences
ICFTU	-	International Confederation of Free Trade Unions
ICIPE	-	International Centre for Insect Physiology and Ecology
ICT	-	Information Communication Technology
IDA	-	International Development Association
IDS	-	Institute for Development Studies
IEA	-	Institute of Economic Affairs
IFC	-	International Finance Corporation
IGAD	-	Intergovernmental Authority on Development
IMF	-	International Monetary Fund
IP-ERS	-	Investment Programme for the Economic Recovery Strategy
IPO	-	initial public offering
IPPG	-	Inter-Party Parliamentary Group
KACC	-	Kenya Anti-Corruption Commission
KAM	-	Kenya Association of Manufacturers

KANU	-	Kenya African National Union
KCC	-	Kenya Cooperative Creameries
KEPSA	-	Kenya Private Sector Alliance
KIA	-	Kenya Institute of Administration
KIPPRA	-	Kenya Institute of Public Policy Research and Analysis
KPLC	-	Kenya Power and Lighting Company
KPU	-	Kenya People's Union
KRA	-	Kenya Revenue Authority
LDP	-	Liberal Democratic Party
MDGs	-	Millennium Development Goals
MMD	-	Movement for Multiparty Democracy (Zambia)
MOU	-	Memorandum of Understanding
MPC	-	Monetary Policy Committee
MPs	-	Members of Parliament
MRA	-	Miscellaneous Revenue Account
MSEs	-	Micro and Small Enterprises
MUB	-	Manufacturing under Bond
NAK	-	National Alliance Party of Kenya
NARC	-	National Rainbow Coalition
NCCK	-	National Christian Council of Kenya
NCEC	-	National Convention Executive Council
NDP	-	National Development Party
NEPAD	-	New Partnership for Africa's Development
NESC	-	National Economic and Social Council
NGO	-	non-governmental organisation
NHC	-	National Housing Corporation
NIC	-	Newly Industrialising Country
NMI	-	Nelson Mandela Institution (for Science, Technology and the Advancement of Knowledge)
NPL	-	non-performing loans
NSE	-	Nairobi Stock Exchange

NSHIS - National Social and Health Insurance Scheme
NUSU - National Union of Uganda Students
ODM - Orange Democratic Movement
OECD - Organisation for Economic Cooperation and Development
OEEC - Organisation of European Economic Cooperation
PEAP - Post Election Action Plan
PRSP - Poverty Reduction Strategy Programme
PS - Permanent Secretary
PSC - Parliamentary Select Committee
R&D - Research and Development
SAL - structural adjustment loan
SDP - Social Democratic Party
TOR - terms of reference
TRC - Truth and Reconciliation Commission
UDM - United Democratic Movement
UNAK - United Nations Association of Kenya
UNDP - United Nations Development Programme
UNECA - United Nations Economic Commission for Africa
UNEP - United Nations Environmental Programme
UNESCO - United Nations Educational, Social and Cultural Organisation
UNICEF - United Nations Children's Fund
UNIP - United National Independence Party (Zambia)
UNRISD - UN Institute for Research in Social Development
UPC - Uganda People's Congress
USA - United States of America
WHO - World Health Organisation
WTO - World Trade Organisation

Introduction

Kenya reached a historic turning point after the December 2002 general elections when a coalition of opposition parties, known as the National Alliance Rainbow Coalition (NARC), defeated the incumbent ruling party, the Kenya African National Union (KANU). The latter had governed the country since 1963. The first president, Jomo Kenyatta, had ruled from 1963 to 1978, and his Vice-President, Daniel Toroitich arap Moi, had taken over and stayed on until the defeat by NARC. With this defeat, an old authoritarian system was replaced by a broad coalition of reformers and non-reformers. It also marked over forty years of presidential authoritarian rule of which I had written in 1989.[1] As it turned out, however, the non-reformers among us would cause the problems that I shall deal with in this chapter and elsewhere in this work.

I played a leading role in putting that coalition together. A few weeks after our victory, the new President, Mwai Kibaki, who had been Moi's Vice-President from 1978 to 1988, formed his cabinet in which I received the portfolio of Planning and National Development. I took up my job with all seriousness and I gave all my energy and intellectual resources to putting in place an economic recovery strategy for our country.

Kenyans received the NARC government enthusiastically and thought the President had done a good job. However, its performance began to be very poorly rated by the Kenyan people in just two years into its administration. Its failure to lead a successful process towards the enactment of a new democratic constitution and the silence over runaway corruption cases like the Anglo-Leasing scandal angered many Kenyans.[2]

Meanwhile, my ministry mobilised the nation as well as development partners and rallied them behind the economic recovery strategy, which eventually proved

---

1 See for example, P. Anyang' Nyong'o, "State and Society in Kenya: The Disintegration of the Nationalist Coalition and the Rise of Presidential Authoritarianism," *African Affairs*, Vol.88 No.351 (April 1989): 229-251.

2 See P. Anyang' Nyong'o, *The Political Economy of Corruption in Kenya* (Nairobi: Africa Research and Resource Forum, 2006). Kibaki's Permanent Secretary for Ethics and Governance, John Githongo, resigned on this issue and escaped to the United Kingdom to expose this scandal at his hideout at St. Anthony's College in Oxford. We shall refer to his exposure documents here as *The Githongo Dossiers* following some mimeograph that he circulated in mid-2005.

to be a major success of the Kibaki presidency. Today, those who did very little to put the strategy in place are laying claim to its authorship. Success, as usual, has many fathers while failure is always an orphan.

I had very good ideas on how we could reach double digit growth within the fifth year of our government, but this required very bold steps: heavy investments in public works, a radical reform in the civil service, and drastic cuts in public consumption. We also needed to take democratic governance seriously and not simply use the language of good governance as rhetoric. Terms such as ending corruption, promoting human rights, institutionalising the rule of law and curtailing tribalism would have created a good environment for development which would in turn greatly improve the quality of life of Kenyans. The cabinet under the leadership of the president and the entire civil service needed to maintain a clear focus and take bold and decisive steps to achieve these objectives.

Crafting the ERS: Process and Content

When we formed government and developed the five-year Economic Recovery Strategy for Wealth Creation and Employment (the ERS) that would ensure that our democracy and good governance led to economic prosperity and the betterment of the welfare of our people, we were confident that we could achieve our objectives enshrined in the following four key pillars of the strategy:

(a) A sound macro-economic management of the economy, which entailed keeping our currency as stable as possible, reducing inflation to single digits, maintaining prudent debt profile by limiting domestic borrowing by the government, and encouraging domestic savings so as to build a solid base for capital accumulation and investment;

(b) Rehabilitation and improvement of our physical infrastructure — roads, railways, harbours, ports, telephony, ICT – through public and private sector investments;

(c) Revitalisation of the productive sectors and service sectors of the economy — agriculture, livestock and fishing, trade, industry, ICT, environment and natural resource use; and,

(d) Democracy and good governance.

We were also conscious that, with better management of our national revenues, we would support better and equitable social provisioning through improvement in education and health delivery (particularly the fight against HIV/AIDS), social welfare services and investment in the arid and semi-arid lands (ASALs). In this regard we developed a special programme for the ASALs and launched it with the Vice-President and Minister for Home Affairs, Hon. Moody Awori, and the Minister for Livestock Development and Fisheries, Hon. Joseph Munyao in Wajir in October 2003.

We realised that these four pillars could not stand without a government that worked efficiently, promoted the rule of law, kept corruption at bay, respected human rights and worked harmoniously and productively with the private sector and development partners within our own civil society and from abroad. That is why, before the ERS was written, we organised meetings with various stakeholders to discuss the translation of our manifesto into a blueprint for a five-year economic recovery plan. These meetings, held every Monday morning from seven to nine, were very well attended. They led to discussions on how the private sector could come together to systematically partner with government in the recovery agenda. Eventually the Kenya Private Sector Alliance (KEPSA) was born as a result of our discussions.

I must commend the private sector in Kenya, both local and multinational, for the positive engagements that we had. But the appointments to the top echelons of the civil service did not reflect the dynamism, resourcefulness and productivity that were required to push through the ERS to fruition. In making these appointments, President Kibaki and his advisors seem to have read from the same script as his predecessors — Moi and Kenyatta — who exercised constitutional powers bestowed on the presidency to award plum jobs to friends, former classmates and kinsmen without due regard to merit.[3]

There was pressure for me to inherit what the previous government had negotiated with the donor community within the framework of the Poverty Reduction Strategy Programme (PRSP) and the KANU government's implementation strategy called *The Action Plan*. Donor after donor came to my

---

3   While I was writing this book, Duncan Ndegwa, Kenyatta's first Head of the Public Service and Secretary to the Cabinet, later Governor of the Central Bank for 16 years, published his memoirs, *Walking in Kenyatta's Struggles* (Nairobi: Leadership Institute, 2006), which shows amazing similarities between the manner in which Kenyatta and Kibaki appointed key people in their administrations from the Mount Kenya communities. I wrote a long commentary on the three presidents, Kenyatta, Moi and Kibaki in the *Sunday Standard*, 30 December 2006 entitled "Kenyatta, Moi and Kibaki in a Historical Perspective."

office on the tenth floor of the Treasury Building asking me what I intended to do with the PRSP and *The Action Plan*. My answer was standard: we had been elected on a NARC Manifesto entitled, *Democracy and Empowerment*. The mandate given to the government by the people of Kenya was to first and foremost implement this manifesto. But if there were some good ideas in the PRSP and *The Action Plan*, we would look at them and incorporate them into our own agenda. But the final product would be a five-year recovery programme that would enable us to fulfil our mandate.

A good number of donors did not seem satisfied with this explanation, and they continued to put pressure through my then Permanent Secretary, rather than on me. Finally, I called all of them into the conference room one afternoon and went through this argument, requesting them to give us time to work through our economic recovery strategy until it was ready. We would then invite them to an open discussion that would lead to what we considered a sound strategy.

I decided to enlist the services of three committed Kenyans to help us prepare a basic discussion document for crafting the ERS. These were Harry Mule, a retired civil servant (former Permanent Secretary) and economist who had worked with both Tom Mboya and Mwai Kibaki at the Treasury; David Ndii, an economics graduate from Oxford University whom I had known as a straight-talking and intelligent young scholar and researcher, and who does not suffer fools gladly, and Caleb Opon, a young former banker who had been my research assistant for some time at the Special Commission on Africa at the African Academy of Sciences.

In January 2003, I met with this team and gave them the terms of reference of what I wanted done. Looking back, we observed that by 2002, the economic growth rate in Kenya had sunk to negative 2 per cent. We needed to restore growth. The agricultural sector of the Kenyan economy was in shambles: people were removing coffee trees from their shambas, cane was rotting in the fields, farmers were hopelessly in debt and did not know where to sell their agricultural produce, the price of milk was at an all time low in the dairy sector, tea farmers in Kisii were watching the green leaves rot on lorries stuck in the mud before getting to the factories. We needed a recovery agenda just to get things moving once more in this sector.

Productivity in the manufacturing sector was at an all time low, due to corruption, poor infrastructure, insecurity and falling consumer purchasing power. In addition, industries had closed as a result of huge indebtedness to the banks following the super inflation and skyrocketing interest rates occasioned by the Goldenberg scam and the huge domestic borrowing by the government

4

that ensued so as to mop up excess money in the economy: both measures simply added more problems to the productive sectors of the economy. In order to get things going in both agriculture and industry, we needed a more disciplined and prudent monetary and fiscal policy; interest rates had to come down, domestic borrowing had to be curbed, nobody must be tempted to print money at all costs, domestic savings had to rise, the tax base had to be broadened while the tax rate had to be brought down, and productive enterprises would not be smothered by the government in accessing credit from financial institutions.

I talked and argued with this fantastic team. They listened, argued back and tried to make sense of my concerns. They prepared drafts of their terms of reference (TOR) and, without even being certain of what we would pay them for their work, they went straight ahead to carry out the one month assignment that became the start of our journey towards crafting the ERS.

During the second week of February 2003, I instructed my staff to bring together a group comprising cabinet ministers, permanent secretaries, heads of state owned corporations, entrepreneurs from Kenya's private sector, consultants, NGO leaders and a few representatives of donor agencies and international financial institutions to discuss the draft ERS at Leisure Lodge on the south coast of Mombasa. We received the generous financial support of the United Nations Development Programme (UNDP) for this seminar and brought in Professor Adebayo Adedeji, former Executive Secretary of the UN Economic Commission for Africa, Professor Adam Przeworski, a political economist from New York University, Thandika Mkandawire, Director of the UN Institute for Research in Social Development (UNRISD), and Kwame Jommo, a distinguished economist from Malaysia for technical assistance during the discussions.

All these deliberations produced excellent results on the way forward. It was also the time when KEPSA was born. The Federation of Kenya Employers (FKE) and the Kenya Association of Manufacturers (KAM) were not strongly represented at this discussion. Tom Owuor, the chief executive of FKE, became agitated about our deliberations and began to attack the government for not coming out with a programme to boost employment in Kenya. We had said in our manifesto that we would create 500,000 jobs a year. Mr. Owuor somehow thought that this would happen within the first two months of our taking over power. I eventually went to his office to explain the process we were going through.

After Mombasa we held many discussions within government and with our team of consultants. The ERS was officially launched by President Kibaki in June 2003. Shortly thereafter the President promoted David Nalo from his position as Director, Central Bureau of Statistics (CBS) to be my Permanent Secretary. David proved to be an invaluable asset: intelligent, hard working, conscious of duty, ready to consult and intellectually agile. He helped a great deal in networking with his fellow PSs in implementing the ERS.

What perturbed me most, however, was that after the launch, the civil servants, in what are called sector-working groups, translated the ERS into the Investment Programme called the IP-ERS for purposes of consumption by donors. This became the basis on which the latter pledged resources at the November Donors' Consultative Conference at the Safari Park Hotel. (This was the first time a donors' consultative meeting was held in Kenya.) At the conference, close to US$ 4.5 billion was pledged to implement the IP-ERS. I was sceptical about this undertaking. In the end little materialised from these pledges partly because of corruption in government, and also because of the lack of seriousness on the part of donors.

In May 2005 another donors' conference was called in Nairobi. At the time, I was in New York and as fate would have it, David was also away in Brussels for another meeting with the European Union. The top brass at the Planning Ministry were, therefore, conspicuous by their absence.

Deep down, however, I felt the meeting was a hopeless venture. The government had already stalled on the fight against corruption. John Githongo, the Permanent Secretary in charge of Ethics in the Office of the President, had left in a huff in December 2004 and the President had offered no convincing explanation regarding why Githongo left. The British High Commissioner, Sir Edward Clay, had lectured the government and Kenyans on how graft was rampant in the Kibaki government, going as far as painting the graphic picture of ministers "vomiting on the shoes of diplomats as they wine and dine begging for more aid while they line up their pockets with corruption and ill gotten wealth." He had dismissed the Head of Civil Service, Francis Muthaura, as an unfortunate bureaucrat "suffering from selective amnesia."

I honestly did not understand how we could, in good conscience, call a meeting with the donors when the reputation of our government was at its lowest ebb. In my own address to the KEPSA after Clay's outburst, I had stated quite clearly that I would not like to belong to a government that condoned corruption and where cabinet ministers perpetrated acts of corruption. I had gone ahead to request for a special cabinet meeting to discuss corruption. The meeting did take place lasting more than four hours. Thereafter, I was surprised at the President's casual treatment of the matter. I challenged the government to show me the door if they knew I was corrupt. At the time, I seriously considered resigning from the government, but some of my colleagues and confidants thought it better to bring about change from within. In an African setting, resigning quite often does not achieve the results that would help move change forward.

Recovering lost ground: The easiest aspect of economic growth

The concept of *economic recovery* bothered many people. Why "recovery?" From my knowledge of Kenya's political economy and economic history it was quite clear to me that we had, along the way after independence, lost some ground in our development process.[44] This occurred some time after 1969 when Tom Mboya was assassinated. I date the deviation from the path of rapid and progressive development to this date because of what Lee Kwan Yew told me in April 1994 when I was in Singapore as a participant in the "Africa-Singapore Encounter" that was led by Retired General Olusegun Obasanjo.

Lee Kwan Yew, then a senior cabinet minister in Singapore, after his retirement from being Premier and founding father of the nation, had just given us a lecture on "What Singapore Can Learn from Africa and What Africa Can Learn From Singapore". At question time I asked him whether he could explain to us why Singapore was able to take off and become a modern developed nation from the late sixties while we, who were at that time at the same level with them, retrogressed. Then came the old man's wisdom in reply to my question: "While we in Singapore decided to march forward together as a nation, you in Kenya decided to assassinate Tom Mboya."

What Lee Kwan Yew meant to convey to us was that leadership matters in development, particularly leaders with clear ideas and vision about the future of their nation, those who can fix their eyes on some distant star that guides their action towards clear developmental goals. One cannot do this while ignorant of the world one lives in, the dynamics of development locally and internationally, and the need to carry the nation with one in a national enterprise into which the majority can buy in enthusiastically and at times with a sense of sacrifice. The presidential authoritarian regimes we have had

---

4   P. Anyang' Nyong'o, "The Possibilities and Historical Limits of Import Substitution Industrialisation in Kenya," in *Industrialisation in Kenya: In Search of a Strategy* edited by P. Coughlin and G. Ikiara (Nairobi: Heinemann, 1985).

in Kenya have, unfortunately, been negations of what we were advocating, and we had hoped that the coalition we had forged in 2002, was going to make a difference. Unfortunately, it did not.

To begin recovering lost ground was perhaps the easiest part of the recovery process. It involved the following:

- Reviving stalled projects in the public sector, most of them government buildings in public institutions;

- Reviving the productive sector, particularly in agriculture and the dairy industry: coffee, tea and sugar growing which led to an almost instant increase in farm gate prices and growth in farmers' incomes;

- Encouraging credit availability to the private sector by reducing domestic borrowing by government in the local market and forcing lending interest rates down; and,

- Taming speculation in the economy by more financial discipline and better supervision of banks by the Central Bank, therefore restoring confidence in the economy.[5]

We debated the best way to tackle corruption, especially in the judiciary. In 2003, fifteen judges and dozens of magistrates were dismissed on the basis of alleged involvement in corruption. The government's onslaught on the judiciary, though hastily and poorly executed, sent shock waves to those who thought they would rely on a corrupt judiciary to cover their tracts of corruption. For a moment, there was "a feel good factor" that the government was on the right path to root out corruption. This encouraged more people to make decisions about investing in Kenya. By the time they realised "business as usual" was returning to the fight against corruption, it was too late to pull out their investments. Hence the economy continued to grow in spite of the failures on governance issues after June 2004.

Recovering lost ground made it possible for milk prices to rise from Kshs. 7 to Kshs 17 per litre within the first six months of our being in government. All we did was to assure the dairy farmer that there was a market for his milk, by reviving the

---

5   For my analysis of the NARC government economic performance see my article in the *Sunday Standard*, 30 December 2006 entitled "Economic Recovery not Economic Growth".

Kenya Cooperative Creameries (KCC) and having it run well. The dairy farmer was now able to bring back the milker to milk the cow; the milk collector went back to work and the banks started receiving their lost clients. That was an important aspect of the recovery programme, which needed to be "grooved into" the rest of the economy so as to stimulate sustainable growth over time.

The government stopped borrowing from the banks by floating treasury bills and bonds whose interest rates were not very attractive. The result was that the banks and mortgage houses became awash with cash. They immediately lowered their interest rates and started hunting for customers to lend the money to. The safest investment for both investors and speculators became brick and mortar in the real estate sector. There was therefore a sudden boom in construction in Kenya, with Nairobi getting the lion's share where illicit money mixed with legal money to create an unprecedented bonanza in housing and office block construction in the republic.

This is the economic growth that the recovery process stimulated. It should be seen as a sector-specific growth whose achievements when averaged, gives the overall national statistic of growth a higher figure. In the Ministry of Planning, we saw it as the bonanza of recovery and not of growth. We were yet to embark on the process of economic growth once we had recovered to the level of growth that the country had known for the last time in 1986.

This process of growth would require much harder choices than the ones we had taken to make the recovery possible. But with the emergence of the Anglo Leasing scandal and other corruption schemes, I began to fear that our government was losing direction and that soon the process of economic recovery would be swallowed by the messy politics of primitive accumulation and self-preservation by the power elite around the President.

Review of the ERS

Notwithstanding my misgivings with the Government of National Unity (GNU) appointed by President Kibaki in June 2004,[6] I ordered a mid-term review of our economic recovery strategy in early 2005 to see how far we had gone with the recovery process as we were heading towards the end of the first half of our mandate in government.

---

6   In June 2004, the President suddenly reshuffled the cabinet and brought in ministers from the opposition political parties: KANU and FORD People.

I engaged a team of three economists: Professor Terry Ryan, former Permanent Secretary, and Harry Mule and Dr. David Ndii since both of them had been involved in crafting the ERS right from the very beginning. Their terms of reference were very precise: to review how far we had gone with the recovery process, the extent to which line ministries and public enterprises had implemented the ERS, what resource gaps had been noticed, and what we needed to do after mid term to ensure the successful implementation of the ERS.[7]

Once more the economists did a sterling job although they handed in their reports after I had left government.[8] As usual there was resistance in the same government and some civil servants refused to cooperate with the reviewers. Nevertheless, they went ahead and ingeniously got the information they needed to make their report with integrity. In brief, their findings were as follows: first, that the ERS as a policy document that envisaged putting together a road map for economic recovery was very realistic and action-oriented. However, it required an enabling political environment of trust, good leadership and democratic governance to succeed. Once there was some political deficit on these governance issues, the ERS would encounter problems in its implementation.

There were two major challenges facing the NARC government, one short-term and the other long-term; one requiring a synchronic approach the other involving a diachronic perspective of development. These were:

a) How to provide relief to the suffering; a vast majority of Kenyans had endured a degree of suffering in the recent past, particularly tremendous social deprivation and political exclusion engendered by authoritarian rule; and,

b) How to tackle the structural problems of an underdeveloped economy in the era of globalisation in order to lay the foundation for sustained economic and social progress.

---

7   Three basic criteria were set for the review: *ownership*, as reflected in the allocation of resources, where resources are defined broadly to include money, materials, managerial effort and political support; *impact*, progress on creating an enabling environment, and evidence of impact on growth, investment, competitiveness and employment; *adequacy*, whether the ERS is adequate response to the stated goals, namely sustained poverty reduction and job creation.

8   I was expelled from the cabinet after we led campaigns against 'the government's position' on the referendum on the draft constitution held on 21st November 2005. The seven cabinet ministers who opposed the draft constitution were: Raila Odinga, Kalonzo Musyoka, William Ole Ntimama, Ochilo Ayako, Lina Kilimo, Najib Balala and I. We acquired a name - "the Orange Seven".

Secondly, the four pillars of the ERS needed to be implemented in tandem. Any attempt to isolate them would run the risk of a non-sustainable path of economic growth in the long run. Key, however, were the issues related to investment in the productive sectors of the economy, rehabilitation and expansion of the infrastructure, and good governance.

Thirdly, it was important to take the title of the ERS seriously. It spoke of an economic recovery strategy for wealth and employment creation. Creating wealth for the few without creating employment for the masses would not lead to a full recovery process for purposes of kick-starting sustainable growth. Such jobless growth models are many in developing economies, and Kenya would not be the first to try economic recovery through the easy way of a growing GDP without the requisite creation of jobs. Tough political choices needed to be made to meet the objectives of the recovery strategy, i.e. wealth as well as employment creation.

Fourthly, allowing the ERS to be turned into a document for shopping for donor funds would not only predispose it to unpredictable capital flows, but it would also limit the government's choice in directing public investments to major employment creating sectors, particularly public works. Indeed, this is what finally happened.

In my own review of the economic recovery process since 2003, I largely concurred with the findings of the three economists. Many other well-meaning reviewers have come to the same conclusion, in particular Osoro in his piece that appeared in the *Daily Nation* of 2 January, 2007.[9]

The pillars and agents of real change

The national democratic front that we had forged within the framework of NARC had had a purpose: to open up political space for democratic changes in Kenya. The most important item on the agenda was to get a new constitution that would lay down the framework for viable and sustainable democracy, good governance, and development in our country. That is why NARC had promised Kenyans that this would be done within the first one hundred days of being in government so that other changes could follow within the framework of this fundamental law. That, too, is why we entitled the NARC manifesto *Democracy and Empowerment*.

---

9   John B. Osoro, "Vision 2030", *Daily Nation*, 2 January, 2007.

I had a lot to do with the crafting of this manifesto and I had given plenty of thought regarding the institutional arrangements we needed to put in place once in government so as to implement our manifesto. Without democracy and political empowerment, no real change in the lives of our people would be realised, and this we could only do if we galvanised the energy of the people into a broad-based democratic government capable of pushing forward a national developmental agenda.

We did not use the word *empowerment* glibly. Empowerment does not simply mean being appointed to a position – although representation is a major aspect of the empowerment process; it essentially means making people have their destiny in their own hands as much as possible. A political dictatorship is the surest form of disempowering the people; democracy, on the other hand, provides the assurance that one can always have the opportunity to change the political destiny of one's society.

Lack of information is also disempowering, so is poverty and lack of self-respect. Hence, when we say that we wanted people to live in a society where they can feel at home and have dignity, we meant taking political, social and economic measures that would change our society fundamentally from its authoritarian and poverty-stricken heritage to a much more prosperous, democratic and open society. We gave constitutional reform high priority because of our conviction that, without democracy and good governance, very little else would be achieved, however glorious our reform agenda sounded.

Major social and economic changes in a society like Kenya cannot be undertaken purely by technocrats implementing proposals derived from consultancy documents. Such changes need to spring from political emotions and concerns; they need to have life breathed into them by men and women who have some passion for their society. Men and women who are committed to a mission and can provide leadership through decisive action rather than procrastination on problems whose urgent solution will determine whether Kenya leaps into the future of development instead of continuing to languish in the quagmire of underdevelopment. Such changes need to be guided by distant stars of hope and aspirations that create visions in people's minds driving them to make great turns in their lives like Saul did on the road to Damascus. After the recovery period, therefore, Kenya needed to come up with an economic strategy for wealth and employment creation that would leap us into the future. This, I am afraid, was not going to be possible under the Kibaki administration given its *false start*.

I

PLANNING TO "LEAP-FROG" DEVELOPMENT

1

To Plan is to Choose: We Choose to Create Jobs

Speech delivered during a public lecture at Taifa Hall, University of Nairobi, 11 February 2003

Somewhere in the Gospels in the New Testament, the story is told regarding some fishermen — Simon Peter and the two sons of Zebedee, James and John — who were the disciples of Jesus, having gone to fish the whole night and catching nothing. This was in the lake of Geneseret that, for all intents and purposes, must have been very humid during the day. So fishing at night made a lot of sense.

In spite of the tremendous amount of work the three disciples had done, and having actually chosen the right moment to do their work, they had caught nothing. When they, therefore, drifted ashore in the morning and met Jesus, they poured out their souls to him with their agonies and frustrations. They were almost giving up — thinking fishing had become a hopeless endeavour.

Then Jesus inquired from them regarding how they had fished. Looking carefully at the sea and observing the movement of the waves, Jesus directed them to set out once more into the waters of Geneseret, going straight into the centre and casting their nets to the right side of the boat. When they did this, they came back with a catch of fish they had never seen in their careers as fishermen. What had Jesus done? He had done the planning for them taking into account the *objective conditions in the lake and the subjective will and commitment of the two fishermen to do a good job.*

The moral of this story is very simple. To work hard so as to produce good and intended results, one must proceed intelligently in a planned fashion. Planning, therefore, is intelligent choice making based on clearly stated objectives that need to be achieved within time and space.

15

Simon Peter, James and John had gone into the lake at night and worked pretty hard, but they had done so without proper planning. Subjectively they were prepared for good results; objectively, however, they had not understood the forces of nature they were up against in the Lake of Geneseret. As Karl Marx once argued, "men make their history, but they do not make it under conditions of their own choice. They make it under objective conditions bequeathed to them from the past."[1]

Many of us have been wondering why we work so hard and get very little from our efforts. We have been wondering why we grow coffee or sugar cane, harvest our crops, take them to the market and yet we continue to be poor, making very little headway in our lives. Quite often we blame ourselves, thinking we are not doing our best. At other times we blame others, saying they do not come to our *harambees* when we organise them to raise some money and invest into our business. And more frequently we blame the government — especially the previous one — saying the powers that be are corrupt and cannot give us an enabling environment to do business and escape from poverty.

But apportioning blame, however justified, is not enough to make us get the just rewards for our labour. While we may, indeed, be right regarding how corrupt the government is and how hopeless the environment of business is, we will not improve our lot until we set sail into the deep blue sea and cast our nets on the right side of the boat. This, we shall soon find out, requires a clear understanding of the objective conditions and hence an intelligent use of our time and efforts. In other words, it requires proper planning so as to make intelligent choices.

Why, therefore, have we remained so poor in Kenya since independence? What choices have we been making? And where did we go wrong? Could we have planned better and attained better results?

Forty years of independence: The lost decades?

Forty or more years after independence, Kenya is still faced with the same problems that we said we would deal effectively with after independence, namely ignorance, poverty and disease. Until the coming to power of the NARC government a few weeks ago, over 2 million Kenyan children did not have the opportunity to go to school; many who went to primary school never made it to high school. The majority of those who went to high school had nowhere to go after that: no jobs, no further opportunity for college, and no resources to start up business.

---

1 Karl Marx, *Theses on Feurebach,* in Quintin Hoare (ed.), *Karl Marx: Early Writings* (London: New LEFT Books, 1974).

Yet we know that soon after independence, the then Minister of Economic Planning and Development, the late Tom Mboya, developed a plan to cater for universal primary education for Kenyan children. Along with this plan was a policy of population control and family planning, the first of its kind in Africa, and one that was hailed by experts the world over as well conceived, realistic and development oriented.

The boom of the first decade

The first decade of independence, 1963-1973, were the boom years of the Kenyan economy:

- The economy grew impressively, hitting an average real growth rate of 5-8 per cent per annum, with per capita GDP that was two-thirds higher in 1980 than in 1963. In contrast, the following 2 decades were characterised by a stagnating economy with average growth rates of 4 and 2 per cent in the 1990/80 and 2000/90 periods. Persistent decline from 1996 onwards culminated in a negative growth rate of 0.2 per cent by the year 2000 in spite of the government's ability to maintain macro-economic stability with regard to rates of inflation, foreign exchange rates, among others.

- The high rate of growth could be explained in part by policies and development plans that favoured the expansion of the frontiers of private property in agriculture as well as trade and manufacture. These were the years of the Million-Acre Scheme, Africanisation of trade, Kenyanisation of employment in the public sector, and import substitution industrialisation. But arable agricultural land was limited and the state could not continue to protect inefficient import substitution industries for very long, especially when they could not produce competitively for international trade in spite of the many lofty pronouncements regarding their virtue.

Decline sets in

With the oil crisis in 1973, emerging corruption and mismanagement in the public sector following the adoption of the Ndegwa Commission Report, and growing adverse terms of trade in the international market against us, the downturn in the economy started to creep in. Except for the brief respite of the coffee boom in 1976-77, nothing really changed to push new life into the

17

economy. It kept on marching on with the momentum of the first decade, with employment opportunities beginning to disappear.

Enter the Nyayo regime in 1978 and the subsequent Nyayo public projects that simply consumed rather than produced things, grew from bad to worse. Public and private consumption systematically went up as domestic savings dwindled — eaten up by corruption or simply stifled in a stagnant economy.

Since the state could not avoid paying the huge public sector wage bill (the basis of its political support), and since the regime developed a culture of cultivating legitimacy through a reward system orchestrated around ethnic elites, corruption, mismanagement and inefficiency went from bad to worse aggravating the ability to service foreign debts contracted to finance public sector investments in agriculture, the energy sector, transportation, etc.

To add insult to injury, Kenya's gold (coffee) was being transformed into iron by the international market. Coffee prices in the international market systematically went down — further complicating the foreign exchange equation. Faced with the challenge to service foreign debt but with decreasing ability for foreign exchange earnings, the government started borrowing heavily from the domestic market.

In the meantime, voices of protest were mounting, men and women who felt strongly that they deserved better in life than living without jobs, going to hospitals and finding no medicine, and wallowing in poverty in a land which should flow with milk and honey. The government would not listen to their protests, or when it listened to them, refused to appreciate let alone understand what was going on. Criticism was taken to be rebellion, challenge of authority interpreted to be treason, and honest discourse on public affairs seen as subversion.

The governing elite, always better off than the people and the direct beneficiaries of state policies — however retrogressive they might have been — fought tooth and nail to maintain their privileges and comfort even when the state was blatantly oppressing the people. Opposition politicians were detained without trial, students and university dons were beaten up by the police, arrested, tortured and even killed — as was the case of Titus Adungosi. Critical citizens — be they lecturers at the university or journalists, priests or fishermen were likewise imprisoned on tramped up charges, tortured, detained or assassinated. Those who escaped the dragnet voted with their feet and went to other lands where they could feel at home: the UK, USA, Australia, Canada, Uganda, Tanzania, Botswana, South Africa and even as far away as Mexico where my family and I sojourned for two and half years in the early 1980s. Thus, Kenya exported capital and skills when it needed them most. To add insult to injury, the export was not voluntary, it was imposed on society by the cruel choices of the then incumbent regime.

Faced with a political environment that was hostile to its people and not very easy to do business with, many investors — both domestic and foreign — chose to relocate elsewhere, further depriving the economy of the capital it needed for economic growth. The geese that lay the golden eggs — labour and capital — were rapidly being estranged from Kenya, and hence disarticulating the development process. For the investors who remained — as many had to do since not everybody could relocate — they moved cautiously into "safe" areas of investment: brick and mortar, treasury bills, land speculation, and self-education.

The Moi regime of the 1980s did not add much to economic growth; it simply kept the lid on and survived on the growth momentum built up in the 1970s. Yes, indeed, substantial investments went into creating new universities, expanding the Nyayo tea zones and the Nyayo wards. But the end result was not really more innovation and discovery from the universities. The end result was more and more unemployed graduates looking for jobs they could never get. In the meantime, universities had eaten up middle level professional colleges that trained skilled human resources for the productive sectors; for example, Egerton Agricultural College had become Egerton University. There was nothing wrong with creating more public universities in Kenya; what was wrong was to do it at the expense of middle level education, which is equally critical to development in Kenya.

The Nyayo wards and the Nyayo tea zones proved more to be conduits for siphoning off resources from the state and establishing funds for primitive accumulation by the powers that be. Later these economic iniquities were to show up in Public Investments Committee reports, chronicling the chains of corruption later to surface in Honourable Kombo's "List of Shame" when he tabled the "Economic Crimes and Anti-Corruption Select Committee Report" in Parliament in the late 1990s.

The challenge of 1992

In 1991, in a world conjuncture that saw authoritarian regimes crumble all over the world, the Kenyan one proved no exception. Challenged by opposition upsurge, the regime printed plenty of money to corrupt the political process and buy its way back to power. It fleeced more money out of the treasury

19

through the now famous Goldenberg scandal. The regime planned to survive notwithstanding the massive public onslaught against it. And to do this, it made choices aimed at its own survival and not at serving the public good.

The end result was hyperinflation—too much money chasing goods that hardly existed. Yet this money was not in the pocket of the majority. It was in the hands of a small group of people the majority of who simply traded in it—producing little or no wealth at all for the nation.

Through what it took to be successful survival techniques, the regime came back to power in 1992, then again in 1997, and all these problems persisted, becoming worse by the year. Kenyans who knew what to do to save the situation continued to talk from the opposition benches in Parliament and civil society organisations outside Parliament. They made little difference to the lives of ordinary Kenyans who continued to suffer. They really had not planned carefully enough to make the strategic choices that could lead them to the successful seizure of power from the oppressive and exploitative regime over which Moi presided.

Enter NARC

Towards the end of 2002, these opposition forces finally came together in one political coalition called the National Rainbow Coalition (NARC) and promised Kenyans that, if elected to form a government, they would do two things:

1. Reverse the trend of political repression and authoritarianism and restore democratic governance, the rule of law, and respect for human rights in Kenya ascertaining the security of both person and property; and,

2. Empower the people economically.

The NARC manifesto was therefore entitled *Democracy and Empowerment*. You cannot empower people who have no food in their stomachs and no money in their pockets to buy this food with, or to seek shelter in a little house when it rains. The unemployed are perpetually vulnerable and the poor get their human rights abused by the rich when there is no court of law to defend them. NARC, therefore, promised those disempowered by unemployment that, once in power, the NARC government would create *500,000 jobs annually* in a political context where the individual citizen is free and has *a place to feel at home*.

Our coalition, therefore, saw good governance and economic empowerment as two sides of the same coin. It also saw economic growth and job creation as also sides of the same coin. Good governance can be achieved at the *subjective level* when good people who are well intentioned form a government with the commitment to democracy and the will to change things. Such people can seek to establish the rule of law in society and ensure that institutions for building a democratic polity are also in place. Thus, the NARC government moved fast on a programme of good governance, establishing institutions for the promotion of the rule of law and human rights such as the Kenya National Commission on Human Rights and the Office of the Permanent Secretary in charge of Ethics. The cabinet also approved the Anti-corruption and Economic Crimes Bill that was tabled in Parliament and became law almost immediately it was passed.

In other words, at the subjective level, the government has the will to bring about all these changes and to put them in place. These measures create the enabling environment for investment activities to increase and for the foundation for economic growth to be created. To translate this environment into actual growth of the economy and the creation of jobs which are our goals, other objective factors come in which the government must carefully plan for so that people can be led to make choices that promote our objectives. To what extent is this possible?

To empower our people economically—given our current objective conditions—we must be prepared to make certain choices with regard to where we invest our available resources for desired returns and impact. We may want to house everybody today, but given our resource base and other equally compelling demands by the people, we may not be able to do so. But we may set in motion other processes of social change that will make housing everybody— by both the private and public sector—a distinct possibility in the next twenty years.

A question of good leadership, legitimacy and team spirit

In 1995 I visited Singapore as part of a delegation led by Retired General Olusegun Obasanjo, then president of the African Leadership Forum, but now President of the Federal Republic of Nigeria for the second time in his life. General Obasanjo led us to what was called the "Africa-Singapore Encounter". This was a group of 15 young African leaders and 15 Singaporean leaders in government and society who were meant to discuss for one week and share experiences.

The first person to talk to us was Senior Minister Lee Kwan Yew, Singapore's first post-independence Prime Minister. Lee Kwan Yew's subject was "What

21

Africa Can Learn from Singapore and What Singapore Can Learn from Africa."
He talked for two and a half hours without notes. He traced the history of the
independence movements in Africa and South East Asia from World War II to
the fall of the Berlin Wall. He told us how Singapore managed to make it from
the Third to the First World in two decades and why he thought Africa could
still make it if we could do a few things right, making some critical choices and
planning better for our future.

During question time, I asked the Senior Minister one question which was,
"Sir: you say that in 1969, when your GDP per capita was the same as ours in
Kenya and Uganda then, you people made a deliberate choice to move rapidly
with economic growth and achieve growth targets which led you to eradicate
poverty, provide full employment and achieve a modern standard of living for
your people. Why couldn't we do the same?" The Senior Minister looked calmly
at me and replied: "While we chose to go forward in Singapore, you in Kenya
assassinated Tom Mboya."

The answer was pregnant with meaning. In Mboya was the planner, the choice
maker, the visionary. In him people believed and people developed around
him an identity and aspiration for the future. He represented the New Kenya,
something that was valued: a place to feel at home. He helped shape minds
and make people plan for the future. He developed a system of governing and
created institutions that could shape the future of society. He could tell Kenyans,
when they had fished the whole night and caught no fish, where to cast their
nets so as to get the big catch. With him gone, the boat became rudderless.

To plan is to choose. We in Kenya chose to go backwards; to fight in defence of
our own ethnic cocoons in the aftermath of Mboya's assassination. In Singapore
they chose to go forward, to build an integrated and multi-ethnic modern nation
where the per capita income stand today at US$ 19,500 while ours remains at its
pre-independence three-digit level of a mere US$350 or less!

In the NARC manifesto, we set out our vision for the Kenya we want and
what we need to do in every sector of the economy to realise this vision. We say
quite clearly that we want to choose a Kenya where every citizen feels at home
because he or she has security of person and property, enjoys his or her human
rights, and is fully protected by the rule of law. We see a Kenya in which people
will live full lives, make and create wealth and maximise their potentials in an
environment where the government is the servant of the people and not the
other way round.

The NARC government cannot realise this vision without eliminating
corruption and all elements of bad governance. It will do this when good

governance becomes the handmaiden of wealth creation and rapid economic growth. But in our manifesto we did not really prioritise the actions we need to take to realise our vision. We, therefore, tried to do so in our Post Election Action Plan where we argued that we must give priority to the economic growth sectors, i.e. those sectors that *create wealth*, or that are vital in providing the enabling environment for wealth creation. We identified the following: agriculture, tourism, energy, infrastructure, and industry and trade.

Agriculture

In making the choice to invest heavily in agriculture, we need to make a paradigm shift. Agriculture should not be looked at in the traditional sense: cash crops versus food crops; large-scale versus smallholder; high potential land versus low potential land. The question we wanted to ask ourselves was: given Kenya and the world as we know it today, where should we invest in agriculture to ensure that our people are fed today and tomorrow and that, when we export, our agricultural commodities are competitive and give us maximum returns for our labour?

Tourism

Our proposal is that tourism, seen in the context of developing a strong service economy, can be a useful growth pole for our economy. It needs to be linked to conference, financial, education and health services; it needs to dovetail with ICT and its attendant forward and backward linkages.

Energy

Although energy is part and parcel of the physical infrastructure, Kenya's history and the objective conditions required us to give it a specific and "own ranger" attention. Without solving the energy equation so many things will not work in the economic growth model we may design, including sensitivity to environmental issues.

Infrastructure

Roads, railways, telephony etc, are all critical to the recovery process. But the choices made in the past have simply compounded the problem of growth: loans contracted without being properly invested, thereby compounding indebtedness; poor maintenance; pending bills, etc; and, tax evasion

Now is the time to come up with building the super highway from Mombasa to Busia and Malaba, through concession to a private developer, thereby creating millions of jobs and stimulating activities in the cement industry, iron and steel works and extending into trading and commerce. Now is the time to ensure that the fuel levy fund is used appropriately for road maintenance, smoking out the "cowboy contractors" and making sure that our people get value for the money that they pay in taxes. Now is the time to net in the tax dodgers, using our watchdog institutions productively and bringing back the people's confidence in government. Now is the time to cast our net on the right side of the boat, fishing in the waters where the catch is plentiful so that our people can get the just reward for their labour.

The targets we have set for ourselves

In setting the targets for the growth of our economy, we aim to provide 500,000 jobs every year. This we can do if we grow at no less than 7per cent per annum; and we can do it. We shall do it. But we hope to do this without necessarily disturbing macro-economic stability. In this regard, we need the cooperation of our development partners to let us access long-term low interest loans as well as generous grants. With the grants we hope to retire our domestic debt so that interest rates can be kept low and affordable credit be made available to entrepreneurs of all sizes: small, medium, big, very big and super big. The government is there to create and sustain the enabling environment for growth, playing the role of a friendly regulator, the provider of law and order and the promoter of human rights.

To plan is to choose. We have chosen to ensure that our economy grows very rapidly so that we can provide for the basic needs of all Kenyans because they work for it in an atmosphere where the rule of law prevails.

2

The State of the Nation's Economy

Address to the Institute of Economic Affairs (IEA), Nairobi, Annual
Lecture Series, 23 January, 2003

Introduction

The Institute of Economic Affairs (IEA) annual lecture serves the purpose of providing a forum to review economic performance in the foregone year and focus upon the policy imperatives of the new year. In the 2003 lecture, the Institute requested me as the Minister for Planning and National Development to make the keynote forum on the government's preliminary assessment of the policy priorities and the direction that the government intends to take.

In addressing the above request I intend to focus on the following:

- The current state of the Kenyan economy;

- The proposed way forward; and

- The expected road map.

The state of the economy

The Kenyan economy over the recent past has been dominated by two inconsistent trends. On one hand, the country has generated a relatively sustainable macroeconomic framework with low inflation (4.3 per cent over 1997-2001 and 2 per cent in 2002), stable exchange rates and acceptable level of foreign exchange reserves (over 3 months by end 2002), and budget deficits that over 1999/2000-2001/03 averaged 1.24 per cent of GDP and would have been sustainable had the country been able to maintain good relations with its development partners. On the other hand, the country has failed to achieve satisfactory performance in the real economy. In particular:

- *Poor economic growth* with GDP growth averaging 1.04 per cent over 1997-2001 by 1.2 per cent in 2002. This means the trend of declining per capita income that begun in the early nineties has continued into the new millennium.

- *Low investment and savings* with the former averaging 19 per cent of GDP over 1997-2001 compared to a targeted 25-30 per cent while the latter averaged just 8.8 per cent over the same period. Kenya has thus experienced insufficient investment co-existing with increased reliance on external funding for investment finance.

- *Poor investment efficiency* as characterised by the high level of investment per unit of increased output. A 19 per cent of GDP over 1997-2001 achieved 1.04 per cent growth while over 1964-73 19.7 per cent of GDP in investments achieved an average GDP growth of 6.6 per cent.

- *Declining export performance* as with export to GDP ratios declining from 32.1 per cent over 1990-95 to 27.5 per cent over 1996-2000 and 26.2 per cent of GDP in 2001.

- *Rising unemployment and poverty* with the latter rising from 45 per cent of the population in 1992 to an estimated 56 per cent in 2002;

- *Net long-term financial outflows* in the balance of payments where in 2001 net outflows totalled Kshs 22 billion. The bulk of these net outflows are from the public sector where, for example, there was a net outflow of Kshs 9.3 billion in 2001/02. Foreign borrowing is thus predominantly short-term making both public and private investment financing difficult and being inherently unstable.

- *Public expenditure skewed in favour of consumption* activities at the expense of investment. Public savings have declined from 2.8 per cent of GDP in 1999/2000 to below zero by 2001/02, while the central government wage bill at over 8 per cent of GDP is substantially above the 5.5-6.5 per cent common to low-income countries. Government investments at 3 per cent of GDP can also be compared to the Newly Industrialising Country (NIC) experience of 8-10 per cent of GDP going to investment. It should be noted that this skewed public consumption has not led to social sector indicators that are superior to the expenditure as not been cost effective.

The coming of the new government has substantially raised expectations. Kenya can no longer afford to have declining per capita income, increasing poverty and unemployment, and poor service delivery. The economic challenge will be to transform the productive sectors of our economy into high performers able to provide the resources to deliver higher performers able to provide the resources to deliver higher quality public services without compromising the macroeconomic fundamentals.

Reasons for economic under performance

Kenya's first decade was characterised by rapid GDP growth averaging 6.6 per cent, relatively high investment efficiency with less that 3 units of investment required per unit of output, growing exports and improvement in service delivery. Macroeconomic fundamentals – deficits, inflation, and balance of payments position were all good. Most important, per capita income expanded by an average of over 3 per cent per year. This economic growth was based on what has been referred to as the 'easy' opportunities, for example:

- Agricultural growth based on bringing more land under cultivation as well as introducing exotic cattle, hybrid maize and export crops to the smallholder sector and intensification of land use through the subdivision of settler farms;

- Industrial expansion based on import substitution which allowed for rapid expansion based on protected domestic demand and postponed dealing with problems relating to economies of scale, inadequate technology, managerial deficiencies and worker productivity that was not internationally competitive;

- Rapid expansion of public services with government services expanding by an average 16.9 per cent over 1964-73. This rapid growth was primarily driven by expansion of educational and health services; and,

- Increasing monetisation of the economy as subsistence production declined and commercialisation of agriculture expanded.

Over 1973-2001, Kenya's economic performance was characterised by secular decline. GDP declined from 6.6 per cent average to 5.2 per cent over 1974-79 to 4.1 per cent over 1980-89 to 2.5 per cent over 1990-95 and below 2 per cent over 1996-2002. Overall, poor performance was due to a failure to adjust to changing

27

economic environment and to find new engines of growth as the old engines run their course. Several indicators exist:

1. Kenya consistently failed to change the policy direction once easy options were exhausted, for example:

    - Agriculture has failed to adjust to a high value added activity. According to *Sessional Paper no. 1 of 1986*, by 1984 over 46 per cent of high potential land was still being used for low intensity milk production while only 3 per cent was being used for high intensity coffee and tea production. Evidence from the *Kenya Rural Development Strategy of 2002* indicates that by 2000, milk production still accounted for 47 per cent of total high potential land use while coffee and tea had risen to 5.2 per cent. This is despite the fact that total land under farms had expanded from 5.6 million hectares in 1984 to 6.8 million hectares in 2000;

    - Manufacturing failed to transform from an inward oriented activity to an export oriented internationally competitive producer. Instead liberalisation led to import penetration without a commensurate expansion in exports;

    - Share of government to GDP has remained high even as social indicators (life expectancy, enrolment rates) have declined;

2. A consistent failure to adhere to adjustment agreements with development partners which has led to tougher (and hence more difficult to achieve) conditionalities in subsequent negotiations. Kenya's structural adjustment borrowing is instructive in this respect:

    - A structural adjustment loan (SAL) was negotiated over the 1979-80 period focusing on export promotion but failed to achieve the targets due to slow implementation.

    - A second SAL was negotiated in 1982 to focus on trade reform, grain marketing, interest rates and energy but was delayed due to strong opposition by vested interests.

    - Adjustment loans for the agricultural sector (1986 and 1990) in the industrial sector (1988), the financial sector (1989) and export development (1990) were largely undermined by government implementation failures.

- It should also be noted that Kenya has yet to complete any ESAF or PRGF borrowing arrangement with the IMF.

Way forward

Following the election of the NARC government in December 2002, Kenyans showed that they had given us a mandate to carry out sweeping economic and political reforms to renew rapid economic growth in a context of democratic governance under the rule of law. An effective recovery and reform initiative will have to be informed by the mistakes and successes of the past. We shall need to build the economic reform framework to ensure that:

- Investors, both domestic and foreign, have confidence in the economy and can put their investments in Kenya.

- Government uses public resources transparently and accountably so as to stimulate domestic savings and domestic capital formation.

- People receive a just reward for their labour and contribute to economic growth through increased individual initiative where mutual social responsibility is an important component of the responsibility of the citizen.

- The sustainable macroeconomic framework that has been achieved at considerable cost to the Kenyan taxpayer is maintained.

- The fundamental reasons for economic underperformance since 1980 are addressed especially the failure of the country to come up with the follow through on a consistent adjustment framework.

- A more consistent partnership with our development partners is pursued to ensure that the external sector does not undermine the overall growth efforts.

Principles to guide development strategy

Several principles will inform the development strategy that we intend to adopt. Critical principles include:

- *Standard of living.* The over arching goal for the country is to achieve a broad based improvement in the standard of living for current and future generation in the country. This requires among others a reduction in the incidence of poverty, reduced maternal and infant mortality, higher levels of educational attainment, more productive jobs for Kenyans and greater domestic control

29

of the country's assets. In other words, a realistic and programmatic pursuit of the UN Millennium Development Goals.

- *Economic growth.* This will play a crucial though not all-encompassing role in achieving the country's socio-economic objectives. Economic growth allows the country to directly tackle the problems of poverty, unemployment and allows a greater number of Kenyan families to meet their basic needs without State assistance. Economic growth also has positive effects on government revenues and thus increases the ability of government to deliver economic and social services to the populace in a fiscally sustainable manner.

- *Conducive business environment.* A business environment that is conducive to both local and foreign investors is a requisite. This will require the core enabling environment consisting of the incentive structure, the infrastructure and the legal and institutional framework that matches international best practice or at least exceeds that available in the region.

- *Private sector involvement.* This will involve enhancing and supporting a responsible private sector as a leading player in stimulating and sustaining economic growth. Not all that the private sector does will necessarily be beneficial to the general population. It will be essential for the government to simultaneously promote the private sector by providing an enabling environment; provide those essential services such as security, law and order, basic education and health that are essential for the country's overall well being but are not often provided by the private sectors; and ensure that even as it promotes the private sector, it protects the national resource base and ecosystems.

- *Fair taxation system.* This calls for putting in place a taxation regime that will be fair, just and equitable, where the base is wide enough to include all taxable incomes, profits and service provided, giving the government sufficient revenue to finance its operations within the context of a healthy economy.

Key economic recovery objectives

The key objectives of the NARC government are contained in the NARC manifesto and the NARC Post Election Action Plan (PEAP). NARC overall goal is to bring about comprehensive political and economic change in Kenya. The manifesto sets out the following objectives:

1. *Governance*: The aim of the government is to put in place a system of governance that ensures leaders remain transparent and that the electorate is able to make demands and receive adequate accountability from those they elect. The focus will be controlling corruption, reforming the system of justice, promoting devolution and decentralisation, strengthening the role of communities, and restoring positive relations with the development partners among others.

2. *Sectoral concerns*: This includes the following:

   - Rethinking the *industrial strategy* and creating a more conducive environment that will promote investor confidence, address the high cost of capital, improve infrastructure, and reduce corruption and red tape.

   - Restoring the *agricultural sector* by adopting a strategy with primary aims of withdrawal of government from production and marketing in the sector, rehabilitation of producer organisations, improving incentives for investment in the sector, increasing utilisation of technology in the sector, and ensuring the sector is protected from adverse competition.

   - Restoring the *financial sector* by putting in place legal administrative and judicial reforms to deal with the non-performing loans (NPL) problem, reducing government appetite for credit and strengthening monetary policy by putting in place an independent Monetary Policy Committee (MPC) to set overall monetary policy.

   - Strengthening the role of *information technology* (IT) in the development process by preparing a national IT policy and using appropriate fiscal incentives to promote the sector.

   - Rehabilitation of the *infrastructure sector* by promoting the role of the private sector in infrastructure provision, allocating increased resources to restoration of the existing infrastructure stock and carrying out the legal, regulatory and institutional reforms necessary to enable the sector to function efficiently;

3. *ASALs*. This aims at fully integrating the arid and semi arid lands (ASALs) into the mainstream of economic life by promoting partnerships between

31

the government, the private sector and non-governmental organisations (NGOs) active in the area; improving infrastructure in the ASALs; and promoting those economic activities, such as beef production, that these areas have comparative advantage.

In the first quota of this year, however, we have decided to lay deliberate emphasis on primary education and the rehabilitation of the battered infrastructure.

The NARC manifesto has a substantial social development agenda as well as clear interventions to ensure the country's ecosystems are protected. There are further proposed interventions in the areas of land, housing, public sector reforms among others. It is essential to appreciate that it is success in the economic recovery agenda that, by providing requisite resources, will underpin reform efforts in these other areas.

Approach to economic recovery strategy

Our economic recovery strategy is based on the following principles:

1. The basic policy thrust must be the implementing of the NARC manifesto since this was the vehicle used by us to sell our vision to the electorate and it was this vision that the electorate endorsed and thus gave the government the mandate to lead.

2. Harmonising the Poverty Reduction Strategy Paper (PRSP), the Government Action Plan (GAP) and NARC Post Election Action Plan with our manifesto. The PRSP document is the result of a comprehensive consultative process that incorporated the wishes of the people of all the districts in Kenya while PEAP is the implementation version of the NARC manifesto. It must be noted, however, that the PRSP lacks the philosophical background of the NARC manifesto hence it can only be useful to us as a source of data and information and not a prescription for development choice-making.

3. The harmonised document will reflect an adequate focus on issues and prioritisation of envisaged activities. For an economic recovery strategy to be credible it must reflect the appropriate sense of urgency as well as provide clear direction on the path to be taken, the measures that will be put in place to achieve desired goals and the trade-offs that will be necessary to achieve the overall policy aims.

4. Available expertise within the public, private and civil society sectors must be utilised as well as international advice must be sought where necessary. This will enable the Kenyan recovery plan to be both a consensus document as well as minimise the errors and omissions, which could have drastic consequences in the future.

5. Finally, to the largest extent possible, already existing commitments and agreements with development partners will be accommodated in the strategy to ensure that the recovery plan remains an all-encompassing policy framework.

3

Roads, Infrastructure and Economic Development

Speech given at the Eastern Africa Construction Conference, Safari Park, Nairobi, 12 May 2005

The link between roads and economic development is quite obvious. One builds a road, particularly a paved one through a region that never had one before, and things begin to happen. First, small markets begin to form, which grow into somewhat larger trading centres if the economy can support these.

Then, other economic activities begin to present themselves. New bus routes are formed along the newly paved road, heavier trucks begin to ferry goods in and out of the region, and before long the area has undergone an economic recovery! On a light note, this may explain why we the politicians are always promising our people paved roads because of all the multiplier effects these roads can have to a given community once they are built. On the other hand, too many paved roads in our country, and probably in your countries too, do not last long enough to fundamentally transform our economies.

Because of substandard construction, maybe as a result of corruption and unethical practices in designing the road, the material used, and the manner in which it was constructed, our beautiful paved roads last less than a decade before you see them rot right before your eyes. This rot is accelerated by a culture of non-maintenance, which I am told comes from a regrettable common feature in many of our languages that do not have a word for "maintenance".

Together, substandard construction and lack of maintenance soon begin to undermine the economic recovery we first described when the road was first built. The potholes, the stripped surface, and the ruts soon become vehicle breakers, so that the passenger and freight transporters who once delighted in a smooth surfaced road and provided cheap transportation become frustrated folks who charge us more in terms of fare and freight to make up for their vehicle maintenance costs.

The trading centres and markets that once boomed because of the heavy traffic begin to wither as people begin to use alternative routes. If the situation is not arrested and the road is eventually stripped of its paved surface and replaced by a rough and patchy earth track, transportation shifts to better maintained gravel and earth roads, or a nearby newly built paved one, to take advantage of the latter before it too goes the way of those built before it.

Thus, a cycle is formed, of paved road built and largely abandoned, and with newer ones built and similarly abandoned and so on. The portfolio of paved roads may expand, but so does the portfolio of badly paved ones! This partly explains why Eastern Africa is so poor. Good roads are few, with most of the networks being in fair to poor conditions. The result of all this is to reduce agricultural productivity, increase transportation costs and the costs of doing business, and generally render the community, city or town, region or country less competitive!

I believe that this conference has been looking at these matters, asking several questions that often cross my mind. For example, why is it so difficult for us in Eastern Africa to build ourselves an interstate grid of roads? This has worked enormously well in the US and Europe, yet here we are with few poorly maintained roads in an area as large as the continental USA!

I often wonder why it is that despite the obvious benefits to our economies and the development impetus such roads would provide, we prefer to build our miserable stock of roads using a timetable largely dictated by the availability of external aid, rather than thinking of how to mobilise sufficient domestic resources for the task. This is so even when we have continental and regional bodies such as NEPAD and the Northern Corridor!

Could we also find out why it is that other rapidly developing countries can design, build and maintain First World infrastructure, while we borrow money to design, build and not maintain Third World infrastructure. Is there anything intrinsically different between a Malaysian road engineer and one from Kenya, Ethiopia, Sudan or Tanzania? If there is not, why then do we have such a problem?

My final question is, why do we continually talk of possible ways of doing things, may be public private partnerships, may be build operate transfer (BOT) and so on – and then gladly go home and do nothing about it? Essentially, why is it that others talk and do, while we from this region tend to talk and shelve?

35

4

Wealth and Employment Creation

Speech given during the 26th African Association of Public Administration and Management (AAPAM) Roundtable Conference, 7-11 March 2005

Kenya is at the moment in the second year of implementing its Economic Recovery Strategy for Wealth and Employment Creation 2003 to 2007, usually shortened as ERS. Therefore, the topic of wealth and employment creation in Africa is of special importance to Kenya.

Indeed, when we were preparing our economic recovery strategy framework early in 2003, we in the Ministry of Planning and National Development were taken to task by many NGOs and development partners over the idea of "wealth creation" as the central focus of our recovery strategy. Against tremendous odds we persisted, knowing full well what the political economy of capitalist development entails in terms of wealth creation and employment generation.

Let me begin by congratulating the AAPAM for joining the paradigm shift towards discussing and implementing "wealth creation" rather than "poverty reduction" or "poverty alleviation". I feel obliged to urge you to shun the use of terminologies like "pro-poor policies" and shift our focus to policies that enable us scale up investments in agriculture, social welfare and infrastructure development so as to create the wealth from which economic growth springs and poverty is reduced and eventually eradicated. This indeed has been the history of many nations since Adam Smith wrote his *Wealth of Nations*,[1] Karl Marx his *Das Kapital*[2] and Milton Friedman his *Capitalism and Freedom*.[3]

---

1   Adam Smith, *The Wealth of Nations*, (London: Methuen and Co. Ltd, 1904).
2   Karl Marx, *Capital*, (London: Penguin Classics, 1992).
3   Milton Friedman, *Capitalism and Freedom* (Chicago: University of Chicago Press, 2002).

I think I should start with some thoughts on this, because I have seen that you have devoted an entire session to discussing wealth creation by poverty reduction or alleviation, a debate that we already had and concluded in this country. This debate has become more than a matter of semantics. In my view, it has to do with a basic understanding of economic history and an appreciation of the political economy of development in the globalised economy of today, replete with the ideologies that seem to be more concerned with the inhuman effects of underdevelopment rather than the eradication of underdevelopment itself. It is the debate on these ideologies to which we have paid more attention in Africa rather than on the much more challenging task of eradicating underdevelopment through wealth creation.

To some people, wealth creation is a bad term, it denotes "trickle down", that is, the wealthy get even richer, and the scraps come to the people at the bottom. For such people, the politically correct "bottom-up" term is "poverty reduction" or "poverty alleviation". Using an analogy, if poverty were a disease, these folks prefer to tell the patients to get themselves less sick (reducing or alleviating the sickness). The result is a handout mentality and worldview that sees governments, development partners and charities handing out "poverty reducing" goods and services to helpless people in the developing countries.

To others like ourselves in the NARC government, we see wealth creation as a good term. We define wealth creation as increase in assets, however modest this may be. When my mother's goats increase from three to five, her liquid assets (or rather assets on hoof) have increased by two thirds! Her wealth status, with five goats, is better than when she had three! The idea is to turn the five into eight, the eight into ten, the ten into twelve and so on! Finally, when the goats are too many, to sell some and use the money to buy shares in the stock market in Nairobi. This is what is called the *accumulation of capital*, a process that cannot be set in motion without wealth creation. The result is an asset building and endowment mentality or worldview that sees governments, development partners and charities working together to reduce poverty in the context of measure, policies and programmes that increase assets (including human capital) and incomes at the bottom of the pyramid.

You must ask yourselves the following hard questions. First, do the poor have resources at their disposal that they can put to better use if they are facilitated? Second, what do the poor lack in order to be productive members of society? And third, who can work with them to address their capacity constraints? Addressing these challenges does not really require "handout approach", but a facilitative and capacity creation approach.

37

I think this difference, between creating a handout culture that comes along with its dependency syndrome and creating an endowments culture that is accompanied by a self-reliance attitude and a wealth creating economy, is critical if Africa is to get beyond the dismal picture that is painted in the Aide Memoire that AAPAM has prepared for this conference. I want to believe that AAPM can make a difference because, as you are constituted from the top leadership in public administration and the private sector, you are the people who make society tick. Some of you here are the heads of public service and cabinet secretaries in your countries, which in effect make you the chief operating officers of your governments. Others are permanent secretaries, while others are top public and private sector managers. If AAPAM, which comprises the cream of African administrative and technocratic leadership cannot make the difference in Africa's transformation from the poorest continent, afflicted by all the apocalyptic horsemen found in the Book of Revelations, then who can?

If AAPAM is to play its role in creating the necessary momentum for the wealth creation paradigm, this conference must be part of the effort in identifying *what works, how it works, when it works* and *where it works* in terms of the critical elements, institutions and instruments that will endow our people with the physical, social and economic capital to become prosperous and take their place in the global market. This is not as formidable a task as it sounds. The elements are known, and you have identified some of them such as owning the wealth creation process ourselves as Africans instead of depending on donors; implementing and upholding the rule of law; having strong and enforceable property rights for all including the informal sector; creating and strengthening the institutions that enable the creation of wealth and employment opportunities; and turning the public service into a vehicle for enabling opportunity, prosperity, equity and good governance for all in Africa.

I hope you do not simply recite these things as a matter of ritual, but that you believe in them and you have intellectually internalised them to the extent that they guide your actions, policy formulation and policy execution. Development is not a routine thing; it is a process that is consciously thought out and expected over time. That is why five-year or ten-year development plans are still a necessity in our development nations, as the Indian case now shows very clearly. Ever since the Nehru-Mahalanobis third development plan of the late 1950s, India has systematically built on her achievements, undertaking reforms within a specifically Indian paradigm, always ensuring that the goal of wealth and employment creation is not lost. The tremendous growth rate, the $130 billion foreign exchange reserve and the 60 million-ton food reserves in a population of 1.3 billion people where nobody goes without a meal is something that Africa should take serious note of.

In reality we know *what works*. Therefore, Africa's problem is not in *not knowing* what it must do; we have listed these things and discussed them in depth in thousands of papers, speeches, workshops, seminars and peer reviewed journals. Our problems begin with the *how to do it, when to do it* and *where to do it*. When it comes to how to do it, we as Africans have abdicated our thinking and doing caps to the development partners and charities from the West.

Let me challenge this distinguished group to tell us why it is so difficult for an African country to determine the "how". Why has it been that Africa's "how" has always been based on donor driven fads and paradigms. In the 1970s and 1980s, we were all excited and funded for "basic needs" and "integrated development", but before we could get our act together, these fellows had the Berg report, and pronto, we were moved to "structural adjustment". We struggled with "structural adjustment" in the 1980s, without adjusting any structures, oil economies remained that way, coffee and tea economies stayed that way too!

Towards the end of the 1980s and into the early 1990s, just as we were getting fed up with these programmes that were impoverishing rather than adjusting our economies upwards, a new fad came by "privatisation". So in the early 1990s we all went into privatisation and for most of that decade undertook privatisation in ways that produced mixed results at enterprise level, but did not change our ordinary people's lives for the better. We closed the twentieth century and entered the twenty-first century with the "poverty reduction strategy papers", most of which have not led to any change in the poverty status of our countries, which is why now in the 2005 to 2015 we will need to be targeting the "millennium development goals" or MDGs which have been declared unattainable for Africa anyway!

If this is not bad enough in terms of the enormous damage wreaked on our economies and societies by the truncated development arising from the conflicting and often contradictory changes in the development fads, we also allowed ourselves to be told "when" to do what needed to be done, and "where" to do it. This often came in the direct form of "conditionalities" that were time-bound, or in the more disguised form of technical assistance that was attached to the loans and grants.

The sum total of this situation is that. while we can truly blame ourselves as Africans for the mess we are in, this is because we abdicated to do the "what", "how", "when" and "where" to develop and prosper ourselves. We as policy makers since the 1960s – that is presidents, prime ministers, ministers, permanent secretaries, and top managers of public institutions, bear collectively (with our predecessors) the greatest blame for the sorry state of the continent. We underestimated our internal capacity to get development right, and overestimated that of outsiders!

Now forty years later, we have the chance to make things right, to rightly estimate our capacities and abilities to deliver democracy, accountability, the rule of law, strong and enforceable property rights that fully include women and the informal sector, sound and well-maintained infrastructure, strong and well-manned public institutions, and equitable endowments and opportunities to all of our people. We know that outsiders cannot do it, and yet we still persist in seeking their assistance. We know that Asians did it by themselves, why are we as Africans afraid to do it by ourselves?

Even if we fail in some areas, we have nothing to lose; we have failed so badly in the past. However, we have so much to gain, because really, we have never exerted ourselves as leaders and managers to do our very best for the people of our countries, which means that our chances of succeeding beyond our expectations are very high if we make a determined, disciplined, diligent and consistent effort to turn our countries around and at least achieve those MDGs! We cannot afford to be the only place on earth where life continually gets worse rather than better with the passing of the days!

Let us go beyond more papers and discussion! Let us propose and recommend deliberate actions that will be used to take back the "what", "how", "when" and "where" to ourselves, which is the essential message of the New Partnership for Africa's Development (NEPAD). What I am suggesting is that let us have Africa's top technocratic leadership which is gathered here reassure us the politicians that "we can do it" by the end of this conference. Let us be assured that we have the capacity to be totally in charge of the development agenda that will create wealth with equity in our societies, and that we can develop our own frameworks that allow external partners to work with us towards our goals rather than us work for them towards their goals, which has been the reality of aid for so long.

I say this because I know that it can be done. Reading Lee Kwan Yew's "Singapore Story: From the Third to the First World",[4] we get to see what it takes to create wealth, abolish poverty and enter the high road towards being members of the First World within a matter of two decades. Singapore has a clear and focused political leadership, from the head of government downwards, with a civil service and political cadre that is well trained and well remunerated, and that exercises its mission free of corruption and is committed to good management of public affairs. Working in partnership with an enterprising private sector, the Singapore state enables wealth to be created and employment to be generated. This is no rocket science; any African state today can become a Singapore just as they can become a Netherlands of Africa.

Malaysia, thanks to the focused leadership of Mahathir Mohammed that spanned two decades, will say goodbye to poverty within the next five years, and meet all the MDGs. In the 1970s, the economy of Malaysia was doing much worse than that of Kenya; when they decided to take off, we decided to retrogress into corruption, the mismanagement of public affairs and the impoverishment of the majority of our people. Over time we destroyed the wealth we had created by looting the National Social Security Fund and most pension funds. We privatised state-owned enterprises not to make them create more wealth, but to enrich the wayward comprador bourgeoisie. Except for the successful story of Kenya Airways, other privatisation initiatives do not have very good stories to tell.

Yet we know that it is from the proper management and investment of pension funds that Singapore built a formidable education system, provided houses for all her peoples and guaranteed retirees life after their retirement. Malaysia, likewise, is currently leap-frogging into the era of information technology through an education system that produces world-class Malaysian engineers as the basis of the success of her multi-media corridor in Kuala Lumpur.

How do we manage what we have? How do we invest it? How do the results of our investments stimulate other investors from within and without?

Wealth and employment creation are the outcome of success in investments, not simply the infusion of aid into our economies. Aid that is not synchronised effectively with investments and capital accumulation remains simply what it is: aid. Aid can help the state to develop the capacity to deliver certain services that improve the environment for private sector investments. For example, the

---

4   Lee Kwan Yew, *Singapore Story: From the Third to the First World, 1965-2000* (New York: Prentice Hall, 1998).

Roads 2000 project in Kenya that is financed by the Swedish Government can help build rural access roads that will make it easier for farmers to deliver their commodities to the market. With improved market access, farmers can be able, like the case of my mother that I referred to earlier, to create wealth and generate employment more successfully.

If we remain focused on wealth and employment creation as the foundation for rapid economic growth in Africa, then we shall be able to remove all kinds of cobwebs from our eyes and see our future more clearly. We shall then also be able to see why we need regional economic integration, and the vital role that infrastructure plays in this, as a way of fortifying the home market for enhancing wealth and employment creation. We shall also seek to reduce the transfer of our wealth to the OECD economies through such sinister processes as debt servicing for debts already more than over paid, tied aid and over valued technical assistance, unequal exchange in the international trade architecture, and the continued pillage of our raw materials by multinationals as is currently happening in the Democratic Republic of Congo.

If indeed the OECD governments accept that the twenty-first century must be a world of global partnership so as to secure the century for all humanity – which we must – then all of us should revisit that speech that Secretary of State George Marshall gave at Harvard University in 1947 with regard to reconstruction and development in Europe after World War II. He called on the USA to grant Europe billions of dollars to reconstruct its battered economy, infrastructure and social services. Marshall feared that if this were not done, Europe would continue to be a threat to global peace and prosperity. But the European states had to be democratic, respect human rights and be properly managed.

I do not think that the devastation that Europe underwent during the War is any greater than what Africa underwent from slavery, through colonialism to imperialist underdevelopment that has continued to bedevil us since the end of that war. Chancellor Gordon Brown seems to have reconciled himself to this historical reality, and has rightly called for Africa's Marshall Plan (or should we call it "Gordon Plan") if indeed the OECD has to graduate from giving Africa inconsequential aid to joining Africa in a massive onslaught to eradicate poverty in our lifetime.

These, I would hasten to add, are issues that we cannot ignore when we are talking about wealth creation and development in Africa. But once more, let not our deliberations be ritualistic; let them be aimed at feeding into our concrete politics of development and the concrete "action plans" that we shall recommend to our governments, private sector and well-meaning development partners.

5

The Economy Will Start Working Once We Understand Its Reality

First published as an article in the Daily Nation, *October 10, 2005*

Jaindi Kisero's bleak statistics column last Wednesday October 8th rang true,[1] but his analysis of the plausible futures for this country fell short of finding underlying causes for the economy's poor performance and therefore solutions to the problems. The column contained several observations, but did not get the cause and effect right. It is true the deficit has resulted in continued government borrowing, but an increase in domestic debt by less than 20 per cent (substantial as this percentage is) cannot be termed exponential. It is true that increased expenditures to a worthy cause (free education) and unexpected recurrent spending increased the public deficit, as did tax shortfall. It is also true that government spends more money than it collects in taxes just as it is true that unlike most countries in the region, the government in Kenya finances its budget shortfalls by borrowing from private savings rather than relying on donor grants. It is also true the economy has been in a secular decline for years, probably since 1973 and cannot be turned around quickly.

However, where Jaindi seems to get mixed up is in explaining the state of today's economic performance. The economy is not performing poorly because there are more bureaucrats at the Ministry of Finance than economists, or the two ministries of finance and planning have been separated. The economy declined most sharply between 1999 and 2002 when there was a single finance and planning ministry. There may be better coordination under one ministry, but some of the most successful economies such as Germany have had separate economy (planning) and finance ministries. The idea of bringing in private sector professionals is helpful, but the sustainable policy making can only take root if the skills and aptitudes are transferred to career technocrats and bureaucrats.

---

1   Jaindi Kisero, "Figures Don't Tell The Whole Story," *Daily Nation,* Oct. 8, 2005

The real issue is a clear and deep understanding of the economy, how it works, and what needs to be done to get it going by the political leadership (the ministers), technocrats (economists) and bureaucrats (administrators). The Economic Recovery Strategy is the beginning of this process, and in it we outline what we think ails the economy and what needs to be done. But understanding the economy is a continuous process, and in disseminating and discussing the strategy with various stakeholders and development partners, an even clearer understanding of what ails it and what needs to be done has emerged, and much of this is contrary to the conventional wisdom that forms the content of Jaindi's article.

It should be clear by now that Kenya is in the midst of a long running deflationary recession. This economic crisis requires a much more subtle treatment than often considered. Take, for example, per capita income and household savings. These have been in decline for the last decade. Following a simple model where my consumption is someone's income, and my savings are someone else's borrowing, as my consumption declines, so does other people's incomes, and as my savings similarly decline, so does the borrowing pool. If this is sustained, a vicious cycle develops where as my income and savings decline, aggregate demand and investment similarly decline, leading to a contraction of the economy with each cycle.

At the same time, on the supply side, the previous regime injected billions of shillings during the Goldenberg crisis and 1992 election into the economy. This created surging inflation in 1993, and sharply depreciated the shilling by nearly 150 per cent, requiring a stringent but largely sterile monetary policy since then to mop up the excess liquidity. While pursuing a stable macroeconomic policy, the previous regime began to pursue a doubly perilous fiscal policy, one in which tax revenues were corruptly plundered in corrupt dealings and public borrowing was undertaken to plug the gaps created. The result is the public debt Jaindi is moaning about, which in the past was mostly about covering up the effects of corruption.

The hot money from corruption (and drugs) created an assets bubble even as the economy was faltering, with prices of land and real estate tripling between 1990 and 2000 when the bubble finally burst. At the same time, both government and private sector fuelled by hot money (either as capital or consumption) continued to borrow even though capital was becoming expensive and assets were overpriced. When the bubble burst in 1999, the results were dramatic. Land and housing prices are now 75 per cent while prices of commercial buildings may have fallen to nearly half of what they were two or three years ago. Most of the private sector borrowing that is interest-rate sensitive (most affected by Central Bank's monetary policy) is either for construction and real estate development or uses real estate as the main collateral. The collapse of cash deposits and T-bills as sources of ready returns is yet another blow to those seeking alternative collateral to real estate. Since 1999, many firms and individuals find themselves doubly exposed, facing declining markets or incomes while having to cope with crippling repayments on declining collateral for money borrowed expensively during the height of the bubble.

The non-performing loans have grown sharply during this period as many firms and individuals simply cannot repay what they borrowed. Several companies have gone bust, tens of thousands of workers have been retrenched, and those companies still in business are now focussing on debt reduction given that real assets are unlikely to recover to 1998-99 prices. T-bills are down to less than 2 per cent, mortgage lending rates between 12-14 per cent away from 18-24 per cent that led to the Donde Bill. Many banks have between 40-60 per cent of available money lying without ready borrowers, leading to sharply falling returns to savings, with the rate from a sizeable fixed deposit dropping from 10-12 per cent in 1998-99 to 2.5-3.5 per cent in 2003.

The reason Jaindi cannot understand why the private sector has not come up to take advantage of the cheap money, is that he may not have understood the real economic phenomenon facing Kenya. What we are facing since the beginning of this millennium is what is sometimes called a "balance sheet recession". Faced with high indebtedness on declining returns and assets, most businesses or individuals prefer to put their businesses and personal finances on a sound footing by paying back debts as quickly as possible. They will cut any costs they can, with individuals reducing consumption and firms retrenching or outsourcing, and use the savings to repay the debt. Companies aggressively pursuing debt reduction will not be in the mood of borrowing, no matter how cheap the capital is. Despite cheap money and willing lenders, most firms and individuals are now in a debt-avoidance mode, reducing outstanding debts while avoiding any new commitments. This explains the paradox whereby money is now at its cheapest ever and yet no one is borrowing.

Moreover, it points to yet another paradox, that a fiscal stimulus is needed and deficit spending is not always bad or fiscal irresponsibility. The low interest rates and high liquidity in banks makes it clear that government borrowing is not crowding the market and has virtually no effect on private sector borrowing but has the added merit of being the only show in town offering some use for the household savings. The composition of deficit spending is the more important factor to consider. Spending on salaries is not the best way to spend this money, but were it's spent on public works, particularly on activities that had an intensive labour input, this would put income into some hands, stimulate demand for goods and services, and in the process create both assets (reducing poverty) and employment. So, the problem is not the financing deficit domestically, it is how such borrowing is used so as to create the right stimulus.

The Economic Recovery Strategy is more than a means to deliver an IMF programme or resume World Bank lending. It is a coherent attempt to begin to deal with the subtleties that underlie the economic difficulties we face, including those I have described above. The government is quite aware of these, and we know that dealing with a private sector balance sheet recession in a deflating economy with serious structural problems and inequities the government must address squarely. At the same time, the public expenditure review will increasingly align policy, taxation, and spending priorities so as to address the structural problems squarely, while the government's investment programme will provide the infrastructural and institutional framework for private sector investment in the economy. The programme will be launched at the Investment Conference to be held on 20-21 November, and to be hosted by His Excellency the President.

Meanwhile the government cannot afford to ignore the scepticism and air of disappointment that characterises media writing and bar-talk. The jaded comments can only be overcome by government's credibility and predictability. The past nine months are just the beginning. I would urge that the sceptics and cynics give us room to establish our credibility through actual accomplishments in the days to come. It may take as many as five years before the results are clearly evident. But it can be done; play your part.

6

Kenya's Economic Recovery Opportunities

*Speech given at the opening of the East African Business Summit, 13
September 2003, at the Mount Kenya Safari Club*

The task of the Kenya Government, like its sister states in East Africa, is achieving high and sustained economic growth that will lead to wealth and employment generation with the overall goal of poverty reduction. This is a monumental task given the status of our economies today.

Reflecting on where we have come from, all the three East African states face a major challenge in improving the welfare for their citizens. Their GNP per capita income levels are currently estimated at about US$ 350, 310 and 260 for Kenya, Tanzania and Uganda, respectively. This compares very poorly with countries such as South Africa and Botswana with a per capita income estimated at $ 2,880 and $3,600 respectively. It is also more disappointing to note that the per capita income for Kenya at independence in 1963, for example, was the same level with that of the South East Asian countries (Malaysia and South Korea) whose per capita incomes are currently estimated at US$ 3,670 and 8,600, respectively.

The welfare of a country is closely related to its economic growth. The Kenyan economy recorded very high growth rates after independence, but the growth momentum was not maintained; for the last two decades the economic performance has been very poor. Kenya's per capita growth rate declined from an average of 3.2 per cent between 1963 and 1972 to a negative growth rate of 1.2 per cent per annum between 1997 and 2001.

Government's reaction

While Uganda and Tanzania recovered in the 1990s and the economies are now growing at reasonable levels, Kenya lagged behind and entered into a low employment-income-savings-investment and growth trap in the 1990s. This is basically what the NARC government inherited in January 2003 when it came into power. In response to this situation, the government has developed an economic recovery strategy referred to as "Economic Recovery Strategy for Wealth and Employment Creation" (ERS) that was launched by His Excellency the President of Kenya, in June this year. The strategy outlines the development strategy and policies that the NARC government plans to pursue in the next five years.

The ERS is based on two main principles. First, respect for democracy. It is recognised that bad governance raises the cost of doing business and discourages credible investors. Second, is the empowerment of the people, particularly with respect to providing them with opportunities to earn incomes and to reduce their levels of poverty. The cornerstone to this strategy is employment creation. These two principles are necessary in providing an enabling environment in order to encourage both domestic and foreign investors. This is important because without investment the desired growth will not take place and without growth there will be no employment opportunities.

The ERS aims not only at breaking the economic growth-investment trap the country is currently in, but also at ensuring social and economic equity to enhance peace, political stability and harmony. Consequently, the government has within the ERS framework identified key policy actions important for ensuring macroeconomic stability, strengthening institutions of governance, improving infrastructure, and raising investment in human capital.

Most important perhaps for the NARC government, is the recognition that the goals of economic growth and employment creation cannot be achieved without the full participation of the private sector. Thus, the private sector has been identified as the engine of growth, wealth creation, employment generation, and hence poverty reduction. The private sector provides the foundation for the government's vision of creating 500,000 jobs annually, achieving an industrialised country status, and enhancing regional economic engagements. The level of interaction between the private sector and the public sector also determines the strides, which our countries can make, not only in improving economic governance, but also in nurturing democratic ideals.

Therefore, the government's vision as defined in the ERS emphasises engagement between the government and the private sector. This is also consistent with Africa's continent-wide vision as prescribed under the New Partnership for Africa's Development (NEPAD). The aim of this strategy is to economically empower Kenyans in both private and public sectors and in all spheres of economic activity. It also aims at providing Kenyans with a democratic political atmosphere under which all citizens can be free to work hard and engage in productive activities to improve their standards of living. The government is also conscious of the fact that achieving economic recovery will require sacrifices, hard work and collaborative effort between the government and the business community. In this regard, the government is ready to play its part and we hope the private sector will do the same.

Fundamentals for investment

The key fundamentals for investment include macroeconomic stability, an environment that encourages competitiveness or reduces costs for doing business, and security both of persons and property. Despite the low economic growth experienced in Kenya in the last decade the macroeconomic fundamentals are currently fairly sound. The key macroeconomic variables such as inflation, exchange rate and interest rate have remained fairly stable and predictable. Inflation rate has declined from 11.2 per cent in 1997 to 7.3 per cent in July 2003 while the 91-day treasury bills rate has declined from 26.4 per cent in December 1997 to less than 1.5 per cent in July 2003.

As a consequence both the overdraft and base lending rates have declined significantly. The overdraft rate, which averaged 30.4 per cent in 1997, declined to 17 per cent in May 2003. The base lending rates have also assumed the same trend and declined significantly within the last 5 years. Although the shilling depreciated between 1995 and 2001, the exchange rate has become stable. The shilling exchange rate averaged 51.4 against the US dollar in 1995, but depreciated to 78.6 in 2001. It has stabilised at this level and the exchange rate in 2003 is expected to average at about 78 shillings per US dollar.

Kenya's investment macroeconomic environment can, therefore, be declared to have improved significantly. However, due to certain constraints, the levels of savings and investments in Kenya have remained pathetically low. The gross investments as a ratio of GDP declined from 21.8 per cent in 1995 to a dismal 13.6 per cent in 2002. This compares very poorly with the 25 per cent gross domestic investments necessary for Kenya to achieve high and sustained economic growth. In addition, the level of Kenya's gross savings as a percentage of GDP declined from 15.4 per cent in 1996 to a meagre 4.6 per cent in 2001 though there was an improvement to 10 per cent in 2002. This is not healthy for an economy that is yearning for industrialisation like Kenya.

Among the reasons for Kenya's poor economic performance include mismanagement and weak institutions of governance, particularly weakening of institutions involved in ensuring public safety, law and order. Security is very important in creating an enabling environment for private sector-led growth and development. Research findings in Kenya indicate that indeed insecurity has been associated with deteriorating performance in leading sectors such as tourism. Furthermore, Kenyan firms spend an average of 4 per cent of their operating income on security, a figure that is fairly high and therefore significantly erodes the profit margins of businesses. In addition, most Kenyan businesses are forced to operate for fewer hours. These factors limit the ability of the private sector in Kenya to create wealth and employment. The situation may not be any better in our sister states within the East African Community. Addressing insecurity has, therefore, become a major concern to the Kenya Government and it is top priority in the ERS.

For the private sector to effectively play its role in wealth creation, the costs of doing business must be reduced for firms to be competitive. For the last two decades, the business community in Kenya has faced a hostile environment characterised by high cost of capital, policy uncertainty, limited market access and poor infrastructure. High domestic borrowing by the previous government was the major cause of the high cost of capital that plunged our economy into the prolonged balance sheet recession we are currently grappling with. This has made it very difficult for the private sector, including micro and small enterprises, to access credit. I am happy to report that this situation is now being reversed and we have seen the rates of interest reducing drastically in the last eight months. I hope the private sector in Kenya, Uganda and Tanzania will take advantage of the low and declining interest rates to expand their businesses or venture into new areas of investment.

The government is also dealing with the issue of access to capital through mobilisation of savings. During the next five years, it will take urgent measures to enhance public savings and reduce public consumption so that substantial resources can be availed for domestic capital formation. In line with this policy, the government will also seek to enhance the confidence of the public to participate in the Nairobi Stock Exchange (NSE). After eight months in office, the government is encouraged by the confidence of Kenyans as underscored by increased investments.

At independence, the government realised that both physical and social infrastructure is extremely vital for the creation of wealth and development.

However, over the years, these arteries of our economy were ignored or run down. As a consequence the costs of transport, water and electricity in Kenya are generally high when compared to the major competitors in regional and international trade.

The government has embarked on a massive physical infrastructure rehabilitation programme to improve the quality of our dilapidated infrastructure. This will reduce the cost of doing business in Kenya and promote competitiveness of our products in the region and in the world markets. The government is determined to create a friendly and affordable environment for investment and doing business in Kenya through increased investments in infrastructure. This will lead to improved efficiency and productivity in key sectors such as agriculture, trade, industry, tourism, mining and other services so that more Kenyans can be productively employed. Just this week, after detailed and prolonged discussions with professionals and consultants, the government took the daring step of restructuring the balance sheets of both the Kenya Power and Lighting Company and KenGen as part of a comprehensive programme to bring down the cost of energy to the consumer as well as to business enterprises. The details are spelt out to the private sector in our investment programme and will no doubt feature prominently during the discussions at the Investment Conference.

Another fundamental pillar in investment is strengthening of institutions of governance. Weak institutions are the breeding grounds for corruption, which is costly not only to business, but also to the government. While this might have been tolerated in the past, the new government is putting efforts to strengthen the institutional, legal and regulatory framework to eliminate this vice. It is important to reiterate that our commitment to stop corruption and mismanagement in government is resolute.

Priority actions on the governance front include implementation of the provisions of the Anti-corruption and Economic Crimes Act and the Public Officer's Ethics Act that were recently enacted; strengthening the security agencies; strengthening the justice administration agencies; and harmonisation of laws. The government also recognises that too many laws and regulations can be an impediment to doing business. As a result, a review of the regulatory agencies, which govern the operation of many business activities, is a major activity to be undertaken in the next five years. The government will submit bills to Parliament to provide the needed institutional and legal framework for reforms. Key among these is the Privatisation Bill. The government will also establish a commission to review all business-related regulations, covering both legal and institutional aspects. The findings will be used to formulate a strategy and action plan to address impediments caused by such regulations.

Many opportunities exist in agriculture for expanding and increasing output for domestic and international markets, particularly horticulture. Interventions in agriculture will focus on providing a single enabling legislation to replace the large number of existing legislations in the sector, rationalising roles and functions of agricultural institutions to empower poor farmers and increase institutional efficiency, strengthening extension services and increasing smallholder access to credit.

Interventions in the manufacturing sector will be built around an Industrial Master Plan, which will lay the groundwork for the first phase of Kenya's industrialisation strategy where small and medium enterprises are expected to grow rapidly. The government will promote micro and small enterprises (MSE) sector on the basis of the recommendations in the Sessional Paper on the sector, which focuses on employment creation, and formalisation of informal activities. The tourism sector will be promoted through increased funding for marketing, upgrading the tourist police force to make it more effective, and diversification of markets, both in terms of geographical distribution and customer base. With Kenya Airways now flying to Hong Kong and Bangkok, we expect an inflow of tourists from Asia coming to visit East Africa.

The government will also be putting in place an Investment Code to consolidate investment incentives, protection and institutional framework in a single legislation to establish a one-stop office for investment promotion activities. We hope that we will also be able to have a harmonised investment code for the East African Community. Export promotion will be carried out within the framework of an export development strategy to ensure maximum export earnings are achieved from minimal promotional costs.

The state of the financial sector is very important in supporting economic recovery. Financial sector reform will be built around a Financial Sector Assessment Programme (FSAP), which will identify the strengths, weaknesses and synergies in the sector. Among the issues to be considered are whether there is adequate justification for an overall financial sector regulator. Financial sector reform will also concentrate on reducing the interest rate spread, enhancing investor confidence and consumer protection in the sector, dealing with the problem of non-performing loans (NPLs) and creating an independent insurance regulator.

To enhance human development and improve literacy levels the government has implemented free primary school education programme, which has registered great success. The next stage is to initiate a National Social and Health Insurance Scheme (NSHIS) that will ensure all our citizens have access to proper and sustainable health care. This is expected to increase labour productivity in our economy.

Investment incentives

The Kenya Government has been providing *investment allowance* in the manufacturing and hotel sectors at the rate of 100 per cent for the period July 2000 to December 2001 and 85 per cent for 2002. Targets for 2003 and 2004 are 70 per cent and 60 per cent, respectively. Eligible capital expenditures have been expanded to include certain infrastructure and environmental protection equipment related to manufacturing activities. The main incentives programmes for investors for export promotion include Duty Remission Facility (DRF), Manufacturing under Bond (MUB), and Export Processing Zones (EPZs) programme.

You may also wish to know that exports from Kenya enjoy preferential market access to world markets under a number of special access and duty reduction programme. In the *regional markets*, Kenya is a member of the East African Community (EAC) with a population of 80 million people and COMESA with a population of about 380 million. Exports and imports within member countries enjoy preferential tariff rates. Kenya continues to enjoy preferential trading arrangements with the European Union countries under the ACP-EU Cotonou Agreement whereby exports into the EU face preferential tariffs. Under African Growth and Opportunity Act (AGOA), Kenya qualifies for duty free access to the US market for a wide range of products including textiles, apparels, handicrafts, etc.

Kenya's manufactured goods are also entitled to preferential duty treatment in the USA, Japan, Canada, New Zealand, Australia, Switzerland, Norway, Sweden, Finland, Austria, and other European countries under the Generalised System of Preferences (GSP). In addition, no quantitative restrictions are applicable to Kenyan exports on any of the 3,000-plus items currently eligible for GSP treatment.

Challenges to the private sector

The government has in the ERS blueprint tried as much as possible to respond to the challenges faced by the private sector in its investment efforts. However, there are also a number of challenges that the private sector should deal with to develop an effective partnership with the government. I now turn to these challenges, which I believe it needs to deal with to take advantage of the opportunities offered by the government.

The biggest challenge to the Kenyan private sector is to respond to the opportunities offered by government, some of which I have outlined. However, the response has been somewhat slower than anticipated. This could point to lack of capacity of existing private sector to invest in large projects like roads; lack of risk mitigation strategies; or due to market fundamentals that may dissuade investment. Unfortunately, there are limited concerted efforts to see how these investment risks could be minimised or spread possibly through private-private sector risk sharing and public–private sector partnerships. At this Business Summit, we need to discuss these forms of partnerships and propose concrete projects.

Quite importantly the private sector can exploit private-public partnership in provision of certain goods and services. Though the government may have the monopoly of providing goods and services of pure public goods nature such as security, law enforcement and defence, private-public partnership in provision of impure public goods such as sanitation, roads and water, is plausible.

Pure public goods like defence — once provided — the government cannot exclude anyone from enjoying the service. Private investment in such goods may not be profitable because production may lead to undersupply and under consumption due to the free rider problem. But, for largely impure public goods (e.g. water, roads, etc.), government provision may also be less than efficient, due to the extra cost and free rider problems. The private provision of such services may also lead to undersupply and the supply may not be efficient in distributive terms, especially to the poor. Thus, private-public partnership in provision of these goods leads to better outcomes, and it is quite desirable to do so.

Thus, alongside some investments being of strategic interest to the state and requiring large capital outlays, there is a strong argument for private-public partnership in provision of services like, air transport, water and sanitation, road provision and transport, security, telecommunications among others. There are some outstanding examples of private-public sector partnership in Kenya today, which are worth emulating. The Kenya Airways is a classic example of a success of private-public partnership in provision of a service. Here, the government sold some of its stake in the company to the private sector as part of its privatisation programme. In such a company the governments role is quite important in that it is able to bail out such a strategic company in times of emergency like the one occasioned by the September 11 terrorist attacks in the United States. The private sector management of the enterprise on its part eliminates government bureaucracy, which can lead to inefficiencies in operations.

Other private-public investments that followed liberalisation of the Kenyan economy and legislative and regulatory amendments include those in the mobile telephone providers, investments in telecommunications and in the energy sectors, where the government is either in partnership or is in close supervision of the provision of such services. In the roads sector, in particular, there are plans for concessioning of some parts of the road network. A good example is the planned Mombasa-Malaba highway, which is earmarked for conversion into a dual-carriage-way. Private-public partnerships can also be explored in other sectors, such as water provision, railway transport and marine transport, and security among others.

So I urge the private sector to explore opportunities for profit-making in agriculture, trade, manufacturing, and in the social sectors. Public-private partnerships in education provision and in health could also be explored without jeopardising quality and access to these services. For example, Kenyatta National Hospital is a case where the government also provides a private doctors section to encourage public-private sector partnership. (But such partnerships can only perform well if both partners are committed to an honest delivery of services and maximisation of efficiency for decently making profits.)

Although private-public partnerships are a great opportunity for the private sector, there are still many hurdles to overcome. For example, there is mistrust between the private sector and the government – stemming from some hang-ups from the previous regime. When the private sector came close to collaboration with the previous government, there is today almost a story to tell about massive corruption. Where there were rather cordial relationships between government and the private entrepreneurs (contractors, suppliers, etc), graft oiled the relationship. The role of international financial institutions in supporting the Independent Power Producers in the early 1990s was a case of literally going to bed with corruption write large. KPLC and KenGen have had to pay dearly for this unholy marriage.

55

Thus, the issues of concern in my opinion are, for example, can the private sector engage the government in a clean and mutually beneficial business? Does the private sector also have the capacity to check its members who may not know fair play? Further, will the private sector muster the courage to invest in low-return projects like roads or railways, without soiling itself in graft?

The other problem underlies a weak private sector advocacy or distortions in such advocacy. Apart from being a little fragmented, the private sector may have little in common thus denying them a common voice. Success of this advocacy needs to spring from strong within-private sector partnerships. The emergence of the Kenya Private Sector Alliance (KEPSA) recently, for example, is important in this respect. A unified voice among different interest groups is useful not only in engaging government, but also in providing a self-regulating mechanism within private sector. The partnership could also foster more useful involvement of the private sector in policy formulation process and in writing laws and regulations.

Interaction within the private sector should also be guided by principles of self-help, self-responsibility, equity and solidarity. Governments also require the private sector to observe greater self-responsibility. For example, though the private sector complains about high domestic borrowing pushing up the interest rates, some sections of the private sector do not pay up taxes, which would seal the fiscal deficits thereby having positive effect on the interest rates. The private sector should establish corporate values that can make it lead in good governance at all levels.

On employment creation, the private sector's role cannot be overstated. For example, with a 20 per cent rate of unemployment, we can underscore the fact that Kenya is a fertile ground for cheap labour and a profitable place for labour-intensive production. Furthermore, the minimum wages are not prohibitive by international standards. But do firms consider labour-intensive production, which will have a dent on unemployment and reduce crime, or to what extent are firms taking advantage of this to pay low wages or deny workers welfare enhancing services?

There has also been a tendency for the private sector to over-interpret the heat in the political environment, not realising that in a post-authoritarian transition, the explosion of freedoms always leads to inflation of political demands.[1]

---

1   P. Anyang' Nyong'o, "Address to the members of the National Assembly of the Republic of Rwanda," Kigali, 8th April, 2003.

Conclusion

The Government of Kenya is determined to provide an enabling environment for investors to help in achieving the objectives spelt out in the ERS. Both domestic and international investors should, therefore, take advantage of opportunities offered by the government, and the position and facilities available in Kenya. Moreover Kenya's macroeconomic and political stability coupled with the existing guarantees for investors should make it an attractive investment destination. The government is willing and ready to listen to investors to know if there are any additional incentives they would like to enable them join us in developing this beloved country.

I wish to report that the government is now determined to reverse the past poor investment environment but the success will require strong partnership with the private sector. This is the spirit behind the proposal to establish the National Economic and Social Council (NESC), which is aimed at strengthening the relationship between the government, the private sector and the civil society. The Council will encourage dialogue between the government and stakeholders in economic management.

7

The Importance of Diversified Financial Systems for African Development

Address given to the Fifth African Venture Capital Conference,
Whitesands Hotel, Mombasa, 7 November 2005

We need to be expressly honest about the role venture capital plays in Africa's development at the moment; it is a very limited one. For instance, there is the now ended Africa Project Development Finance (APDF) set up by the International Finance Corporation (IFC), and other private equity firms, yet their overall effect, at least in Kenya, has not been substantial. Let me explain what I mean by this. It is my understanding that there would be no Microsoft, Apple Computers, Google, Yahoo, eBay, and a host of other globally acknowledged names, if it were not for the role played by venture capitalists when these firms were in their formative stages.

Today, it is hard for me to think of African firms that have grown and become big and stable companies because of the support of IFC or any other venture capital organisation. Instead, the venture capitalist tends to be government, in the form of investing in poorly managed and financed parastatals which were started a generation ago, to give the Africans a foothold in the modern economy, a promise that has unfortunately not been well-delivered in the majority of cases. To be honest, the promise has not been well delivered because the government in most cases is a particularly poor venture capitalist, with a limited understanding of commercial value and practices, and even less of how to make money from the initial investment made. This situation is not made any easier by our chequered history of political patronage that makes it impossible to select the best managers for public corporations. Indeed, even where the government has been eventually forced to privatise, either through private threat with its business partner, or outright sale, or through an initial public offering (IPO) on the stock exchange, it never realises the type of value and return a private equity firm may have earned.

It is my submission that without venture capital, many of our small and medium-sized entrepreneurs who could have grown into national and continental icons have either shrivelled and died because commercial banks would not support them or they have remained stunted, growing largely on profits and shareholders loans. The continent is actually full of these dwarfed enterprises, an embarrassing testimony to colossal waste of entrepreneurial talent and a terrible catastrophe of jobs and skills not created which in turn is a major contributor to the menace of poverty that we face in the country. It is in this connection that I must single out the importance of one recent initiative that my ministry has been associated with: the Kenya Business Incubation project designed to nurture small businesses into successful enterprises. In similar breath, I also do hope that the noble idea of Science Parks already mooted by the community of scientists at our national universities will receive the necessary support from the government, and in turn from venture capitalist so that some of the promising scientific research can be nurtured into viable inventions and enterprises.

I want to note that our other source of finance has been aid, which as you all will appreciate, is probably the most inefficient way to support small and medium enterprises (SMEs). The gains from the various SMEs and private sector programmes have been minimal, and again, in the Kenyan context, these have barely been noticed by the majority of the 20,000 plus SME owners. In my view, aid as a means of supporting the business community is better off spent doing the non-business things such as infrastructure, institution building and educating our people. Surprisingly, it is exceedingly rare for any donor to provide scholarships for MBAs, probably with good reason that such scholars may not come back home, but the question must be asked: without sound business knowledge, how will Africans ever become competitive entrepreneurs on the global scene?

With government and aid money providing the bulk of business and enterprise development finance, one can say that opportunities for growth in Africa are highly limited unless one has access to commercial bank loans or unless one has one's firm listed in a dynamic stock exchange or is able to attract private equity partners. The latter three financiers are poorly developed. The commercial banks rarely touch African businesses, and when they do, they charge interest rates that make the return on investment difficult.

In addition, few locally owned firms are listed on bourses, either because the conditions are too tight, or they are too small, or the owners are not keen on giving up ownership. Alternative listings also do not work that well. The market for commercial paper and other debentures is limited, and venture capitalists are few, sometimes, even communally selective, and not a major player for the majority of businesses in our countries. With perhaps the exception of South Africa, there are few African countries where the conditions I have enumerated do not prevail.

The foregoing should not be a cause for despair, rather it is meant to challenge you over the next two days, to seriously ask yourselves several questions; for instance, what is the role of venture capital in countries with poorly developed economies and systems? Does this require innovative forms and risk-taking not undertaken in other parts of the world to reach and support SMEs in Africa? How do we get venture capital to support African entrepreneurs in equal measure? Is there any role for government to making venture capital a reality for African SMEs, and what should African governments do as an absolute minimum to encourage such ventures? Also, can aid really play a constructive role in achieving these desired outcomes?

The whole issue of microfinancing is important but still misses the point about nurturing and growing SMEs. Microfinancing through group-based lending of small amounts of money is of course great for the informal sector, but it cannot really be the way for SMEs. Commercial banks that are only interested in already established large firms do not have much time for SMEs either. If this seminar finds the answer to the missing middle puzzle on who will finance and nurture SMEs who are too big for microfinancing and too risky for commercial banks AVCA will have made an important contribution towards a brighter future for Africa.

In conclusion, unless the financial systems in Africa are diversified, deepened and widened to include financing for the entire scope of enterprises, Africa's future development will remain stunted.

II

THE CHALLENGE OF DEVELOPMENT

8

Who Will Speak on Behalf of Kenya?

*Speech given at the launch of UAP Insurance at the Carnivore
Restaurant, Nairobi, 14 June 2005*

Many years ago, at the dawn of the history of colonial Kenya, a young man called Delamere arrived in this country intent on making a success career as a farmer and a cattle rancher. History has it that he arrived without much more than his determination and some family fortune to fall back on. But he was ready to risk much to realise his dream. Let us not forget that he was also lucky: the land that was key to his eventual success was more or less a Christmas present handed over to him by colonial authorities.

Having lost a good part of his herd and after many years of frustration, Delamere became a leading Kenyan farmer, and his name lives on today, either to be celebrated by the high and mighty within the Kenyan elite, or to be looked upon as part of an out-of-date colonial culture that is best tucked away in the pages of history. The question worth asking is: when Delamere made his daring moves and investments, what insurance did he have? Who insured his risks?

I dare say that the answer is likely to be "Nobody", at least in those early days. And even now, few farmers enjoy the luxury of insurance that modern industry and services enjoy. Indeed, there is something that the business community call "investment climate". This, indeed, is a form of insurance that businessmen usually seek to ascertain before risking their capital into any venture.

But when Delamere came to Kenya, I wonder whether he asked about the "investment climate" in Kenya. I remember addressing an investment conference at Marlborough House in London last year. After a whole morning of talking, and I was with my colleagues Mukhisa Kituyi, John Githongo and Ongong'a Achieng', I felt satisfied that we had successfully sold Kenya to this audience. But just before lunch, a hand shot up with an urgent question. The question was: can you assure us, Mr. Minister, that our investments would be safe in Kenya?

I felt frustrated because I thought this is what we had been doing the whole morning: giving these white people assurances about Kenya by talking to them in detail about the government, the laws, the investment code etc; a luxury that Delamere never enjoyed. My answer to this fellow was: I am surprised that we no longer have risk takers and real entrepreneurs among foreign investors like in Delamere's days.

I believe that those of you who are in the insurance industry do not see insurance as an end in itself but as a means to an end. You must see insurance as surviving only when the people of Kenya are surviving. You must see insurance as thriving when the people of Kenya are thriving. You must regard the insurance industry as growing when the economy of Kenya is growing. So you cannot be in the industry and be a real insurance entrepreneur if you are not, at the same time, a person who has an abiding faith in your country and her future. You are not the kind of person who, at the end of the day, will begin doubting whether it is worth it putting your bet on the future of Kenyan industries, Kenyan farmers and Kenyan workers.

To be in the insurance industry is to be able to stand up and speak for your country. By speaking for your country I do not mean defending your country even when things are going wrong, but being able to stand up and be counted for both the good and the bad that we go through as part and parcel of our own history of becoming a nation — modern, prosperous, just and fair. We live at a time when scepticism about ourselves and our potential to achieve lofty goals is becoming a venerable religion of the faint hearted. We live at a time when appearances are fast giving way to reality in the daily discourse about what goes on around us that we are almost making scientists superfluous and the analytical minds irrelevant.

I say this because it is shocking to see how the elite and the press usually speak about important things in the life of this nation as if they are trivia; and trivia, on the other hand, is elevated to the level of big news and momentous happenings. I suppose such level of discourse is quite excusable in advanced societies where many important issues were settled many decades ago, and public discourse can occupy itself with trivia without substantially affecting the history of such societies.

We, however, are yet to make important decisions in the making of our own history, such as the constitution, national values, the status of the citizen, the province of private property, the creation of wealth and so on. We cannot, therefore, have the luxury of playing with words by trivialising social discourse.

I do not, thereby, mean that we cannot indulge in amusement, entertainment and light talk. Far be it for me to suggest that. But I seriously want us to insure our future by building on solid rock rather than shifting sand. And we cannot build on solid rock if we do not cultivate some level of seriousness in discussing public issues, some level of commitment to certain values that we cherish and that create the ties that bind us as a nation.

Somebody, therefore, must stand up and speak for Kenya. Somebody must become a Kenyan even when others are reluctant to do so. Within the mosaic of our beautiful national cultures: the various languages, jokes, music, physical talents etc, we must weave a political order that respects individual and people's rights. It is this positive attitude that the insurance industry and its entrepreneurs need to cultivate because your industry is about the future. Your industry builds on positive scenarios not negative ones. Your industry cannot sit at the same table and dine with sceptics; it must, per force, entertain the gods of optimism and the soothsayers of good fortunes.

I am, for that matter, very disappointed by the finance ministers of the G8 who are reported to have decided to cancel the debts of the Highly Indebted Poor Countries in Africa while leaving the burden of debt repayment to those countries, like Kenya, which have been faithful in servicing their debts. I do believe, like I stated to the African group in the House of Commons last year, that debt is debt whether by the lowly indebted or the highly indebted for it aggravates poverty in both countries. The enemy of humankind today is poverty. Indeed, the biggest threat to global peace and security is poverty and not terrorism, since terrorism needs the environment of poverty and relative deprivation to survive.

Kenya has done all she can to bring peace within the East African Region and the Horn of Africa. For this task, carried out patiently for many years, and with a great deal of sacrifice, the OECD governments should have helped Kenya carry on the struggle for peace by cancelling the debt. In any case, the US and the UK Governments have already shown the world that they are very capable of mobilising Coalitions of the Willing against threats to world peace when necessary. They have done this in the case of terrorism. A coalition of the willing against poverty as a threat to global peace is long overdue. I hope it will be born at the G8 meeting in Gleneagles in Scotland early next month.

For those of us who believe this, let us stand up and speak for Kenya to insure and guarantee our common future in a world that is threatened by scepticism and almost grounded in the lamentations of the past.

9

Technology, Culture and National Development in Africa

Speech given at the Bassey Andah Memorial Lecture, University of Calabar, Calabar, Nigeria, 5 January 2006

I am now reminded, many years after I graduated from primary school in a rural homestead in Kenya, somewhere around Lake Victoria perched right on the Equator in a little village called Ratta, that the colonial chief warned us that we would never become an independent nation. His reasoning was quite simple: the black man has never learnt even how to make a needle. How could he pretend to know how to run a modern government?

The District Commissioner, who was a white man, made matters even look gloomier regarding our future in colonial Kenya. He gathered the people in what is known as the chief's *baraza* (meeting) and warned us that natives must know that the white man has the superiority of the gun; bows, arrows and spears, may be weapons of war and defence in Africa, but they are no match to the smoking pipe from which bullets fly with fury to finish anybody on their path. To add insult to injury, he reminded us that the Mau Mau rebellion in Kenya in the early 1950s had become a cropper against the white man's technological might! Technology, therefore, was associated with power, might, superiority, political oppression, dominance and the white man when I was growing up. It was something "out there" to which we could aspire but might never get. It was part of an alien civilisation.

In school we were taught Mathematics, Religion, History, English, Geography, something called Rural Science and Civics. These were things that one had to learn to be able to go about as a "modern man" in colonial Kenya. These things would make one get a job, stand for elections to parliament or the district council, go into the post office and send a letter to Nairobi and, of course, listen to the radio and read newspapers.

The science and technology behind the publication of the newspaper did not worry us. How the postal system ran was the headache of the postmaster and not us. The train that took one to Nairobi was an alien machine that made travelling easier than walking. Why we never had it in our own societies did not really worry our minds. These were the results of Western progress that made it possible for them to cross the oceans and "discover us", bringing us — by force as well as persuasion — into their own "civilisations."

Yet when I later read Basil Davidson's many historical treatises on Africa,[1] and I added to them Walter Rodney's *How Europe Underdeveloped Africa*,[2] I realised that the origin of man was in East Africa, at a place called Olduvai Gorge, and the Kenyan anthropologist Louis Leakey had gone to great lengths to provide evidence to this effect. As man developed beyond being a mere ape, he used tools and started conquering nature for his own survival. These tools were the results of conceptual thinking, not of the white man as such, but of man the *Homo sapiens*, the descendant of the *Homo habilis* and the *Homo erectus*, essentially a creature of Africa. The development of technology and culture, as Marx and Engels[3] remind us, has nothing to do with racial superiority, but with *man the producer*, whether in Africa, Europe or Asia. But when the story of man came to be written, albeit by various people at different times and seeking to achieve different objectives, they brought in racial biases that sought to demarcate certain races as having advanced (progressed) much faster than others because they were better masters of "modern technology".

A close look at European history, as Professor Andah observed in his 1992 study of *Nigeria's Indigenous Technology*,[4] reveals that the modern Western concept of progress is pragmatic, empiricist, scientific, exploitive and elitist. It is *pragmatic* because this view of progress is mainly preoccupied with material gains and practical improvement for the immediate future. It is *empiricist* because the world is viewed through the empiricist spectacles as basically made of physical matter interacting in a mechanical fashion. It is *scientific* because the laws of (physical) science are thought to be of supreme importance, being the tools of which men manipulate the physical universe to their advantage. It is *exploitive* because the natural resources and subtle balances of the ecosystem

---

1   See, for example, Basil Davidson, *The Black Man's Burden: Africa and the Curse of the Nation-State* (New York, Times Books, 1993); *The African Genius: An Introduction to African Culture and Social History,* (Boston: Little, Brown and Co., 1970).

2   Walter Rodney, *How Europe Underdeveloped Africa* (Dar es Salaam: Tanzania Publishing House, 1973).

3   See, for example, Yujiru Hayami, *Development Economics: From the Poverty to the Wealth of Nations,* (Oxford: Oxford University Press, 2005).

4   B.W. Andah, *Nigeria's Indigenous Technology* (Ibadan: Ibadan University Press, 1992).

have been taken for granted and indeed treated in a nonchalant, ruthless and high-handed manner characteristic of *conquistadors*. It is *elitist* because this progress has actually benefited very few at the expense of very many and at the expense of natural resources belonging to all.[5]

We in Africa did not escape the impact of this empiricist, exploitive and elitist model of progress. Our societies grew on this template, and far-reaching economic, social, political and cultural impacts followed. Frantz Fanon saw how the psychology of the colonised was messed up by the growth of society on this template. In *Black Skins White Masks*,[6] he observes how the black man's inner world of thought, images, values and perception is taken over by this Western mode of thought and "civilisation". The black man, as it were, is dehumanised and cannot really discover for himself his own future unless he decolonises his mind. This psychological colonisation inhibits the African from advancing technologically, giving up on science as something beyond his reach, and being content to go only as far as administering the instruments of oppression that white colonialism has put up to keep him in positions of servitude.

Walter Rodney, in analysing the history of Africa from pre-colonial to post-colonial times, sees the incorporation of Africa into European development through imperialism as essentially a process of under-developing Africa.[7] This process has not really come to an end. It continues given the technological superiority of the West over Africa, and the unequal trade and exchange that globalisation imposes on Africa. Combined with the psychological oppression, this objective underdevelopment creates a much more burdensome situation for Africa to develop than can easily be discerned from casual observation.

Thus, both at the subjective level of conceptualising reality and the objective level of interacting with other human societies through trade, politics and economic well-being, the African person has to deal with this historical past and structural intermeshing with Western civilisations. It comes in the form of language and modes of thought. It comes in the form of ceremonies, dress and perceptions of success. It comes in the form of institutions and what we regard as modern. It comes, finally, in terms of what we regard as belonging to the public domain and the private one; what governments exist to do and what families, individuals and communities should do for themselves.

---

5   H. Skolimowski, "The Scientific World View and the Illusions of Progress", *Social Research,* 41 (1974):52-82.

6   F. Fanon, *Black Skin White Masks* (London: Penguin, 1967).

7   W. Rodney, *How Europe Underdeveloped Africa* (Dar es Salaam: Tanzania Publishing House, 1973).

Progress, at its barest minimum, means improvement. Going from good to better is making progress. Thus, humans progressed from being scavengers on nature using simple tools to exploiters of nature using labour saving devices called *machines*. But in that process of making progress, they started subjugating others to servitude and to force them to survive below human existence. This is the misgiving we now have about the Western heritage of progress and its cultural and ideological expression in capitalism and what Max Weber called *the protestant ethic*.[8] Karl Marx and Friedrich Engels went further than that. They saw the inequality and social injustices that capitalist progress brought to Europe as essentially a breeding ground for revolution.[9][25] To avert this revolution, Lenin later argued, Europeans exported their class contradictions to their Third World colonies through imperialism.[10]

Yet science and technology need not be used permanently as tools of domination, exploitation and under-development. In attempts to restructure the production and use of knowledge, the United Nations, after World War II created organisations that had the aim of making technology and the fruits of progress *to serve humanity, to turn swords into ploughshares* as it were. Where there was war, mankind had to sow peace; where there is hatred, love; where there is sadness, joy; where there is disease, health; where there is poverty, plenty; and where there is backwardness and inequality, progress and social equity.

A global political culture of mutual social responsibility and shared progress was expected to be promoted by such UN bodies as the United Nations Development Programme (UNDP), the Food and Agricultural Organisation (FAO), United Nations Educational, Social and Cultural Organisation (UNESCO), United Nations Children's Fund (UNICEF), the World Health Organisation (WHO), and many others. The Bretton Woods institutions, which include the World Bank and the International Monetary Fund (IMF), were both meant to fund development and to stabilise the international financial system respectively, all with the aim of creating a global culture of progress for all humankind irrespective of race, history or cultural heritage.

The history of the world since World War II has not been written according to the optimists who established the UN system. Here we are in Africa, after contributing so much to the world economy and global civilisation, still lagging

---

8   M. Weber, *The Protestant Ethic and the Spirit of Capitalism*, translated from the original German by Talcott Persons (New York: Scribner's Press, 1958).

9   The idea by Marx and Engels that Capitalism breeds its own "grave diggers" — the working class — is poignantly expressed in *The Manifesto of the Communist Party* (Moscow: Progress Publishers, 1968).

10 V.I. Lenin, *Imperialism: The Highest Stage of Capitalism* (Moscow: Progress Publishers, 1968).

behind as technologically the most backward continent in the world. Plagued by famine, ravished by floods, invaded by diseases that were eliminated by science from the face of the earth some years ago, and wasting our environment with little concern nor knowledge that it is in our interest to sustain it, Africa seems to languish in the past as other societies benefit from technological progress in improving the livelihood of their peoples.

The technology of irrigation cannot be rocket science thousands of years after Hammurabi; the Egyptians have made effective use of it so as to turn the waters of the Nile into the lifeline of desert agriculture that makes it possible for Egypt to be her own bread basket. Egypt stands out as a lone example in Africa. Kenya could follow suit so as to make this irrigation technology banish drought-induced famine to the museum of its history so that no more human and animal life is lost simply because the rains fail.

It is ironical that when it rains, western Kenya suffers from severe floods making people flee from their homes leaving behind hard-earned wealth and turning to emergency aid as their only source of livelihood as they move into camps for internally displaced persons. When the sun strikes with a vengeance these same people face drought and have to beg for external aid to survive on the very environment they fled from when water was in plenty. In either case, a more appropriate taming of nature by technology and a scientific management of nature's predictable changes would make these same people live more stably.

It is quite often said that such progressive use of technology has not occurred in many parts of Africa because of poverty. The culture of poverty confines the poor to live almost fatally in a pre-technological environment, marking time in a vicious cycle of poverty. Yet this cannot be really truth since from these so called *cultures of poverty* emerge men and women with doctorates of philosophy in some of the most sophisticated scientific subjects. Within these so-called backward societies people tune on radio stations listening to news in diverse languages from many corners of the world. The lack of rapid advancement in development, science and technology needs to be explained by other variables other than poverty itself, or the so-called inability of these cultures to absorb and use technological innovations. We need to look at the history, the global environment, the political power structures, and the cultural predispositions as some of the key variables.

First, of course, is our history: if Africa had been allowed to develop the way she was doing under the kingdoms in West Africa and the savannah civilisations her levels of technological achievement would be different today. But these are the *ifs* of history that would not help us much today to shape up and get on with the job. If slavery and the slave trade had not disrupted socio-economic progress in the vibrant parts of Africa, maybe matters would be different today in terms of development and technological advancement. After all, Great Britain, with so much superior military might, could not subdue the Kingdom of Buganda at the end of the 19th century and had to banish the *Kabaka* (Buganda's king) to the Seychelles to get a foothold in the kingdom. Where would Buganda be today had the British not interfered with its forward march into the modern world? Such questions and arguments may be good for putting our case for "reparation" from the Western imperialists, but they may not be very useful in getting our acts together today to galvanise our cultures and peoples in the fight against poverty and for development based on technological advancement.

Second is our current location in the globalised village called the *world economy* that makes us start off as underdogs in world trade in goods and services as well as in international politics. What Samir Amin once called *accumulation on a world scale* still lives with us.[11] Its effects are dramatised everyday, either on the floor of negotiations at the World Trade Organisation or when IMF/World Bank missions visit poor African countries to rescue them from "balance of payment crises". One only needs to read Joseph Stiglitz to see how these "economic missionaries" hardly solve the problems of the poor and merely do "rescue operations" in the interest of global capital.[12]

Third is our own cultural and political inertia to confront and deal with these problems in a way that can rescue Africa from the current predicament through what Mahathir Mohammed, once Prime Minister of Malaysia, called *smart partnership* with the globe. Prime Minister Mahathir's idea was that the developing countries can actually leap-frog from their present predicament of backwardness and underdevelopment if they related to each other as smart partners, and if they adopted internal policies and programmes that are consciously aimed at pushing them into the same levels of development as their imperialist adversaries in the long run. In less than twenty years Malaysia has developed from a poor Third World country into a medium income modern society that will say goodbye to poverty before 2015.

What is the secret behind Malaysia's success? A political leadership capable of putting science and technology at the forefront of national development and ensuring that all national potential for development are optimally utilised, chief

---

11 S. Amin, *Accumulation on a World Scale* (New York: Monthly Review Press, 1974).

12 J. Stiglitz, *Globalization and Its Discontents* (New York: Penguin Books, 2002).

among these is the development of human resources. Malaysia's investment in education: primary, secondary, tertiary and university level education is something that should be a lesson to Africa. Second is her investment in infrastructure and national integration, making sure that agriculture and industrial production is stimulated by a home market which works, first and foremost because the people can feed themselves and produce enough for domestic consumption as well as for exports. Third is her use of science and technology to position Malaysia strategically in the global market, particularly in the telecommunications sector and the out-sourcing business. These are all the results of conscious planning by a *political leadership* acutely aware that poverty can only be fought with concrete policies at a particular conjuncture in history.

When the African Academy of Sciences (AAS) was founded in the mid-1980s, I had the privilege of serving as its first Head of Programmes. Our aim was, among other things, to champion a *science-led development process in Africa* believing full well that without science and technology, little would happen in Africa in terms of eradicating poverty. The founding President, Professor T.R. Odhiambo, was himself an entomologist and had specialised in research that aimed at improving agricultural productivity in Africa by scientifically controlling insects and pests destructive to animal and plant life while also improving plant and animal varieties that are more resistant to hostile environments while being amenable to high yields. The International Centre for Insect Physiology and Ecology (ICIPE) that Odhiambo founded in Nairobi in the sixties is now a well-known centre for insect science research as well as a leading R&D outfit in Africa. It has developed a science and technology park, and works with peasant farmers to improve honey, cereal and tuber production using environmentally friendly technology among other things.

It is to be noted that the Nigerian Government recently gave the AAS an endowment of US $5 million because, in the words of President Olusegun Obasanjo, "of our belief in the Academy and the power of science and technology as the engine for national economic growth and development for African countries, and to assist in the transformation of Africa, to improve the quality of life of our people, create jobs and wealth, and become more competitive in an emerging knowledge-based, science and technologically-driven global competitive economy."[13]

---

13 Message delivered by the President and Commander in Chief of the Armed Forces of the Federal Republic of Nigeria at the 20th Anniversary of the African Academy of Sciences in Nairobi, Kenya, 11th-15th Dec 2005.

President Obasanjo himself had been closely associated with the Academy, both in his capacity as the President of the African Leadership Forum and as a person with keen interest in science and technology and their role in development. Currently, as chair of the Implementation Committee of the Heads of State and Government of the New Partnership for Africa's Development (NEPAD), President Obasanjo has been keen on NEPAD's "Africa Consolidated Science and Technology Plan of Action" bringing to the fore priority areas and flagship projects that should catapult Africa into faster development in such areas as ICT, biotechnology, SMEs, energy, basic research and space technology. For example, the energy consumption per capita in many African countries — except Egypt, Libya, Morocco, South Africa and Tunisia — is miserable. This level of energy consumption cannot possibly guarantee poverty eradication in the next ten years. Only 4 per cent of Kenya's rural dwellers have access to electricity, which means that value addition in agriculture is severely curtailed while agricultural management skills can hardly be improved in the absence of the use of electrical gadgets such as computers. In Tanzania electricity outreach in rural areas is hardly 1 per cent while Uganda is just about 2 per cent.

The low use of electrical energy means that domestic consumption of energy is based largely on wood fuel or kerosene fuel. Reliance on wood fuel means more destruction of forests, environmental degradation and lower rainfall volumes. And with less rainfall comes the drying up of riverbeds, the lowering of the water level in lakes, such as Lake Victoria, and the ecological imbalance in such lakes that affect fish breeding and production. In the end even the generation of hydroelectricity may become a problem when rains fail. Thus, it can be seen, in this simple example, why it is more than imperative that Africa has to move towards a science and technology-led development process if we have to progress while also sustaining our environment.

The use of kerosene as a source of light in rural homesteads using wicks, though popular, has environmental and health hazards. The smock that comes from the wicks is a pollutant and when inhaled in the poorly ventilated houses can be detrimental to human health. Moreover, kerosene-based energy is infinitely more expensive than electrical power. Thus, the struggle to reduce the cost of living among rural dwellers needs to include the use of cheaper and cleaner forms of energy other than kerosene. In this regard, where possible, wind-based energy has proved the most preferable where the technology can be developed locally so that costs associated with foreign sourcing and over invoicing are reduced to a minimum if not totally eliminated.

73

In his epic poem, *Song of Lawino*,[14] Okot p'Bitek writes extensively about the conflict between modernity and tradition in post-colonial Uganda. But he only castigates modernity in so far as it is an apish imitation of what he calls "the white man's ways" without any meaningful content, and at the expense of *uprooting the pumpkin in the African homestead*. By using the symbol of the pumpkin, Okot refers to the lifeline of cultural as well as productive life. Culture, in other words, should not be sacrificed for apish imitation of what is considered as modern. Modernity, on the other hand, should come in to improve the productivity of the pumpkin that was usually planted at the centre of the homestead in Okot's Acoli society in northern Uganda.

The African cultural heritage that is found in languages, marriage practices, various forms of communal living and mutual social responsibility, inheritance, transfer and use of knowledge, music, dance, architecture, authority structures and religion, while they need not be petrified in the past, need to be infused with science and technology for the aim of improving livelihoods and not simply venerating the past. A visit to the Buganda kings' tombs in Kisubi in Kampala reminds one of how rich and meaningful this past was, but how much it now needs to be incorporated into the modern requirements of putting together various nationalities into one progressive political community where regional integration will produce better results in terms of improving the people's standards of living.

Do not uproot the pumpkin is Okot's constant refrain in his epic poem. Yet many an African leader has uprooted this pumpkin in the name of progress and simply returned us to the quagmire of political suffering and economic backwardness where neither cultural life nor modernity could be encountered. Such was the predicament of Zaire under Mobutu's *euthenticite*. Such was also the unfortunate history of Chad with Tombalbaye's *chaditude*. These military dictators gave a bad name to state-led cultural renewal in Africa such that any subsequent talk of an *African cultural renaissance* has since then been looked at with some amount of scepticism and suspicion.

But we have now reached an era where the African leadership feels more confident to speak of a cultural renaissance in the middle of championing a science and technology-led development. This, perhaps, is the positive outcome of the spirited NEPAD debates, something that Africans should take as a point

---

14   Okot p'Bitek, *Song of Lawino* (Nairobi: East African Publishing House, 1967).

of departure for building a twenty-first century African civilisation(s) that will rise above the nationalist resistance era of the post-War period. Hopefully, this should take us to a new African reconstruction era that should be the true inheritance of those born after World War II and tempered by the vicissitudes of neo-colonialism.

The establishment of the Nelson Mandela Institute for Science, Technology and the Advancement of Knowledge (NMI), aimed at promoting centres of excellence in Africa for Research and Development (R&D), comes at an opportune moment. NMI is conceptualised along the Indian institutes of technology experience started during the Nehru years. The Indian ITs have played a key role in propelling India into the era of advanced technology and the cutting edge of information and communication technology (ICT) while, at the same time, integrating a uniquely Indian ethos in technological advancement. This includes the sending of Indian nationals abroad for training and learning and then being reincorporated into Indian industries, research institutions and government to spearhead the development process.

The aim is to have four campuses of the NMI in Africa: in Abuja for West Africa, Arusha for East Africa, and two other places yet to be determined for Southern and North Africa respectively. African scholars and scientists would have the opportunity of sharing knowledge and initiating research together with the single aim of overcoming the debilitating underdevelopment and poverty through scientific and technological advancement. If the twenty-first century is to be different from the previous twentieth century, politics alone will not do it; politically driven and science/technology led development will do it. I emphasise "politically driven" because politics will take into account the needs of the people, the aspirations of the people and the goals towards which communities aim. There will, obviously, be struggle over these goals, over which needs are paramount and how they should be met. This is where the issues of democracy, justice and social equity come in.

When Bassey Andah says *our traditional and technological systems were and still remain viable systems on which we can build our future,*[15] he essentially means that these systems were compatible with local cultures. They were not alienating; they were woven into the social fabric of seeking to fulfil communal concerns based on shared knowledge, or knowledge driven from culturally legitimate

---

15   Andah, op cit, p. 124.

institutions. It is this integrative aspect of science and technology that should be borrowed from traditional systems into modern systems which, rather than being seen as alien and imposed, as I observed at the beginning, should now be domesticated into our systems and ways of life. This is, among other things, one of the objectives of the Nelson Mandela Institution for Science, Technology and the Advancement of Knowledge.

What Professor Andah observed in 1992 remains valid even today. The educational system is central in this process. Our educational system should be such as to help fashion a technology appropriate to our needs. It can do this by making us thoroughly conversant with our environment, the resources contained in it and how we can use these resources to develop without upsetting the ecological balance. The term *environment* does not simply mean the physical environment in which we live (land, air, water and the resources, but also the social and cultural, what the Spanish call *ambiente*.

When human beings interact and work to transform this *ambiente* for the better, so that each and every individual enjoys a better and higher standard of living, then development occurs; and that is only when the fruits of science and technology become useful to the human being. Professor Andah went a long way to indicate how a sustainable and balanced *ambiente* needs to be maintained in this process of development, with resources being optimally used within the context of ecological balance.

I know, for example, of a case where the Kenyan Government, in the 1980s/90s, decided to expand a sugar mill in the western part of the country. An American firm was contracted to do the job. The firm imported technology from the USA lock, stock and barrel, including "experts" to undertake the expansion process. The imported technology included tractors that were meant to haul the cane from the fields. The wheels of the tractors were so big that they could neither travel on the access roads in the farms nor could they fit on the bridges! Ten years after the expansion process began, not a single extra ton of cane had been processed through the factory. The tractors and all other machines lay in the compound that now looked like a cemetery of abandoned metals.

This is a perfect example of development through inappropriate technology, apish imitation and misuse of resources. Kenya could still have expanded its cane production through a process of learning that would have led Kenyan engineers and technologists fabricating some much more appropriate technology incorporating knowledge from outside. This, I think, is where the African renaissance in science and technology will come from: applying knowledge to solve our problems through learning, research, discovery and innovation. Not surprisingly, when we started the journal of the African Academy of Sciences over twenty years ago, we called it *Discovery and Innovation*, and its first editor was, not surprisingly, Nigeria's current Minister for Science and Technology, Professor Turner Issoun.

10

The Political Economy of Corruption in Kenya

This essay is based on a public lecture given at the African Research and Resource Centre, Nairobi, Kenya, on 16 March 2006

Introduction

Corruption has always been an issue in Kenyan politics. The degree of concern about it and the intensity with which it occupies public discourse have, however, varied since independence. In the 1960s the official records in the National Assembly (the *Hansard*) show very few debates on the issue.[1] It was not until a minister was engaged in a major scandal that had to do with the marketing of maize that pressure in Parliament forced the President to look into the matter by establishing a commission of enquiry.[2] From this report, it became evident that both the maize marketing board and the minister were engaged in conflicts of interest and the use of public office for personal gain.

But the inquiry also revealed that people in public office were very reluctant to discuss issues of corruption even when they were not themselves involved. This led a writer in the *Sunday Nation* to comment, "by and large Kenyans seem to adopt the time-honoured philosophy of hearing nothing, seeing nothing and saying nothing about corruption in public life."[3] But with the annual publication of the reports of the watchdog committees in Parliament — the Public Accounts Committee and the Public Investments Committee — even within the confines of the one-party state, discussions of corruption in Parliament started to increase.

1   See, for example, C. Gertzel, M. Goldschmidt and D. Rothchild, eds. *Government and Politics in Kenya* (Nairobi: East African Publishing House, 1969), 91-97.

2   Republic of Kenya, *Report of the Maize Commission of Enquiry* (Nairobi: Government Printer, 1966).

3   *Sunday Nation*, 20 January 1968.

Part of the pressure for democratisation in the 1970s and 80s arose out of increasing concern about corruption and the defiant use of public resources by state officials and politicians for largely personal gain and political aggrandisement. Indeed, if there is any one pillar of support on which the authoritarian regime, particularly under the presidency of Daniel arap Moi, relied for sustenance it was corruption. It has also been a major contributor to Kenya's underdevelopment.

This essay seeks to trace the roots of corruption in Kenya and the road it has travelled in Kenya's political economy since independence. It notes that one of the key policies in government that institutionalised corruption in the public service was legalising the engagement of civil servants in private business. With substantial use of discretionary powers within certain echelons of the public service, the culture of corruption took deep roots, becoming almost acceptable as the norm of "eating where you work."

Attempts to establish institutions to fight corruption have not been very successful even after the transition to multiparty politics since 1993. Indeed it was with the advent of multiparty politics that mega corruption in the form of the Goldenberg scandal hit Kenya, and this was subsequently followed by the Anglo Leasing scam at the turn of the millennium. This essay, therefore, goes deeper into analysing the relationship between mega-corruption and the demands of sustaining authoritarian rule threatened by popular pressures for democratisation. It concludes by attempting to answer the question, "What is to be done?"

Corruption: What is it and why do we abhor it?

Corruption is akin to cheating, but it goes beyond that. It is cheating in the use of public office so as to achieve personal gain in terms of resources such as money, services and other goods. Corruption is also akin to bribery; when a public official receives payment in any form in exchange of some service rendered to an individual or the public that is tantamount to corruption. In short, corruption is the misuse of public office for personal gain. The important word here is *misuse*, (putting to wrong use).

In democratic systems of government, public affairs are conducted in accordance with the rule of law by both civil servants and elected officials. In both cases, there are laws and regulations, which guide public conduct and the delivery of services. When an act of corruption is alleged to have been committed, it must be subjected to, and proven in a legal process. As we shall subsequently realise, when the legal process is itself flawed, or subject to injunctions that border on filibustering, punishing corruption can at times be a daunting task.

It has quite often been argued that when civil servants and elected officials do not receive sufficient remunerations for the work they do they may be tempted to *supplement their wages* through corrupt deals. The logical outcome of such arguments leads to the conclusion that public officials should be paid well enough to protect them from the temptations of corruption. Judicial officers are included here.

Yet even in situations where very well-off people are elected to positions of leadership and public officials are well remunerated, incidents of grand corruption still occur. Thus, to avoid corruption in public offices, more is needed rather than a good pay package and terms of service. Laws, regulations and procedures must be both strong and enforceable to ensure that any act of corruption is severely punished to deter public officials from the corrupt use of such offices. But more than that, a political culture and a political leadership that frowns on corruption is necessary to reinforce the legal process. For example, when civil servants are allowed to engage in private business, they will easily be tempted to use public procurement systems to their advantage, (giving their own companies preference in providing goods and services to the state), quite often at inflated prices. Thus, the Ndegwa Commission 1972 that allowed Kenyan civil servants to engage in business provided a big loophole for corruption in Kenya. It was indeed after the Ndegwa Commission Report that corruption in public offices started to escalate.

When laws are loose and leave room for too much discretion in decision-making and the application of the same laws, public officials may also tend to abuse the discretion so as to get personal gain. For example, during the days of foreign exchange allocations and import licensing, too much discretion was given to the Minister of Finance to make such allocations and give such licences. Obviously, it is such discretionary powers that led to the schemes such as the Goldenberg scandal,[4] and others of equally astounding magnitudes before then. Discretionary powers in the judiciary, the tax collection system, the public

---

4   As the pressure mounted for multiparty politics in 1992, the one-party government of Daniel arap Moi decided to organise a shady scheme of exporting fictitious gold and diamonds from Kenya for which the trading company called Goldenberg International would receive export compensation from the Treasury of close to 30% of the total money "earned" from such exports. Kamlesh Pattni, the regime's operative behind Goldenberg, received monumental sums of money from this deal which led to an inflationary spiral in the economy lasting several years. The effects of this scam greatly undermined Kenya's economic growth during the last ten year's of Moi's rule.

vehicle inspection system and many other branches of government have also encouraged corruption.

Thus, substantial public resources have been diverted from the public domain to private hands, visibly crippling government activities, undermining the delivery of services, and deepening underdevelopment in the economy as a whole. Cumulatively, corruption makes the public lose faith in government, and this often leads to, among other things, avoiding tax paying, and encouraging a shadow economy and flight of capital. Many professionals whose skills are internationally marketable are also likely to leave their own countries for foreign countries where their services are not only better appreciated, but also quite often better remunerated. Such professionals also put a premium on the improved governance environment in which they find themselves when they escape from their corrupt *home environment* to societies they consider as better governed.

Kenya has lost hundreds of doctors, nurses, lawyers, accountants, engineers, surveyors, university dons and even clergymen to the Southern African countries and the West, not to mention Australia and New Zealand, over the last two decades. In effect, we spend billions of shillings developing rare skills only to lose them to more developed countries such as the USA and Great Britain. This process of draining our brains is part and parcel of the process of underdevelopment that corruption aids and abets.

But much more ominous is when corruption destroys the productive capacity of our nation and subverts the process of development towards a mercantile economy and pure speculation. Between 1991 and 1994 when, as a result of the Goldenberg scandal involving the fictitious export of gold and diamonds from Kenya, billions of shillings were paid out from the Treasury leaving behind a big hole in the public purse, the Treasury was then forced to borrow heavily from the domestic market through treasury bills and bonds, driving interest rates for these bills and bonds to close to 76 per cent per annum.

Many banks, rather than lend to the productive sector and stimulate economic growth as well as create jobs, preferred to trade in these government monies, and hiking up their own interest rates as well, making it very difficult for manufacturers, industrialists and traders to service their bank loans. Many industries and businesses were soon foreclosed during this period, and Kenya, to this very day, has not really recovered from the adverse shocks of the Goldenberg scandal on the economy.

Going back to the colonial times

Let it not be said that corruption is a uniquely African disease, nor would it be correct to assert that it is an affliction of post-independence Africa. The white settlers in colonial Kenya made their fortunes through corruption. Without cheating in collusion with colonial officials, stealing from the coffers of the colony, appropriating land for which they paid next to nothing, sacking the blood of poor peasants for labour not paid for and literally getting public transport for free for their farm products, the Blundells and Delameres of colonial Kenya would not have built their fortunes and "moved to better things" when the nationalists finally took over political power.

In a recent book written about the Mau Mau called *Histories of the Hanged,* David Anderson unearths corruption in the then City Hall of Nairobi involving white administrators and Asian contractors during the construction of Ofafa and Mbotela residential estates for what was then regarded as the African middle class. He says:

> Never had a commission of enquiry been less welcome in Kenya than was that led by Sir Alan Rose. A distinguished barrister of the Inner Temple, and a confirmed bachelor with a reputation for probity, austerity and sternly conservative values, Rose was hardly the kind of man likely to find many kindred spirits among the robust, hard-drinking and womanising white highlanders...
> The scale of corruption unearthed by the Rose Commission surprised even Kenya's most cynical observers. The operation of the City Architect's office and its supervision of the Ofafa and Mbotela contracts in particular, came in for savage criticism...On inspection, numerous contraventions of the building specifications came to light—shallow excavation footings, under-strength concreting in floors and lintels, substandard joinery, the use of cheaper, weaker materials throughout, and generally poor standards of workmanship. Yet, throughout the contract this work had apparently been inspected and approved by City Council officers...
>
> The implications of these revelations soon became clear. European officials had accepted 'gifts' from building contractors before and during the Ofafa and Mbotela contracts, entering false specifications and logging inspection reports when no inspections had taken place. Malpractice was found to be widespread in every aspect of the tendering and management of the Council's building contracts, and had evidently been so for many years.[5]

---

5   David Anderson, *Histories of the Hanged,* (New York: W.W. Norton, 2005), 226-229.

Sounds very much like today, and it is as if Kenya really never became independent. And if she did, we decided to inherit from the colonialists the good, the bad and the ugly in governance; corruption remaining at the centre of what subsequently came to be known as *neo-colonialism*.

But the civil service, though corrupt in colonial times, had its avarice kept to a minimum by the vigilance of the white settler community that it served. It was not as avaricious as its counterpart that emerged after the Ndegwa Commission legalised official corruption. It was a service that was meant for the white society to deliver goods and services at the least cost to the master. It had to be small, lean and efficient, and any corrupt deal was carefully tugged away under some justifiable expenses at the senior levels dominated by the whites, therefore kept to a minimum. If it was discovered that one was taking advantage of an administrative office for personal gain, and hence passing the transaction cost to the master, the punishment was prohibitive at junior levels where most of the officials were Africans.

Civil service after independence: Lost virginity?

The much spoken about clean and efficient civil service at independence was, therefore, not an accident; it had its own origin in the political economy of colonial Kenya. After independence, the service became an employment bureau, an arena — quite understandably — of rewarding the boys and girls with jobs and new opportunities. As it expanded, it demanded more wages and more services for itself — houses, clinics, schools, holidays, pension schemes, and so on. These salaries and services were to be paid for from the taxes levied on ordinary Kenyans.

The Kenyatta government opted for the easier, though more sinister, option. Rather than raise taxes to sustain a bloated civil service, it was allowed to supplement its own wages through private business; this was the essence of the Ndegwa Commission Report, a commission set up to review salaries and terms of service of civil servants in the early 1970s, but a Commission which, for all intents and purposes, legalised official corruption. From then on, the civil service lost its virginity of cleanliness, and entered the ranks of the police and provincial administration in corruption and the most debilitating forms of rent seeking that soon brought the whole administrative edifice to its knees as far as both service delivery and economic growth were concerned.

A political culture of corruption

What Ndegwa brought to the civil service was already an acceptable and quite noble practice in the world of politics. Jomo Kenyatta and his courtiers had no qualms whatsoever of translating their ascendancy to state power as also meaning immediate inheritance, if not at times, usurpation, of economic power from the departing colonialists, in what was justified as the *Africanisation of the economy*.

There was, of course, nothing fundamentally wrong with the Africanisation of the economy, especially when it meant the opening up of the frontiers of private property to Africans in terms of agricultural settlement schemes, trading licences, small and medium enterprises supported by the Kenya Industrial Estates, and new business empires financed by bank loans from the Industrial Development Bank, housing estates put up through Housing Finance Company of Kenya and so on.

What was wrong, however, was when some people used their proximity to state power—particularly the presidency—to access these business opportunities for themselves and their friends in a corrupt manner in exclusion of the others, and quite often disregarding the wider interest of society. They also indulged in corruption when they used their *discretionary powers within the state* (powers to license, to allocate foreign exchange in the Treasury and the Central Bank, to approve and award contracts, to procure goods and services, etc) to enrich themselves and their friends, and to accumulate power and wealth, to "Africanise" businesses and enterprises to themselves. Many of the economic and political potentates who today stride the streets of Nairobi as successful African businessmen trace their steps to these corrupt deals of this era. It is not surprising that they are averse to any talk of Truth and Reconciliation and the dismantling of the authoritarian presidency.

Amendments to the independence constitution that heaped more and more powers on the presidency had a lot to do with the material interests of the power elite around the president who found an authoritarian presidency a ready tool for aiding and abetting their accumulation of power, property and wealth. This phenomenon was not unique to Kenya; it has been the cause of corruption and underdevelopment in Indonesia, the Philippines, Mexico and Nigeria among many other low-income developing nations.

Very early in the life of the independent Parliament, cries of corruption started to be heard. One of the key issues that the Kenya People's Union (KPU) raised in breaking away from the KANU government was corruption. A substantial

84

section of the *Wananchi Declaration,* the KPU's manifesto of 1966, is devoted to a discussion of corruption in Kenya, which the party billed as "the biggest drawback to the country's future development." Even the Minister of Economic Planning and Development, Tom Mboya, Kenyatta's ablest and perhaps least corrupt ministers, decried corruption and nepotism in the following words in a speech at the University of Nairobi: "I find it appalling that some of us in positions of power and authority quite often resort to cheap clannism in making appointments to public positions, and very often this is done to aid and abet corruption."[6]

When Paul Ngei, then Minister of Marketing and Cooperatives, diverted maize meant for food relief to Emma Stores, a shop belonging to his wife, thereby inviting tremendous public disapproval, Kenyatta was quick to change the law and allow him to retain both his parliamentary seat as well as his position in the cabinet. Kenyatta perhaps saw nothing wrong with what Ngei had done because for him this was a way of Ngei "improving himself", helping himself to something that did not belong to any particular person, something that was not owned by "anybody's mother".

Thus, when KPU cited corruption as one of the ways by which KANU misruled Kenya, Kenyatta chided Kaggia in that famous speech at the rally in Nairobi in 1966 where he accused him of having failed to build a house for himself while he, Kenyatta, had put up a mansion in rural Gatundu. For Kenyatta, it was not corruption that was the issue, it was the inability of some "leaders" to make use of "opportunities" open to them within the state to improve themselves. In this public and dramatised setting, a tradition was set from the highest level of political authority that made public officials enjoy *impunity against the law* should they be accused of corruption.

When corruption goes thus unpunished it soon becomes rooted in a society's political culture; Kenyatta aided and abetted the institutionalisation of corruption in Kenya's political culture. Moi and Kibaki followed in the tradition, quite often more than excelling in the art, much to the chagrin of ordinary Kenyans.

Fight against mega corruption under Kenyatta, Moi and Kibaki

It is not as if Kenyans have sat by and saw corruption happen without doing something about it. Struggles have been waged; resistance has been put up, but

---

6   Tom Mboya, in a panel discussion with Prof. J.J. Okumu and Ceere Cerira, at the Education Lecture Theatre No. 2, University of Nairobi, on 7 April , 1968 to discuss "African Socialism and Its Application to Planning in Kenya."

the forces of corruption have always ignored, removed, pushed aside or totally eliminated those who have fought against the vice. The student and staff revolts in the public universities, the Saba Saba uprising and the popular struggles for democracy dating back to the 1960s are part and parcel of Kenya's history in the quest for good governance.

The Public Accounts Committee, the Public Investments Committee and many other parliamentary reports and debates have sufficiently documented corruption during the Kenyatta, Moi and Kibaki presidencies. The statute books are full of laws seeking to keep corruption in check, the Anti-Corruption and Economic Crimes Act being the latest addition among the legal speed governors. Books, treatises and articles have been written analysing and drawing attention to the debilitating effects of corruption on economic growth, poverty eradication and democratic governance. Politicians and other leaders have been detained, imprisoned, killed and assassinated for no other reasons other than speaking about, investigating or opposing corruption in society and high places. We can remind ourselves of Pio da Gama Pinto, Tom Mboya, J.M. Kariuki and Robert Ouko.

Lawyers have been killed in broad daylight in the streets of Nairobi while dealing with cases of corruption in the courts; arrests have rarely been made that lead to conclusive prosecutions. University dons were thrown into police cells and detained; students were butchered while demonstrating and violence meted out against their parents, as they demanded transparent use of national resources in the development of the nation. Recently, a policeman, hot on the trails of drug traffickers, was gunned down in his compound; the police do not seem to be making much progress on that case either.

In the end, law enforcement agents begin to operate under fear, and fear leads to conscious omission of performing duties that will lead to apprehending criminals engaged in corruption or complicit in such affairs. An ineffective and compromised law enforcement agency becomes a weak and ineffective speed governor. If anything, it becomes a speed governor checking people intent on fighting corruption; it joins the chorus of those calling for *going slow* in dealing with corruption cases and investigations.

If law enforcement agents had not been ignored, compromised, derailed or stopped from performing their duties, such mega corruption cases as Ken Ren, Kisumu Molasses Plant, the expansion of Nzoia Sugar Mills Phases I and II, the Turkwell Gorge, the many botched privatisation schemes, etc, would not have gone unpunished to the extent that, finally, such mega rip-offs like Goldenberg and Anglo Leasing came as nothing to be surprised about. A culture had been set in the civil service and the high echelons of government that *it became normal to make money this way!* And, as John Githongo soon found out, being a law enforcement agent under such circumstances can easily earn you a ticket to the gallows, courtesy of the engine of high-level corruption.

When the hunters become the hunted

When the hunters become the hunted, then the fight against corruption in government is hijacked by a mafia of plutocrats who in public speak against the vice, but in private urge that the hunters go slow in their job, or abandon it altogether. Even the judges before whom corruption cases appear, engage in the game of filibustering, adjourning cases endlessly, losing files deliberately and even excusing themselves from hearing a case when many months have gone down the drain as evidence is given and witnesses grilled to no avail. The rich and powerful are quick at filing injunctions in courts to delay, and even completely obstruct corruption cases against them while the poor are punished severely for receiving or giving tiny little bribes.

Lawyers following up witnesses in corruption cases have been bought off or bumped off. Prosecutors have been threatened. Witnesses have been made to disappear without a trace. Wrong people have been deliberately arrested and brought to court, charged with corruption or drug smuggling, when the law enforcement agencies know exactly what they are doing; pulling the wool over the faces of the people of Kenya in a make believe exercise of fighting corruption.

The Anglo Leasing Affair

What is now known in Kenya as the Anglo Leasing scam,[7] had it been allowed to travel the full journey as Goldenberg did, it would have had an equally devastating effect, if not even worse, on the Kenyan political economy. Like the Goldenberg scandal, it involved both public officials and private wheeler-dealers who entered into the affair for two purposes. One was for those in politics to

---

7 Sometime in 2000, the government of Daniel arap Moi worked out a scheme of purchasing security-related equipment and services from abroad under "lease financing" contracts with certain companies. One of these companies called Anglo Leasing Financing Company gave as its home address somewhere in the United Kingdom. When NARC came into power President Mwai Kibaki appointed John Githongo as his Permanent Secretary in charge of ethics. The new government decided to implement the scheme and to use it, like Moi had done with Goldenberg, to access money from state coffers under the guise of lease financing for the procurement of security goods and services from abroad. It was Githongo's thorough inquiry that revealed that Anglo Leasing was a fictitious company, and that the billions of shillings that the government had either paid or committed to these contracts were fictitious. Attempts by Githongo to get into the bottom of this affair put him in great conflict with the "president and his men" and Githongo had to flee the country in December 2004 for a safe haven at St. Anthony's College in Oxford, England.

87

make "easy money" from the state for purposes of buying and keeping political power. The other was for the wheeler-dealers to make money for private gain as well as for access to, and control of, high-level public officials and politicians in the Kibaki government.

For both groups, this scam could not succeed if the rule of law was to be respected. And yet to carry it out in the name of the state, some form of legality had to be respected. Hence certain public officials had to be used with powers to "sign documents" so as to pass the test of legality notwithstanding the criminality of the scheme.

Under the previous regime of President Moi, such schemes could be carried out provided the name of the President was invoked to compel public officials to do what they knew was illegal. Since the presidential authoritarian regime was still very much in place, few people feared too much that they would be found out. Even if they were, the President's name was enough to protect them. This is why Kamlesh Paul Pattni moved with so much ease within the corridors of power, and why he could sit and scheme with Vice Presidents, Ministers of Finance, Permanent Secretaries and customs officials.

Under the current regime of President Kibaki, presidential authoritarian powers, though still intact in the constitution, had been substantially eroded in the sphere of politics. Following the December 2002 elections, the people had asserted their power against the political order; society would no longer simply be ordered around by the politicians. It was now an open and free society. Secondly, Parliament had itself become increasingly assertive and independent of the executive since the IPPG reforms of 1997; the 2002 coalition politics simply crowned this independence by counterpart departmental committees in the august house. And thirdly, a free, independent and fierce mass media was now a menace to the corrupt, and their victim as well at times.

So, undertaking a scheme like the Anglo Leasing one would have to be done much more carefully and much less ruthlessly with regard to the law with authoritarian politics now in the wane. This is what the schemers in the President's office and their civilian underworld contacts in the Anglo Leasing Company did not fully appreciate. But they knew, however, that in order to retain political power after usurping the power from the coalition by trashing the MOU, they needed some muscle to push their way through. This muscle, they concluded, was to be found by building a financial war chest with which to control NARC, the constitutional review process and votes in Parliament. What they did not factor in was an unusual man of integrity as a law enforcement agent who was working in State House as the Permanent Secretary in charge of ethics, John Githongo.

The men and women who were involved in wheeling and dealing as politicians and "businessmen" under Moi were still around—Kamlesh Paul Pattni, Deepak Kamani, Keterring, Pereira and now their running dogs abroad. Some had been elected to Parliament under the NARC arrangement while some had even financed the NARC campaigns without necessarily revealing their underworld identities. Those who were looking for "easy money" to buy and control political power did not, therefore, lack advisors or partners with whom to do business. In any case, these partners came forth and offered their useful services, and the new NARC clients were only too eager to play ball.

The Anglo Leasing deals had been started but not consummated under Moi. The wheeler-dealers advised that here was an easy area where easy money could be made provided the scheme was consummated, and the NARC officials could actually do so under cover of "legal procedure". The wheeler-dealers would make their money by selling fictitious goods and services to the state while the politicians would raise enough cash to buy and keep power. All this was done under the name of the President.

Unfortunately for both the politicians and the business tycoons, John Githongo discovered the scam and reported to the President. In no time, monies that had been paid out to the non-existent Anglo Leasing Company were returned to the Treasury into what was called the Miscellaneous Revenue Account (MRA). The ministers and government officials involved argued that since the money had been returned—close to US$ 15 million—the matter needed to end there and no further investigations were necessary. Githongo thought otherwise; thorough investigations were necessary and all involved had to be prosecuted in accordance with the Anti-corruption and Economic Crimes Act. A constellation of these politicians and their counterparts in the business underworld now threatened Githongo either to shut up or risk the gallows. By the end of 2004, Githongo had decided to quit when the opportune moment presented itself.

Presidential involvement in corruption

Many questions have been asked regarding the involvement of the President himself in this scam. Did the President know what was going on? Did he sanction it? If he did not know, was it because information was kept from him? If he did, why did he not stop it?

From Githongo's published diaries, it is quite clear the President was informed and he knew what was going on. The question to ask, therefore, is why he did not do anything to stop it or to bring the culprits to book. One possible answer is that he did not do something to stop it, nor did he quickly punish the wrong-doers because he sanctioned the scam. If this is the case then Kenya is facing a Watergate type situation. The other possible answer is that the President knew but was mentally and physically unable to do anything, in which case the responsibility must be put squarely on the cabinet, the Chief Justice and the Speaker of the National Assembly.[8]

From Githongo's diary, by June 2004, it was quite clear that ministers and high officials in government were involved with fictitious firms in procuring fictitious security-related services and equipment under the names of several fictitious companies, chief among which were Anglo Leasing and Finance Company and Infotalent Company. When Githongo pressed the relevant officials about these fake contracts, monies were paid back to the Treasury equally mysteriously. He comments in his dossier to the President:

> I found this unsettling. First Euro 956,700, on 17-05-04 and then US$ 4.7 million is repaid on 07-06-2004, by a company that does not have legal status and no indication from within the government who its owners were. Only Hon. Mwiraria's admission to me on the 14 June 2004 that J. Oyula, then Financial Secretary, had called up Kamani who had then repaid the money gave an indication as to who Anglo Leasing was. Now another bogus company, Infotalent, had 'repaid' Euro 5.2 million.

> Your Excellency, I informed you of these developments on this day 16 June 2004. We agreed that we were talking about the 'refund' of almost Kenya shillings 1 billion and no one was celebrating; those making the refunds were not making themselves known; none of the civil servants involved were saying they knew who Anglo Leasing was.

> Anglo Leasing refunded US$ 4.7 million (Kshs 370 m) on the Forensic Laboratories project; Anglo Leasing refunded Euros 956,700 (Kshs 95 m.) on the Immigration Security project and Infotalent Ltd refunded Euros 5,287,164 (Kshs.506 m) on the E-Cops Security project.[9]

---

8   Section 12 of the Constitution of Kenya regarding the "Removal of the President on grounds of mental or physical incapacity to hold office" gives the Chief Justice the powers to appoint a tribunal to look into the matter after an appropriate cabinet resolution requesting him to do so. The report of the tribunal is then handed in to the Speaker for further action.

9   See John Githongo, *Report on my Findings of Graft in the Government of Kenya,* submitted to President Mwai Kibaki, Nov. 2005, p.11.

Why didn't the President take any action on these anomalous repayments? Why did he continue to say nothing one year later when Githongo finally submitted to him this report after the referendum on the proposed new constitution for Kenya?

These questions remain pertinent, and will need to be addressed by the relevant organs of government, particularly Parliament and its select and departmental committees. No doubt this process is underway, and may soon answer questions that bother every Kenyan that has sought for long to have good, clean and democratic governance that can deliver on the rule of law, human rights and development.

Corruption: What is to be done?

"Philosophers have explained the world in various ways; the point, however, is to change it." That was Marx's invocation to the revolutionaries of the 19th century when he wrote the *Theses on Feurbach*.[10] Likewise, it does us no good to analyse and describe corruption in all its forms and historical evolution in Kenya if we do not use this knowledge to do something about it.

Kenya has the institutions and laws with which to fight corruption. The Anti-corruption and Economic Crimes Act was well crafted and gives Parliament, the courts and other law enforcement agencies sufficient powers and institutional leverage to investigate, apprehend and prosecute corruption. As the Mexican novelist, Carlos Fuentes says, "The question is not whether there is corruption, it is whether corruption can be exposed and punished".[11] To expose and punish corruption, three interdependent factors, institutions and processes are necessary: a political leadership with the vision, programme and will to do so; a political culture that encourages, nurtures and reinforces exposure and punishment; and, law enforcement agencies, particularly the judiciary, that will try and punish corruption.

We have seen the pitfalls in the past and present Kenyan political leadership in the fight against corruption. Since 1992, however, with the tremendous growth of an open society—freer press, political pluralism, aggressive assertion of civil liberties and press freedom—the public fight against corruption has been heightened. In

---

10 Karl Marx, *Theses on Feurebach,* in Quintin Hoare (ed.) *Karl Marx: Early Writings,* (London: New Left Books, 1974).

11 Carlos Fuentes, *The Years with Laura Diaz* (Mexico: Farrar Straus Giroux, 2001), 39.

2003, soon after NARC came into power, the Minister of Justice and Constitutional Affairs carried out what was seen as a surgery in the judiciary. It was meant to root out compromised, incompetent and corrupt judges and magistrates. In their places were to be recruited new people on grounds of merit. As it turned out, the exercise was infiltrated by favouritism and nepotism, promoting people who could not deserve those positions if merit were to be applied, and victimising others on fictitious charges or mere suspicion.

Yes, there was indeed a tremendous effort made to turn the judiciary upside down, but it has not led to improving performance in the institution. It is not simply a question of "fighting the good fight" in trying to bring about changes in the judiciary; it is more important to ensure that this good fight delivers in terms of performance in the administration of justice and the fight against corruption.

The same can be said of the Kenya Anti-Corruption Commission (KACC). Since it was revamped during the NARC administration, with a Director and a bevy of officials earning tremendous sums of money to justify their "heavy duties" and "to keep them away from temptation", the number of people who have been prosecuted for corruption in high places is not terribly impressive. A recent advertisement published by the government communication officer in the dailies showed hundreds of Kenyans apprehended for corruption involving embezzling 200 - 20,000 shillings. While we would not want to forgive such sins off-hand in the fight against corruption, they really cannot be paraded, in good conscience, as major achievements by KACC in three years.

What is the implication of our argument? First, that good institutions and laws are not enough in the fight against corruption; qualified, committed and *independent* people are needed to work in these institutions and to exercise these laws for the corrupt to be duly apprehended and punished. By *independent* we mean independent from undue external influence, by the powers that be or any other party interested in subverting the cause of justice. But *independence* is tough and costly; it requires high resolve and tremendous competence and courage in the Kenyan context, as Githongo's experience has shown.

Second, that getting the right individuals into the right institutions is not enough. A society needs to develop a *political culture* that discourages corrupt practices, or makes it difficult for the corrupt to parade the proceeds of corruption as signs of success or social status. With the recent Anglo Leasing revelations and the call for ministers to resign from office following their being implicated in the scandal, we may have started on the road towards effectively *shaming corruption and the corrupt.* But as long as the corrupt of yesterday are capable of successfully pausing as the saints of today for election and appointment to public offices, then the enabling political culture for fighting corruption is yet to be built.

Such a culture will not be borne spontaneously; it has to be cultivated through struggle, and it is a struggle which will not, at the moment, be led from the top; it has to be engineered from below, whether we are talking about government, the religious order, civil society or the business community. At the top of all these institutions in Kenyan society are men and women intertwined by webs of interest and relationships that have been compromised by corrupt practices, knowingly and unknowingly, over time. While a few may *commit class suicide* like Githongo did and fight bare knuckles against the vice, the majority will compromise themselves through silence as an easy option. The usual middle class sin: *complain and do nothing; partake of the benefits of corruption but blame others for it.*

But the realm of the political is always the most visible and the quickest to activate. It concentrates experiences of society and aspirations of the people into one act: the vote. If, in that one act, the issue of corruption and how to fight it is condensed, if in that one act the true soldiers are selected with the armour and the spirit to fight bereft of the compromises of the past, then a political leadership can take up the mantle of the fight against corruption and move it a notch further. Good, committed, visionary and truly democratic political leadership is what Kenya needs to successfully keep corruption at bay.

In this regard, civil society organisations that are ready to go beyond the rhetoric of accusation into the realm of constructing a future that zero tolerates corruption must now take up their crosses and make this history. The next general election in Kenya needs to be fought on the corruption platform. Parties need to qualify and disqualify candidates given their corruption credentials: corruption free ones to run and those blemished by the vice to decline from contesting for any elected office. That having been done, we shall change history for the better, and not simply continue to explain the causes of our underdevelopment woes, including corruption.

From colonial days to Anglo Leasing: Lessons gained from corruption

The following lessons are important from the issues we have addressed above as we look at the political economy of corruption in Kenya from colonial times to our day, now confronted not only with Anglo Leasing, but also with the menacing Armenian brothers as well. First, any repressive regime prepares a fertile breeding ground for corruption. From colonial rule through Kenyatta to the darkest days of the Moi government, corruption and authoritarianism rose in tandem. In fact, it was during the most repressive time of Moi, from mid-1980s onwards, that mega corruption became a feature of bad governance in Kenya.

Two, it is the struggle for democracy and the advancement that the popular national forces have made in opening up society that has provided the biggest onslaught against corruption. A few brave foreign envoys like the late Smith Hempstone, Mutzelburg and Edward Clay must indeed be congratulated for their contribution, but these laurels cannot be bestowed on the so-called donor community in general. The victory of the popular national forces in the 2002 elections is what has opened the democratic political space for transparency, free debate, an aggressive press, independent parliament, a vibrant civil society and now the exposures on Goldenberg and Anglo Leasing. We still need to know more about the Halal Meat Factory scandal, the Ken Ren saga and many other such scandals that happened under the single party regime but could not be exposed because of the severity of political repression then.

Three, if it had not been for John Githongo, Anglo Leasing would have gone the way of Ken Ren with very little exposed and hence very little known. We therefore need public officers of unquestionable integrity and patriotism in the fight against corruption; men and women who will implement procurement procedures and laws in public interest.

Fourthly, we need to eliminate the culture of impunity in our political system and government as a whole. Big or small, public officers indulge in corruption because we have set a poor precedence – the corrupt are left to vaunt their wealth and are serenaded as 'development conscious leaders" in ostentatious *harambee* gatherings. A competent and homegrown rule of law culture must prevail.

Fifthly, a politically committed leadership with a clear democratic and national developmental vision for Kenya is a *sine qua non* for fighting corruption. As Githongo has shown, the fight against corruption must begin from the very top of government and be seen to begin there. Sixthly, transparency in government expenditure and procurement, including the hitherto sacred defence and security expenditures, is vital.

Seventhly, we must, as Kenyans, believe in ourselves and congratulate ourselves when we do something good. Those who have given so much for the democratic struggle in this country need to be recognised and encouraged;

we quite often overstate the role of donors in the fight against corruption. It is to be noted that aid to Kenya was at its highest when the country was most repressive and corrupt (1988-91). It was cut when Kenyans ashamed donors by coming out to the streets on Saba Saba and several times in the early 1990s. Even with Anglo Leasing, it is the loud and clear voice of Kenyans that have now compelled significant changes in government that will, finally, herald a truly democratic and clean government.

And finally, there are international networks of corruption as the Anglo Leasing saga has revealed. To fight corruption effectively there is need for a global approach, with governments in the developed countries effectively supporting measures in the developing countries to deal with the issue. Where substantial evidence has been put in the public domain regarding public officials who are corrupt — even when their governments are reluctant to prosecute such persons — foreign governments should constrain such persons from making use of their wealth kept abroad in banks and other assets.

That, however, is addressing "the after effect" of corruption. To take a much more proactive stance, we need to look at the relationship between development assistance (or aid) and the propensity for governments in developing countries to be corrupt. Both Devarajan *et al.* and Swaroop *et al.*[12] argue convincingly that foreign aid merely substitutes for already earmarked government spending; the central government spends funds freed by aid on non-development activities, and we dare add "on corruption." This implies that government expenditure choices are unaffected by external sources of finance. Aid merely softens the government's budget constraints and increases the ease with which it can dream of corrupt ventures to finance politics and other non-core budget activities.[45] Development partners will, therefore, need to give assistance of a new and smart kind where core programmes are agreed to between partners in the context of the budget as a whole, and given a capable, democratic and developmental state.

---

12 S. Devarajan et al. *What Does aid do to Africa Finance?* AERC/ODC Project on Managing a Smooth Transition from Aid Dependence in Africa (Washington, D.C.: AERC, 1998); V. Swaroop et al., "Fiscal Effects of Foreign Aid in Federal System of Governance: The case of India," *Journal of Public Economics,* Vol. 77, No. (2000): 3007-30.

11

Why Did We Walk While the Asians Ran?

A Case for Future Cooperation Between Kenya and East Asia

Speech given at the luncheon of the Asian Ambassadors and High Commissioners in Kenya at the Lord Errol Restaurant, Nairobi, on 5 August 2004

I do believe that we can leap into the future in terms of development, and in this we have something to learn from the East Asian countries as well as China. I think Africa-Asia cooperation will become one of the most significant developments in international economic relations and the diplomacy that goes along with that – provided we initiate the right policy and strategies to achieve that goal starting now. And yet, we have not devoted anything close to the attention that this topic deserves. This is true of government, our private sector, the press and academic research institutes that address Africa's international relations. This is a pity.

Japan is the second largest economy in the world today. Considering the current, unprecedented pace of industrialisation in the Peoples Republic of China and the other leading South East Asian states – like South Korea, Taiwan, Singapore, Hong Kong – in the closing decades of the last century, the twenty-first century has been dubbed "the Asian Century." The US, some Latin American states (like Mexico and Chile), the European Union, and Australia are positioning themselves to the realities of the Asian Century. This is what we see coming out of the Asia-Pacific summits. We in Kenya, and the rest of Africa, cannot afford to be complacent about this. We probably have a greater stake in what will happen in East Asia than most other nations. If Kenya is to reconfigure her economic strategy to overcome a poverty rate that now afflicts 56 per cent of our population, it must engage the fastest growing economic region in the world today – those in East Asia, and also the Indian subcontinent with which we have long trading and cultural ties.

I have just come back from a trip to Lankawi in Malaysia, organised by the "Smart Partnership Movement" of the Commonwealth Partnership for Technology Management and Technology, or CPTM. Do not be deceived by the title into thinking that the Commonwealth Secretariat in London – which brings together former British colonies – was responsible for the meeting. No, the CPTM is an initiative of the Malaysian Government under Dr. Mahathir Mohammed and like-minded African, Asian and Caribbean states, and international corporations, to rework the dominant development paradigm that we all have inherited from the West so that we can arrive at a locally-grounded and practical alternative that stresses dialogue, local-foreign partnerships, and rational response to market failure and the excesses of the unrestricted competition in free markets.

And I was struck by the awesome progress that Malaysia has made in the last 25 years! It is not just the splendour of Lankawi Island as a holiday resort that truly impressed me. It was also the road network, housing in Kuala Lumpur, commercial buildings in Kuala Lumpur, new industries (including automobile production), infrastructure and most important of all the fact that Malaysia today has full employment and like most OECD states, she has to deal with the problem of illegal immigrants coming from less developed neighbouring states. You all know the grave problems we all face in Kenya on all those fronts.

Yet in a way, Malaysia was returning the favour. Malaysian leaders told me that when they visited Kenya in the mid-1970s, they were similarly struck by the progress Kenya had made since independence compared to where they were at the time! Kenya's economy was then growing at 7 per cent annually. She had just won the right to host the first United Nations agency in the developing world, namely UNEP. The first ever World Bank-IMF annual conference in a developing country was held in 1974 in Nairobi. But what had struck the Malaysians most was that at the time, Nairobi (and Kenya) had better infrastructure than Malaysia, and it was also better managed. At the time, Nairobi was clean, traffic moved efficiently and there was a public bus transport system (the Kenya Bus Company) that met commuter demands adequately.

Kuala Lumpur was nothing like this. So Malaysian leaders decided they would make their capital as good as – or better than – Nairobi. They requested the Kenya Government to allow Malaysian planners and civil servants to take courses at the Kenya Institute of Administration (KIA), then Kenya's premier public service training institution, and the Kenya Government obliged. Today we call this technical assistance – in this case from Kenya to Malaysia. I am informed the records are actually available in KIA archives.

Today, we could do with technical assistance from Malaysia. You all know the story because comparison between economic performance of East Asia and Africa has become the staple of many studies from the World Bank, most prominently the 1993 study entitled *The East Asian Miracle*, but also from journalists, scholars, and *soi-dissant* "experts", many of whom engage in wholesale denigration of African capabilities without any knowledge of the kind of story I have just narrated, proving that African states can also perform and *have* performed in the past. People with their noses so deeply buried in statistical number crunching that they are oblivious of the world around them. People devoid of any nuances understanding of the economic history of Africa, who unfortunately have had a greater influence in economic policy making in Africa than they deserve.

It is sufficient to observe that, while the Kenyan economy grew at 7.9 per cent between 1965 and 1969 – the figures are from the World Bank – East Asia, home of the future "Asian Tigers" only managed an average of 4.2 per cent in economic expansion – about half that of Kenya. We had a slightly higher per capita income than - in 1965. Today, Malaysia has a per capita income of US$ 4,000 that is rising. We in Kenya have one estimated at US $330, which has been falling! In 1970 Ghana and South Korea had a similar per capita income (about $500). Today, South Korea has a per capita income thirty times higher than that of Ghana. This is the kind of raw comparison to which we have been treated *ad nauseam*.

What went wrong?

Let us begin with dispelling some popular myths. First, it is not cultural differences! Much has been made out of cultural stereotypes between East Asians and Africans, especially by Western scholars. But this cannot tell us why Kenya was doing better than Malaysia in the 1970s. Neither the Kenyan nor Malaysian culture has changed between 1970 and today. The cultures are the same old ones.

Second, it is not geography about which so much has been written especially in the policy and academic circles. Africa indeed lies mostly in the tropics, where diseases are endemic and climatic changes unpredictable making agriculture perilous.[1] But not all African states fit the stereotype. In Eastern Africa, for example, we have a huge variety of climatic and topographic zones – the cool Ethiopian and Kenya highlands, the tropical coastlands, the African savannah, semi-deserts, snow-capped mountains, etc.

Third, it is not just a matter of pursuing the right macro-economic policies, and then letting the free market to deal with "micro" (i.e. sectoral and specific project) issues. To give just one example, Ghana made exceptional progress in meeting most of the macro-economic and economic deregulation targets required by the donors. But look at the Ghanaian economy today. Per capita income is at just about where it was before reforms. Worst of all, there has been no *structural* change in the economy. Ghana is basically still an exporter of raw materials – agricultural-based (like cocoa), or minerals (like gold). Is it any wonder that Africans are so sceptical about old-fashioned neo-liberal economic policies?

What I deduce from this is that market-driven deregulation and macro-economic stability are necessary but not sufficient conditions for rapid economic transformation. Hard-nosed innovation in selected economic sectors through private-public partnerships of the type we discussed at Lankawi seems to be the key to our problems in Kenya. A profit-making state intervention in support of selected local-foreign enterprises so that they are cost-efficient in international markets is the key. Comparative advantage in the international markets is created by purposeful human innovation, not natural resources (as the textbook says). This is true of the Asian experience and it is true of Kenya if she wishes to industrialise.

I wish to use the conclusion to identify some priorities in the cooperation between Kenya and Asia in future, which are:

1. We must begin to learn more about each other's experience. CPTM's Smart Partnership is a fine example of this. Whether in Asia, or Africa, our countries have long been tied to a North-South economic and political relationship between Africa and Europe (or the US). We cannot undo that overnight. Some aspects of it are good. But we must now look to a new age of Kenya-Asian ties. I would propose an annual meeting between Kenyan economic and trade ministers with their ASEAN counterparts.

---

1   See, for example, David Landes, *The Wealth and Poverty of Nations: Why Capitalism Succeeds in the West and Fails Everywhere Else* (New York: W.W. Norton, 1998).

2. Kenya should seek new sources of direct foreign investment in Asia. There is ample room for expansion in the Kenyan market. In addition, Kenya is the gateway to the East African and COMESA markets – of over 100 million people.

3. There are prospects for expansion of the Kenyan tourist market to serve the middle class in East Asia. This requires publicity and public education on both sides — Kenya and East Africa.

4. Cross-fertilisation of ideas through policy research institutes and national economic councils. We in Kenya are in the process of creating a National Economic and Social Council.[2] We could learn a lot from its counterparts in Malaysia, Indonesia, South Korea, etc. There is such a thing as an East Asian model of development, which is not the same thing as what is often prescribed to us by the technical experts we receive each year from the West. Remember that Africa has received more advisers in the last 30 years than any other region in the world. And to what effect? Should we not be looking at other models of development in addition to the ones we have?

5. Kenya could use East Asian experience, technology and investment in the development of her infrastructure. I cannot stress enough that Kenya needs world-class infrastructure if she is to make progress in reviving productivity in agriculture, industries, services, and indeed even in internal security. Nairobi is no longer what it used to be in the 1970s because infrastructure and law enforcement has failed to keep pace with the rate of urbanisation. This must now change. We could learn a lot not just from Kuala Lumpur, but also from Bangkok, Singapore, Djakarta, Seoul, Manila, Shanghai and other cities whose conditions were like ours (or even worse) not too long ago.

In 1955, the Bandung Conference united us – Africa and Asia in rejecting colonialism. Let us now use the same spirit to infuse greater cooperation between Kenya and East Asia.

---

2   When the NESC was finally formed, I got the President to appoint a Malaysian engineer who had been President of the World Council of Engineers and advisor to President Mahathir Mohamed, Professor Lee Chong.

III

FROM AUTHORITARIANISM TO DEMOCRACY: THE POLITICAL CONTEXT OF DEVELOPMENT

12

The Challenges of Transitional Politics in Kenya

Essay based on a paper presented at the conference titled, "In Quest of a Culture of Peace in the IGAD Region: The Role of Intellectuals and Scholars", held in Nairobi, 2-4 March 2006, and organised by Heinrich Boll Foundation

Introduction

A few books written on Kenyan politics since the multiparty elections of 1992 bear the words "transition" or "change" in their titles. The word "transition" is quite often used to mean "change" in a number of the essays in the edited volumes. For example, "transition from the Moi to the Kibaki regime" may mean "change" from the Moi to the Kibaki government. While the word "transition" implies "change", the word change does not necessarily imply transition.[1]

The two concepts, "government" and "regime" also need to be distinguished. On 30th December 2002, there was indeed a change of government in Kenya from KANU to NARC, with substantial changes in the people who run the country politically. A new president was elected and he proceeded to form a new government. *But the regime continued.* Here, perhaps, is where the puzzle lies: with the change in government in December 2002, did Kenya undergo any significant *transition in its politics?*

Notwithstanding the several essays that have been edited on Kenyan politics talking about "transition in Kenyan politics" since 1992, this essay intends to

---

1 See, for example, W. Mutunga, *Constitution Making from the Middle: Civil Society and Transition Politics in Kenya, 1992-1997* (Nairobi, Sareat and Mwengo, 1999); Winnie Mitullah et al *Politics of Transition in Kenya: From KANU to NARC* (Nairobi: Claripress, 2003); L.M. Mute et al, *Building and Open Society: The Politics of Transition in Kenya* (Nairobi: Claripress, 2002); A. Bujra (ed.) *Democratic Transition in Kenya: The Struggle from Liberal to Social Democracy* (Nairobi: ACEG and DPMF, 2005).

103

argue that *a process of transition is still underway within an essentially competitive authoritarian regime.* The structural basis on which this regime has been erected remains essentially the same. It is a structure of extreme economic inequalities where *oligarchic* interests tend to rely essentially on violence and the monopoly of violence to maintain political power and stem the tide of political changes towards democracy and an open society.

As such, when we are discussing political transition, we need to discuss transition in terms of *regime change* not simply changes in government. Regime change can occur at the level of a *political break with the past* without necessarily having an *economic break*, which involved substantial shifts in property relations and improvements in the well being of the poor.

When political breaks occur without substantial economic break—which is the usual character of transitions from authoritarian to democratic regimes— various forms of resistance and conflicts will occur during the transition period, quite often tempting those with state power to resort to the repressive tactics of yester years to maintain what they regard as "political stability". Authoritarian regimes are therefore usually conflict and violence prone, although they tend to suppress contradictions and conflicts inherent in them by using the armed might of the state. That is why when authoritarian regimes break down violent conflicts usually follow as injustices, which have been suppressed over time "burst out" and as legitimate political arrangements emerge through the ensuing struggle.

More specifically, this essay seeks to discuss the challenges of transitional politics in Kenya and the unfulfilled promises of independence nationalism that have always been at the root of the conflicts that have erupted from time to time in the history of the nation since independence. It argues that the failure to break the *structures of inequality* inherited from the colonial political economy have reinforced the structures of conflict in post-independence Kenya. We further note that attempts to break with this past *politically* have aborted twice: first with the 1966 failure of the left wing of KANU to assert hegemony over the right wing, and second, in 1992 when the Forum for the Restoration of Democracy in Kenya (FORD) failed to keep the broad *national democratic front* together in the political onslaught against the authoritarian KANU regime. The essay therefore advances the argument that a *political break* that entails a transition from authoritarianism to democracy and an open society is already under way since the December 2002 elections in which the NARC government came into power.

Authoritarian regimes and structures of violence

Sometime in the mid-1980s, I wrote an article that was published in UNESCO's *International Social Science Journal* that was entitled "An African Perspective on Peace and Development in Africa."[2] In this article I argued that peace was a necessary condition for development in Africa. But my concept of peace was not based simply on the cessation of hostilities among warring or conflicting forces, but the establishment of what I called *structures of peace in Africa,* particularly the region that has now come to be known as the *Horn of Africa.*

Apart from this region having been home to regimes riddled with violent and internal conflicts such as in Ethiopia, Uganda, Somalia, Rwanda and Burundi then, it was also home to regimes that, on the face of it, looked politically stable, but underneath were essentially brittle or conflict prone. These were the authoritarian states of Kenya and Tanzania. These regimes did not, in my view, have sustainable structures of peace in so far as they were authoritarian with substantial socio-economic inequalities.

I do not think that I was making a tremendously new argument. In any case Johan Galtung and his Peace Institute in Oslo (covering the Scandinavian countries)[3] had inundated international discourse with this kind of argument from the mid-1960s. Nonetheless it was then important to think of structures of peace in the discourse on peace and development in Africa because of the emphasis being put then on *blaming* insurgents for disrupting development in such countries like Uganda, and looking for states strong enough to put such elements of insecurity sufficiently under the armed might of the state so as to guarantee development.

Yet my point was that it is not the repressive strength of the state that can guarantee peace, stability and development, but the dynamic potential of society released by democratic governance that is much better at ensuring peace, stability and development. Indeed, this is the point that I later developed in the exchange we had in the *CODESRIA Bulletin* and *Africa Development* with Thandika Mkandawire and Shadrack Gutto among others.[4] The point is now much better appreciated: the

---

2   P. Anyang' Nyong'o, "An African Perspective on Peace and Development in Africa," *International Social Science Journal* (1986).

3   See, for example, J. Galtung, "A Structural Theory of Imperialism," *Journal of Peace Research* 8:2 (1971): 81-118.

4   Anyang' Nyong'o, "Political Instability and the Prospects for Development in Africa," *Africa Development, XIII* (1988): 71-86. See also Thandika Mkandawire, "Comments on Democracy and Political Instability," *CODESRIA Bulletin,* No. 1989.

much touted development encouraged by the stability in authoritarian regimes is more of an exception than a rule. In general, authoritarian regimes tend to be inherently more unstable politically, and stifle development through corruption and discouraging entrepreneurial initiatives.[5]

As we subsequently argued in our book *Arms and Daggers in the Heart of Africa*,[6] conflicts arise not because people are inherently prone to violence, but because of economic, social, cultural and political injustices that *historically* predispose people to such conflicts. For example, there would perhaps have been no violent conflict in Kenya in the early fifties had the colonialists not forcibly removed the Gikuyu peasants from their land, and the latter having no other option but to take up arms and reclaim their birth rights from the indulgent Happy Valley adventurers masquerading as commercial farmers in the exciting heat of tropical Kenya.[7]

Likewise, Desmond Tutu warned, after concluding the work on the Truth and Reconciliation Commission (TRC) in South Africa, that the poor and the downtrodden would most likely turn once again to violence if their hopes were not met after the so-called liberation from *apartheid* South Africa. Freedom, Tutu observed, only makes sense to the ordinary South African if it means a job from which to earn a living, a school in which to send the children for education, a house to live in and some safe drinking water with which to quench thirst. In other words, South Africa was not to be guaranteed peace after the fall of *apartheid* unless and until the structures of peace — in terms of economic growth with redistribution — was put in place.

Conflict — or the absence of peace — can be *latent* or *overt*. When violence breaks up in the open then conflicts are overt; they are seen, guns are shot, arrows fly around, machetes cut off people's heads and dead bodies are counted. That was overt conflict *a la* genocide in Rwanda in the mid-nineties. Latent conflicts, however, are those that simmer beneath the surface of what we may regard as *normal society* as people go about their daily business oblivious of the seething anger of those who recent social deprivation, neglect, dishonour,

---

5   The literature on this is now extensive, but see, in particular, M.H. Halperin, J.T. Siegle and M.M.Weinstein, *The Democracy Advantage: How Democracies Promote Prosperity and Peace* (New York; Routledge, 2004); S.M. Lipset and J.M. Lakin, *The Democratic Century* (Oklahoma: University of Oklahoma Press, 2004).

6   P. Anyang' Nyong'o, ed. *Arms and Daggers in the Heart of Africa: Studies in Internal Conflicts* (Nairobi: Academy Science Publishers, 1991).

7   See, for example, James Fox, *White Mischief* (New York: Random House, 1983).

political repression, inequalities of wealth and crass arrogance of those wielding political power "in the name of the people" as it were.

Societies which emerge from long periods of authoritarian rule into "political freedom" and an open society usually face the danger of not matching this political freedom with the economic liberation of the economically downtrodden which are the majority in society. When this freedom is then accompanied by the continued impoverishment of the majority while a small minority of the politically powerful wallow in tremendous wealth and good living, a structure of violence will remain inherent in such societies, and any economic growth achieved may be prone to social explosion from below. The violent robberies that occur in Johannesburg and Nairobi, the butchering of families by the male head who has just lost his job as state corporations are downsized and the inter-ethnic skirmishes over land ownership and grazing pastures so frequent in Kenya today are the living examples of the external expression of latent conflicts in transitional societies such as Kenya.

The IGAD countries together present this paradox of countries where overt violence has characterised internal conflicts and attempts have been made to solve these conflicts militarily as well as through social, political and economic reforms with very limited success so far. These are the countries of Somalia, Ethiopia, Eritrea, Sudan and Uganda. Then there are the two countries, Kenya and Tanzania, where latent conflicts are to be felt as a result of inequitable economic systems, unfair political dispensation, and — in the case of Kenya — an unfinished transition towards democracy and an open society.

The aborted "NARC revolution" of December 2002, did finally usher in the long delayed political transition from authoritarianism to an open society, but the delayed transition to competitive democratic politics remains, hemming society within the armpit of essentially authoritarian competitive politics much within the interest of the traditional ethnic and oligarchic political forces.

But the NARC government, like the previous Moi government, is still essentially a *presidential authoritarian regime that renews its legitimacy through competitive politics*. This break, further, should not be confused with an *economic break* that would entail a major shift in public policy towards meeting the basic needs demands of the masses through the politics of redistribution. It is precisely because the structure of the economy remains essentially the same as developed during the 40 years of authoritarian rule that the objective conditions for the transition are themselves a problem, and therefore require much more complicated *political alliances* than the populists would have us believe.

Political transition in an economic *status quo*

The transition from authoritarian rule to democracy actually started with the independence struggle. Colonialism was essentially an authoritarian system of government. The nationalists challenged it successfully; but they were also acutely aware of the dangers that independence faced. The eventual political and economic dispensation may not please or satisfy all the social forces that coalesced together into the nationalist struggle. There were seeds of authoritarianism latent within the emerging "ruling parties" even before they came to power after independence.

In his autobiography, *Freedom and After,* Tom Mboya argued that *uhuru,* or freedom, meant many things to many people: to the unemployed it meant a new opportunity to find jobs, to the landless access to land, and to civil servants promotion and better salaries.[8] The nationalist party had to mobilise all these diverse interests and hopes into one formidable movement focused on nothing but *uhuru* so as to win independence. But after independence then the crisis of meeting these expectations, given the limited resources available to the state, or limited opportunities in the economy would, no doubt, produce strains in the nationalist movement as some interests would be satisfied while others disappointed. Authoritarian politics might follow to stem rebellion and discontent.

Nonetheless, if the people see that opportunities available are fairly shared out, if they see that decisions are made in the interest of the majority and not on the basis of favouritism, tribalism or other discriminatory practices, the people are likely to accept inequality of access to opportunities and services and not necessarily revolt against structures of inequality.[9] The problem, however, is that politics in post-independence Africa has been replete with governments presiding over social injustices and maintaining such injustices through political oppression. No doubt political crises have been frequent as such injustices have been resisted, with such resistance manifesting themselves as military coups, secessionist movements, inter-ethnic conflicts, popular insurrections and even collapse of the state precisely as a result of dissatisfaction with political patronage, discrimination based on race, ethnicity, religion and region, extreme inequalities, political repression, wanton denial of human rights and so on.[10] In certain countries these crises have led to open and violent conflicts lasting

---

8   Tom Mboya, *Freedom and After* (New York: Andre Dautch, 1963).

9   Tedd R. Gurr, *Why Men Rebel,* (Princeton, New Jersey: Princeton University Press, 1970).

10   See, for example, our own study, P. Anyang' Nyong'o ed. 1992.

several years. In others they have been kept simmering beneath the surface of presumed stability due to a more successful use of the armed might of the state or its ideological manipulation of antagonistic social forces through tribalism, religion and regionalism. Kenya belongs to this last genre of presumable political stability.

In 1965, following prolonged disagreements over land policy, foreign policy, appointments in the public service and the running of the ruling political party, the less than two years old government of Jomo Kenyatta was headed for a split between what was regarded as the left wing (more populist) and the right wing (centrist and pro-big property ownership). Led by Jaramogi Oginga Odinga and Bildad Kaggia, the left wing favoured distributing land free to the landless, putting a ceiling on the amount of land an individual could own, opening up more job opportunities to the unemployed through major public works, adopting a less pro-West foreign policy, and filling up civil service positions on grounds of merit rather than nepotism and patronage.

In 1966, the left wing was kicked out of the ruling party by a clever process of reorganisation and restructuring that made the party depend on the political patronage of ethnic leaders as its vice presidents, while the president wielded authoritarian power at the centre. The outcome was the birth of the Kenya People's Union (KPU) as a party of the left in opposition to KANU, a situation that only lasted three years before the authoritarian might of the state came down heavily on the party and its followers, throwing its leaders in prison and banning the party altogether in 1969. It was in July of that year that KANU's Secretary-General, Tom Mboya was also assassinated, thereby eliminating him as a serious contender to succeed the ailing Kenyatta as Kenya's second president after independence.

As Colin Leys has ably shown in his path breaking book, *Neo-Colonialism in Kenya: The Political Economy of Underdevelopment*,[11] the structure of an economy whereby a small group owned the most fertile land, controlled industry, was the biggest employers of labour, earned over 90 per cent of the nation's income and monopolised political power, characterised Kenya in colonial as well as post-colonial times. The only difference was that, in post-colonial times, this *power elite* was largely African, albeit in alliance with an enclave of Asians in the commercial and manufacturing sectors, and Europeans in financial and industrial sectors. The African peasantry remained largely untransformed, except for the

---

11 C. Leys, *Neo-Colonialism in Kenya: The Political Economy of Underdevelopment* (Nairobi: Heinemann, 1973).

fact that the frontiers of private property in land and agriculture was open to a limited number of the rich, middle and poor peasantry through settlement schemes and "land-buying companies" after independence. Otherwise the land issue and landlessness remained a problem.

It was this structure of the economy that the KPU challenged and failed. By 1970, the authoritarian regime had reconsolidated itself, finishing the fusion between business power and political power when the Ndegwa Commission allowed civil servants to indulge in business in 1972. The symbiotic relationship between occupying positions in the state and making it in the world of business was never to be broken again; any attempts to do so in the guise of fighting corruption, either in Parliament or outside in civil society, met with severe political repression, including detention without trial, murder and assassination, by the authoritarian regime.

In 1975 J.M. Kariuki, a populist politician from Nyandarua, was brutally assassinated for challenging the authoritarian regime. Subsequent to that, a series of detentions without trial followed involving dissident politicians, university lecturers, journalists, priests and trade unions. When Moi took over power from Kenyatta in 1978, the trend of repression did not change, but internal disagreements within the regime on how to dispense with state patronage after the death of Kenyatta led to an aborted temporary rebellion by the armed forces in August 1982. The attempted coup, however, gave Moi the excuse to purge the state machinery of individuals not loyal to him and to entrench his own personal rule.

The brittleness of authoritarian regimes lies in the fact that they do not lend themselves easily to political change, either in terms of elite circulation or regime changes. Since authoritarian systems are prone to personal rule, which is further solidified by political patronage, any change will be resisted by individuals who find it difficult to transfer or renew personal loyalty. That is why both resistance and attempts at change have frequently invited the intervention of the armed might of the state, in the form of the armed forces or the secret agents of the state. This was the drama that played itself from August 1978 when Kenyatta died to August 1982 when there was an attempted coup against Moi.

In actual fact, Moi never really recovered from this attempted coup. He lived in awe of his own shadow, always suspecting somebody to be plotting against him, and reshuffling his cabinet, senior civil service officers and personnel in the armed forces with immodest frequency. In the business community, doing well in a new venture was a recipe for being invited to give shares to the oligarchy around the president, for money was associated with political power, and its monopoly by the oligarchy was its best recipe for retaining power by denying it to others.

Precisely as a result of this fear of insecurity for his regime, the 1980s became years of extreme political repression. The regime erected a one-party state by law. It banished any formal opposition to its rule. More detention without trial of opponents followed. Torture chambers for dissidents were opened in Nyayo House. The president and his cronies frequently talked the language of violence in warning their real or perceived opponents.

This inherently unstable system, prone to crony capitalism and surviving on political patronage, was also inherently un-developmental. Financing its political machinery through corruption, it depleted into wasteful expenditure of public resources, which could otherwise have gone to social provisioning such as education, health, housing and social security.

With the fall of the Berlin Wall in 1989, there was a major shift in the balance of political power globally. Not having to put up with the so-called communist threat globally, the West suddenly found they no longer needed undemocratic and oppressive client states in the Third World as buffers against communism. Such states, like Zaire and Kenya in Africa, lost their lustre of anti-communism, and found themselves nakedly facing democratic pressures from within. We had, in 1987, published a book on *Popular Struggles for Democracy in Africa* in which we presented cases of people's movements and organisations that had been organising for democratic change in many African countries.[12] With the new international conjuncture, they found a "breathing space" against these oppressive governments as the West started to openly support and encourage democracy in the Third World, with many Western NGOs appearing in the scene in the Third World to monitor democratic elections, support political party organisations and spell out democratic conditions for disbursing aid.

It is in this context that the Forum for the Restoration of Democracy (FORD) was born in Kenya in 1991, after the Moi regime had brutally murdered its own foreign minister, Dr. Robert J. Ouko in February 1990, for investigating corruption in his own government, and for daring to communicate with Western capitals on the same. Ouko was challenging the staying power of the authoritarian regime, corruption and the politics of patronage, he had to go. But his death at such a volatile international conjuncture exposed the regime, and

---

12   Anyang' Nyong'o (ed.), *Popular Struggles for Democracy in Africa* (London: Zed Books, 1987).

made it vulnerable to the mounting pressures for change now receiving more overt support internationally.

The upsurge of movements, organisations and political parties in Kenya after the 1991 sudden amendment of the constitution to allow for multiparty politics brought into being limited competitive politics in an essentially authoritarian system, what has now been called *competitive authoritarianism*.[13] This depicts a civilian non-democratic regime with regularly held elections that are competitive but extremely unfair, as indeed the elections under Moi in 1992 and 1997 were extremely unfair in many counts.

In such regimes, Way argues, democratic institutions exist and are regarded as the principal means of obtaining and exercising political authority, *but power holders violate those rules so often that the regime fails to meet minimal democratic standards*.[14] Incumbent's regularly harass opposition leaders, censor the media, and attempt to falsify election results. Yet elections are regularly held and remain competitive, and opposition candidates can and sometimes do win.[15]

Such regimes are also usually presidential, with those exercising that office dependent largely on an array of clients within and outside the state apparatus who provide political support, loyalty, the largesse for buying and maintaining political power and the running of state machinery on a highly personalised basis. Throughout the nineties, Moi gave in to competitive politics grudgingly and sought, in many ways, to circumvent the competition and ensure the survival of his regime. But the system also weakened gradually as competitive politics in Parliament also brought about legal and constitutional changes that deprived the presidency of some of its authoritarian powers. For example, the Inter-Party Parliamentary Group (IPPG) reforms in 1997 that made changes in electoral laws, led the ruling party KANU to lose substantial control of Parliament to the Opposition.

This gave Moi, though an authoritarian president, a slim majority in Parliament, compelling him to seek allies in the opposition to ensure the passing of government business in the House. The effort led to cooperation

---

13 See, for example, A. Lucan, "Way's Description and Analysis of Ukraine Under Kuchma's Presidency in Kushma's Failed Authoritarianism," *Journal of Democracy*, Vol. 16, No. 2, (April 2005): 131-145.

14 Steven Levitsky and Way, "The Rise of Competitive Authoritarianism", *Journal of Democracy*, 13 (April 2002): 51-65.

15 In the post 1990 "democratic wave" in Africa, most countries that held competitive elections, with the exception of South Africa and Botswana, were essentially authoritarian regimes that were largely undemocratic but allowed competitive elections for purposes of gaining legitimacy locally and internationally.

with the National Development Party (NDP), which eventually dissolved itself and joined KANU. This move was to prove the beginnings of the break-up of the authoritarian regime and the lead towards ample democratisation and the birth of an open society.

But why was Moi so intent on controlling Parliament?

Competitive authoritarian politics finds its locus of expression usually in key representative institutions such as parliament. It is in parliament, with its rules of immunity and its special powers and privileges, that the enemies of the authoritarian regime, particularly the democratic opposition, finds its widest freedom to express itself, expose the iniquities of the regime and seek to supplant it from power. Indeed, parliament gives the opposition the chance to exploit all available opportunities in the constitution and democratic practices internationally to bring about political change legally and by peaceful means.

The records of the Kenya National Assembly show how, between 1993 and 2002, a lot that was previously unknown to Kenyans regarding corruption, misuse of public office, the denial of basic freedoms and the lies of the regime were exposed through debates in Parliament and the works of the parliamentary watchdog committees. Although the regime tried to intimidate Members of Parliament (MPs) with arrest, police harassments and the banning of political rallies, it could not altogether shut down Parliament where all the talk and the exposure was done. It could not stop the formation of such select committees as those set up to look into corruption and the grabbing of public assets by the regime. It could, however, strive to control decision-making in Parliament by bribing MPs to vote in its favour when crucial bills and motions were tabled in the House.

Finally, when Moi's term in office constitutionally came to an end in 2002, his attempts to orchestrate his own succession by the so-called "Uhuru Project" led to the break up of his own party as politicians desirous of high office resisted Moi's imposition of a presidential candidate over them. The rebels, forming themselves into a Rainbow Alliance, broke out from KANU and sought alliance with the then opposition to come up with a new coalition to oppose Moi that was to be called the National Rainbow Coalition (NARC). It is this formidable coalition that finally trounced KANU in the December 2002 elections to form the new government under the presidency of Mwai Kibaki.

The frustrations of the transition to democracy under NARC

As a pre-election coalition, NARC brought together diverse political parties representing regions, ethnic groups, personalities and business interests. These parties were ideologically amorphous and were used mainly as "vehicles" for entering parliament. But as vehicles, they had to assure their members of getting "better things for their supporters" once in Parliament. These "better things" included cabinet positions, appointments to jobs in state corporations, directorships in such corporations, ambassadorial appointments and so on. All these were agreed to in a pre-election Memorandum of Understanding (MOU) between the Liberal Democratic Party (LDP) and the National Alliance Party of Kenya (NAK), the key members of the coalition. There was also an understanding regarding the programme that the government would undertake once in power.

But once Kibaki was sworn in as President, he quickly did away with the MOU, avoided any further discussions of its contents with the LDP leaders and went ahead to appoint the cabinet and other officers of the state without much regard to the views, opinions and preferences of his coalition partners. Using the powers conferred upon the presidency by the essentially authoritarian constitution, Kibaki preferred to rule legally rather than politically; exploiting these constitutional powers even when they went against the *political spirit of coalition politics* that had brought him to power That is the summary; let us now tell the story in full as follows.

Between 1992 and 2002, several political developments had occurred in Kenya's political culture that had substantially undermined the authoritarian presidency without necessarily being translated into constitutional provisions. Some, through the IPPG reforms of 1997, had been translated into law and had affected amendments to the National Assembly and Presidential Elections Act, for example. Precisely because the constitution was now out of step with the political culture and the popular mood that frowned on authoritarian politics, popular pressure escalated for the reform of the constitution to be more democratic and more accommodative to the politics of an open society.

In the run-up to the elections of December 2002, while the opposition political parties were campaigning to remove the Moi regime, the people were looking back to the experience of 1992 and 1997 and observing that without the coalition among the opposition political parties, Moi's Kenya African National Union (KANU) would still win the elections. A popular demand for the opposition to unite followed, and the leaders responded by coining a united front of the parties called the National Alliance Party of Kenya (NAK) that brought together the Democratic Party (DP), the Forum for the Restoration of Democracy-Kenya (FORD-Kenya), the National Party of Kenya (NPK), the United Democratic Movement (UDM), a faction of the Social Democratic Party (SDP) and SPARK. The leaders of these parties respectively were Mwai Kibaki, Michael Kijana Wamalwa, Charity Ngilu, Kipruto arap Kirwa, Anyang' Nyong'o and Shem Ochuodho. They formed a joint forum that gave leadership to the united opposition and held rallies across the country committing to endorse one presidential candidate among them, a feat that was achieved by October 2002 with the support of an array of civil society organisations, which were also part of the Alliance. Key among these civil society organisations were the Green Belt Movement, led by Professor Wangari Maathai and the National Convention Executive Council (NCEC) led by Professor Kivutha Kibwana.

In the meantime, in Moi's attempt to impose Uhuru Kenyatta as his successor in KANU and the sole presidential candidate for the party, a major disagreement arose among the KANU presidential hopefuls who demanded an open and democratic nomination process. Remaining adamant, Moi found himself defied by these gentlemen who immediately marched out of the party in a huff, grouping themselves in a powerful pressure group called the National Rainbow Alliance. One after the other they resigned from KANU and from cabinet positions to carry their message to the Kenyan people, again promising that they would name one among them to contest the presidency on the National Rainbow Alliance ticket. This group was led by Raila Odinga, then KANU's Secretary-General, George Saitoti, the then Vice President, and Stephen Kalonzo Musyoka, then Minister for Environment and Natural Resources. Others included the then Deputy Speaker of the National Assembly, Joab Omino (who became the chairman of the Rainbow group), Fred Gumo, David Musila and George Khaniri.

As the two opposition groups moved around the country appealing for popular support, the message came loud and clear from the people: please unite if you really want to remove Moi and KANU from power. The Kiswahili phrase, *nyinyi muungane*, meaning "you people unite", was heard everywhere from the crowds as they shouted back to the political leaders of the two groups addressing them from various platforms around the country. The response was quick: consultations started between the two groups, and these consultations were extended to other opposition groups like Simeon Nyachae's FORD-People, leading to the agreement in mid-November to endorse Mwai Kibaki as the sole presidential candidate of the opposition under a pact of sharing power enshrined in a Memorandum of Understanding. The new united opposition was given the name National Rainbow Coalition (NARC).

NARC developed two structures of governing itself: the Summit, which brought together all the presidential hopefuls from the two groups as the key political decision-making body; and the Strategic Committee, which discussed policy, logistics and acted as the executive committee of the Alliance. There were other subsidiary committees like the Mobilisation Committee, for mobilising resources for the campaign, the Economic Committee which worked on the manifesto, and so on.

Within the Summit were all the presidential hopefuls including Moody Awori who was its chairperson. One of the most important things that the Summit did was to agree on a power-sharing formula among the summit members, especially cabinet positions in the event of winning the elections. This formula was contained in a Memorandum of Understanding, which was subsequently deposited with lawyer Ambrose Rachier of Rachier and Amolo Advocates of Nairobi. This particular MOU was only known to Summit members and not to the general leadership of NARC as a whole.

NARC, therefore, ended up with two MOUs: one, more elaborate and containing policy commitments and key principles of forming the coalition government, and this was read to the public when NARC was launched at the Hilton Hotel in November 2002; and the other secretly signed by the Summit leaders at the Nairobi Club, detailing the power sharing formula for the two parties coalescing in NARC, the Rainbow Alliance (now called the Liberal Democratic Party-LDP) and the NPK. The key beneficiary of both MOUs was Mwai Kibaki, for in both he was endorsed as the flag bearer of NARC. Thus, one was read out publicly (in full view of the Kenyan people) at the Hilton Hotel, and the other privately (in full view of his peers and cohorts in the leadership of the new coalition) in the secret chambers of the Nairobi Club.

Soon after the NARC election victory of 29 December 2002, Mwai Kibaki formed his cabinet with scant respect for the terms of the Nairobi Club MOU. The LDP leadership cried foul. Attempts to get him to explain his action at the Summit did not succeed. The then controller of State House, and the President's private secretary, advised that such matters be discussed at Cabinet level, as the President was now exercising his constitutional powers which now took precedence over temporary political arrangements. Other partisan groups argued that the president could not be bound by *secret agreements among power-hungry leaders*. They went further to observe that the people of Kenya had elected Kibaki as *the* President and not these others who were now making *selfish claims* on him.

Two issues are pertinent here. One, *constitutionally*, the President was indeed right to appoint his cabinet in accordance with the powers conferred upon him by the constitution. But this constitution was, for all intents and purposes, *an authoritarian constitution* which NARC, under his leadership, had promised the people of Kenya to change for a more *democratic one* within one hundred days of coming to power. In other words, to give the authoritarian constitution more legitimacy in forming his government than the promise he gave to his peers in the Summit and the people of Kenya of forming a government on a more consultative coalescing principle, was to undermine the trust bestowed on him to initiate democratic governance from the word go.

Two, *politically*, it was through the process of pre-election coalition building that he had been elected President, and not through the authoritarian framework of the constitution that actually made it difficult to form post-election coalition government. That is why the opposition parties had to go through the political gymnastics of their candidates being endorsed by *a political party called NARC* in order to legitimately enter the National Assembly. All this was made possible by agreements *which he himself signed* so as to access presidential powers. The root to these powers was not therefore the constitution which he was now using to justify his choice of the cabinet and other appointments; the root was a *political process.*

Frowning upon this political process while crowning himself with the authoritarian powers from the constitution, revealed one thing very early in his presidency: Kibaki was more at home exercising presidential powers from the authoritarian political templates of the Kenyatta and Moi eras rather than embracing reform and crusading for it under a *democratic* NARC government. Under him the transition from authoritarianism to democracy would stall. Rather than deliver the new democratic constitution within one hundred days as promised in the Hilton Hotel MOU, he preferred to forgo the honeymoon with the open society within these same one hundred days as he nonchalantly ignored his promises and went about business in accordance with the existing constitution. The constitution gave him the authoritarian powers that are unpopular with the people, but very acceptable to him and his entourage grouped together within the presidency or what came to be known popularly as the *Mount Kenya Mafia*. Rather than institutionalise coalition politics by strengthening NARC as the ruling party, he preferred to disband the NARC governing organs and, like Kenyatta and Moi before him, run politics through the state apparatus.

What explains the stalled transition?

Authoritarian regimes usually destroy organisations, particularly those that try to organise civil society politically in the arena of competition for power or for the control of state power. That is why, very early on in the emergence of authoritarian regimes in Africa, they all established *one-party rule*. Very often this became no-party rule as presidents ruled through the state apparatus or as the military took over to run political affairs through command. Where political parties existed or were deliberately created by the civilian or military rulers, they functioned as branches of the state apparatus, with personnel moving in and out of both as the president so appointed.

Sooner rather than later, the art of political organisation is lost by civil society. In Kenya, for example, the Maendeleo ya Wanawake, a purely women's organisation that dated from colonial times, was made a branch of the ruling party KANU, with its leaders enjoying support and close proximity with the President. Elections to its organs became KANU affairs, and the autonomy vis-à-vis the state was rapidly lost. In Uganda the National Union of Students of Uganda (NUSU) in the late sixties went through the same experience with Milton Obote's Uganda People's Congress (UPC) government, creating tension between NUSU/UPC and the more autonomous Makerere Students' Guild.

That is why when popular pressure begins to mount against authoritarianism in such developing societies it rarely comes through political parties as such since these do not really exist. The pressures emerge from a whole array of popular movements and civil society organisations that arise in stiff opposition to the regime, with leaders and members very often going through repression, torture, assassinations, exile life, and so on. In the event that a conjuncture arises where competition for political power is possible through elections, the regime always makes it very difficult for such forces to organise politically through parties. Innovative leaders are therefore useful at such moments in coming up with *points of entry* or *appropriate organisational forms* that can lead the reform movements to capture political power through elections.

It is quite often said that organisations, in the abstract, do not innovate; individuals and people, however, do. In 1992, faced with the repeal of Section 2A of the Kenya Constitution Act that finally allowed for the formation of political parties other than the ruling party, KANU, the opposition formed a mass movement called the Forum for the Restoration of Democracy (FORD) as a broad united front of the forces opposed to the regime. When FORD split following the competition for leadership of the various ethnic elites, the resulting political parties, devoid of both the numbers and the art of organisation, lost the elections to the state-backed KANU. The same predicament followed in 1997 as even more political parties in the opposition confronted KANU in the presidential and general elections of that year.

In 2002, through the *innovation* of the opposition political leaders, a more successful united democratic movement against KANU called NARC was forged and the opposition managed to form the government on a pre-election coalition. But taking power under a largely authoritarian constitution, the innovation should not have ended with winning the election; it needed to have been carried out even more vigorously in the post-election period.

The tragedy with NARC is that the innovative leaders who crafted the MOUs, the Manifesto and the campaign slogans handed over power to a non-innovative President with enormous powers under the constitution, and with his mind grooved in the political routines of his predecessors at State House. As we have observed earlier, Kibaki looked back and resurrected the templates of governing from the Kenyatta and the Moi years, re-canonising authoritarian rule atop the innovative ideas on which NARC was erected, banishing politics to the cupboards of a demobilised NARC, and leaving state power to be wielded by political novices who now averred to rule in the name of the President as their erstwhile incompetents had done under the outgoing Moi government.

The end result – and indeed the outcome of this – was, among other things, disarray in the judiciary as these novices sought to appoint their men and settle political vendettas in the name of a surgical reform in that vital branch of democratic and constitutional government. Impasse followed in the urgent task to reform the civil service so as to deliver on the reformist mandate of NARC as these same novices impressed upon the President that only the "politically correct of *our men*" could keep key places in the civil service. Retirees were called back to occupy key positions in the civil service not because they were the only ones qualified to do so but more because they were politically correct from a loyalty or ethnic point of view. Again Kibaki went the same route as his two predecessors at State House had done, and reform was stillborn since there was no enabling environment for it in the civil service.

As opposition amounted within government to these reactionary moves by the President, the cabinet became less deliberative and more key decisions were made within the small group around the presidency, some individuals in this group having no formal positions in government but wielding substantial influence on policies and public appointments. So irate were leaders in NARC that a meeting was soon called to chart the future of the coalition in early April 2003 under the chairmanship of the then Vice-President, Michael Kijana Wamalwa.

At this meeting, held at the Mount Kenya Safari Club at the foot of Mount Kenya in Nanyuki, the Vice-President decried the lack of progress in the reform process, the sliding back to the old ways, the apparent settling into power for power's sake and the rapid loss of confidence in government among the ordinary Kenyans. The Vice-President asked a poignant question: "*If elections were held today, would NARC win?*"

The Vice-President received a standing ovation from those who attended the retreat when he finished his very eloquently delivered speech. But the more important question was what the NARC leadership gathered in Mount Kenya was going to do following the VP's entreaties. It was resolved that NARC be revitalised, the organs become operational, that the Summit's membership be expanded so as to be more inclusive and effective, and that the President be informed of the deliberations and he takes heed of the concerns of the Members of Parliament and the leaders. Keeping faith to the reform process was emphasised, particularly the constitutional reform process and the fight against corruption. A committee to follow up the implementation of the Nanyuki agreements and another one to work on the constitution of the party were set up. Subsequently, these committees did do their work but, tragically, the President paid scant attention to the Nanyuki deliberations as well as the work of the committees that were set up.

While all these debates, retreats and arguments about NARC and the reform process were going on in the open, something much more serious was going on within the presidency in the background. This was the plan to amass financial resources with which to buy and maintain political power in NARC and to build a financial war chest in readiness for the 2007 elections. Having decided not to be bothered with building the ruling party as a coalition as decided in Nanyuki, the President decided that financial power would be needed to turn NARC into a state party and to retain the state in its authoritarian form by financially influencing the constitutional reform process at the Bomas of Kenya. He therefore comfortably announced in Mombasa on New Year's evening in December 2003 that anybody in NARC who thought they belonged to any other party was dreaming. Again, using his constitutional authoritarian powers, completely oblivious to the political process that had brought him where he was, he ordered the social and political forces under him to organise in accordance with his command: once more back to a one-party state.

As history would later reveal, this thing that was going on in the background was the Anglo Leasing scam. This was an arrangement whereby government officials in the President's office and the security branches of government sought to procure security goods and services for the government from fictitious companies through the mediation of equally fictitious financial institutions. One such financial institution came to be known as the Anglo Leasing Finance Company. The President's office — inheriting a scheme already hatched under Moi's administration--arranged that this company facilitate the building of a forensic laboratory for the Kenya Police, the buying of tamper-proof passports for the Immigration Department and the building of a ship for the Kenya Navy. The total sum of money involved in these and other deals was close to a quarter of a billion dollars. A good part of this money was paid well in advance but returned mysteriously to the Treasury when the Permanent Secretary in charge of Ethics in the President's Office, John Githongo, questioned the deals.

From Githongo's diaries, it becomes clear that the Kibaki regime was stalling on the reform process and disengaging from the process of transition from authoritarian rule to democracy precisely because they needed the political shell of authoritarian presidency to undertake these corrupt deals. Further, these corrupt deals were also needed to finance the politics of sustaining presidential authoritarian rule. Who says corruption, therefore, says authoritarianism and who says authoritarianism beckons corruption as a necessary bedfellow.

In January 2005, confronted by the British High Commissioner in Nairobi, Sir Edward Clay, with 20 or so cases of corrupt deals in his administration, the President handed the Clay dossier to the Director of the Kenya Anti-Corruption Commission, Justice Aaron Ringera, for action. In April of the same year, in a submission to the development partners at a Nairobi meeting, Justice Ringera categorically stated that the government had either investigated or concluded all the Anglo-Leasing related scams that Clay was concerned about.[16] When I raised the issue during the campaigns on the referendum on the draft constitution, both Ringera and Mwalimu Mati — the Executive Officer of Transparency International in Nairobi — dismissed my claims of the covering up of corruption as "mere politicking". At the beginning of 2006 when Githongo

---

16 The Director/Chief Executive, Kenya Anti-Corruption Commission's *Status Report on the Anti-Corruption Agenda of the Government of Kenya*, Nairobi, 5 April , 2005.

released his diary, it was quite clear that the President had mobilised all organs of government to facilitate the cover-up.

The referendum on the Draft Constitution and the stalled transition

Two key issues dominated the debate on the drafting of the proposed new constitution throughout the constitutional review conference at the Bomas of Kenya from the beginning of 2003. These issues were on the executive branch of government and devolution of power to local or subsidiary authorities. Quite understandably so for the essence of authoritarian government is the concentration of executive power at the centre, usually the presidency, and where presidential rule is the key repository of authoritarian power, then it is equally unlikely that any other branch of government will exercise much executive power. Hence local authorities, under presidential authoritarian regimes, usually become mere appendages of the centre, with little power over their finances let alone the employment of their key officers.

Juan Linz, the American professor of political science at Yale University, argues that *"presidentialism"* is the curse of the politics in many low-income countries. From it arise substantial denial of human rights to most citizens in these countries, the perpetration of corruption, the stunting or blocking of the growth of the private sector and the general underdevelopment.[17] It is therefore understandable, he goes on to argue, for pressures to mount in such countries for political reforms in favour of *parliamentary* systems of government and the *dispersal, de-concentration or devolution of power* from the centre to local authorities so as to enhance possibilities for development. In other words, such reforms would enhance more democratic governance, and more democratic governance stands a better chance of stimulating development; the use of resources not for corruption but for investment in economic growth, human development and social provisioning.

The draft constitution as amended by the Parliamentary Select Committee on Constitution Reform, the so-called Nyachae Committee, and as finally drafted at the Kilifi Retreat of the Committee and presented for a National Referendum in November 2005, rejected the parliamentary system in preference for the highly presidential system of government as enshrined in the constitution whose reform had been called for. It also greatly reduced the financial powers that were to be devolved to lower units of government, reserving the very survival of

---

17   Juan Linz, "Presidentialism versus Parliamentarism", *Journal of Democracy, 16:3 (Winter 1990): 51-69.*

these units to decisions at the centre. When the referendum debates started, two contending schools of thought therefore came forth: the one for a parliamentary system of government and substantial devolution whose campaign sign was the *orange (chungwa* in Kiswahili) and those for a presidential system of government and very limited devolution whose sign was the *banana* (or *ndizi).*

While there were obviously other issues on which the two sides differed and argued passionately for their points of view, and while propaganda and mudslinging played their usual role in such vote-wooing campaigns, the key ideological and *reform* issues that created a meaningful divide between the two were these two: the structure of the executive and devolution of power. For maintaining the current system of presidential rule with limited devolution, the *ndizi* side submitted the following points:

- A strong central authority is needed to maintain political stability and promote development in a new nation that is developing and in which ethnic diversity needs to be handled carefully as people compete for development resources.

- To have a president as head of state and a prime minister as head of government is to bring confusion in government. This amounts to creating two centres of power, which is unnecessary, expensive and prone to conflict within the executive branch of government.

- In order to fight corruption and put in place a lean and efficient government, devolution is not really necessary. It is possible to disperse centres of corruption to local authorities and hence end up wasting even more resources through "devolved corruption."

- For doing away with the presidential system of government, bringing in a parliamentary system and de-concentrating power from the centre to lower levels of government through devolution, the *chungwa* side advanced the following argument:

- A parliamentary system of government makes it possible for the leader of the party with majority in parliament to form the government. If no single party wins a majority, then parties can form a post-election coalition. Such a government is likely to be more responsive to popular pressure for reform as decisions are not concentrated in the hands of one man called the president but dispersed among political parties which will constantly be bargaining in parliament.

- A decision needs to be made on how both the president and the prime

123

minister are elected to their positions. If the president is directly elected by the people, as in France, and then he appoints a prime minister who leads the government in parliament because he can marshal a majority in parliament, then the powers of the president and those of the prime pinister need to be very carefully spelt out in the constitution. On the other hand, in a purely parliamentary system like India and Great Britain, the presidency is a mere ceremonial position and that office can be filled through an election in parliament. In either case, there is less likelihood of having the kind of imperial presidency with all its excesses that Kenya has had since independence.

- Devolution need not lead to dispersing centres of corruption if there are strong regulatory institutions, the rule of law is enforced and the judiciary is fully operational. The problem at the moment is that local authorities are not only under financed, but they also operate outside the purview of strong regulation and quite often oblivious to the rule of law.

- With the experience of the Constituency Development Fund (CDF), it has now been proved that when the people have a say on how resources are to be used at the local level and when there is room for social auditing, devolution actually works much better than centralisation. The CDF resources have reached the people much more successfully than the District Development Committee (DDC) resources of yester years.

The draft constitution was soundly rejected at the referendum, with 152 constituencies out of 212 voting "NO", a total of just over 3 million votes out of 5 million cast ballots, and delivering victory to the Orange side. The government reacted by crying foul: the opposition, it claimed, had rigged the voting; people, they further averred, had been told lies about the draft constitution; and even more devastating to the intelligence of the 3 million Kenyans who voted against the draft, the government argued that these voters had merely cast "protest votes" against one community which was seen as being "for" the draft. Research is yet to be carried out to determine to what extent the outcome of the vote was due to these reasons. But it is indeed true to reason that people do cast votes in elections for diverse reasons – fear, group dynamics, personal convictions, partial information, fulfilling obligations, party and individual loyalty, and so on. Whatever the case, such motives would influence voters on either side of the divide, and in the case of this referendum, both *ndizi* and *chungwa* spared few arsenals for vote catching that were at their disposal.

After the 21 November verdict, the President dissolved his entire cabinet, appointed a new and highly enlarged one comprising 95 ministers and assistant ministers in a parliament of 222 members and excluded all those ministers and assistant ministers "who had gone orange" during the referendum. The "Orange Seven" in the dissolved cabinet were Raila Odinga (Roads and Public Works), Lina Kilimo (Office of the President in charge of Immigration), Ochilo Ayako (Gender, Youth and Sports), Najib Balala (Office of the President in charge of National Heritage), Kalonzo Musyoka (Environment and Natural Resources), William Ntimama (Office of the President in charge of Public Service), and Anyang' Nyong'o (Planning and National Development).

The new cabinet was appointed from among members of parliament in all parliamentary political parties who the President considered as having remained loyal to the government during the referendum. It was called the Government of National Unity (GNU), thereby debunking once and for all the idea of a coalition government under NARC. The LDP reacted by formally announcing its leaving of the government side and joining the opposition in Parliament. The stage was therefore set for a new round of struggle over the pending issue of the constitution, the important agenda for the Kenyan people as far as urgent reforms that were still needed for the transition to democracy. So far, with Mwai Kibaki at the helm of the state and still bending over backwards to rule from the political templates of the authoritarian past, this transition will remain stalled.

13

Elections and Democratic Transitions in Africa
The Kenyan Experience in the African Context

An address to the Nigerian Association of Political Science in Lagos
Nigeria on 28 June 2004

Introduction

We know that democracy is something we in Africa expected in our form of government after colonialism. We would rule ourselves and not be subjected to alien rule. We would, therefore, be free to elect those who govern us under the slogan "one man one vote" that the nationalists used to mobilise us at independence.

Freedom, social justice, respect for human rights and government by the rule of law came naturally to the lips of the nationalists, and the post-colonial state was heralded as the home of this democracy. Then came military coups and political dictatorships justified by diverse ideologies mouthed by many demagogues who straddled the continent like colossus. Some one-party states were run by patriots and humanists like Nyerere and Kaunda, men who meant well but perhaps used wrong methods to pursue their good ends at times. Other one-party states were run by rascals like Mobutu and Siad Barre.

The popular struggles for democracy in post-colonial Africa has therefore been the subject of many theses and books, and we can only here mention ours, *Popular Struggles for Democracy in Africa,*[1] and hope that the knowledge acquired in it can lead us directly to our subject matter of today. And that is the recent electoral victory of the opposition parties in Kenya and what it tells us about transitions from authoritarian regimes to democracy in Africa.

---

1 See P. Anyang' Nyong'o (ed.), Popular Struggles for Democracy in Africa (London: Zed Books, 1987).

The December 2002 elections in Kenya

On 27 December 2002, a general election was held in Kenya to choose a new president, 212 Members of Parliament and thousands of councillors in local authorities. The result was a major victory for the opposition political parties and a removal from power of the authoritarian KANU regime, which had been in power since independence in 1963. Much more important, however, was the defeat of Daniel Toroitich arap Moi as President since he had put up Uhuru Kenyatta, Jomo Kenyatta's son, as KANU's presidential candidate to continue with the system he had presided for a quarter of a decade.

The nomination of Uhuru as KANU's presidential candidate proved to be Moi's undoing. In March 2002, Moi had formed an alliance with Raila Odinga, leader of the National Development Party (NDP) to bolster KANU's chances of winning the December 2002 elections. NDP had actually been dissolved and fused with KANU, as Raila became the Secretary-General of the new KANU while Moi retained the party's chairmanship. The tacit understanding was that Raila would become the party's standard-bearer come the general elections at the end of that year. Moi, however, had different ideas. He did not trust Raila with the leadership of KANU, nor did he trust any of the other contenders for the presidential slot. These included Vice-President George Saitoti, Education Minister Kalonzo Musyoka, and a host of others.

While KANU was busy jostling who would become their presidential candidate, the opposition political parties were busy bridging the gaps among them and working on a common platform in readiness for the elections. The leader of the Official Opposition in Parliament, Mwai Kibaki as chairman of the Democratic Party, Michael Kijana Wamalwa of FORD-Kenya, Charity Ngilu of the National Party of Kenya, Kipruto arap Kirwa of the unregistered United Democratic Movement (UDM), Anyang' Nyong'o of the Social Democratic Party and Shem Ochuodho of SPARK all came together to support one presidential candidate from among themselves. It was tacitly understood that this candidate would be Kibaki, and a carefully worked out pact bringing together all the top leaders endorsed Kibaki to be the standard bearer of what became know as the National Alliance Party of Kenya (NAK). Several smaller parties and civil society organisations endorsed NAK, and the movement now appeared formidable enough to cause Moi some nightmare.

It was in the wake of this opposition unity that the rebels in KANU, ganging behind the disappointed possible presidential candidates, started to hold rallies

127

across the country to drum up support for their case. They contended that, while they supported KANU as a party, they refused to recognise Uhuru as KANU's presidential candidate. And if Moi insisted on this undemocratic choice, they would have to think twice about their support for KANU. But wherever they went in the country campaigning against Moi and his "Uhuru Project", the people urged them to unite with NAK against Moi. And wherever NAK held rallies, the people urged the leaders to unite with the rebels from KANU who now called themselves "the Rainbow Alliance." Everywhere the people said "*muungane*", Swahili word meaning "you people unite."

The call for unity became irresistible. The people could not listen to anything else. In 1992, during the first multiparty elections, the opposition parties got 67 per cent of the popular vote and still lost both Parliament and the Presidency to KANU. This is because the votes were split among 4 key opposition parties, and a number of other smaller parties. In 1997, a similar thing happened, although this time Moi had to go overboard in rigging the elections to get both Parliament and the Presidency. In 2002, the people of Kenya – majority of whom were opposed to the Moi regime – did not want to take another risk with a multiplicity of opposition parties at the polls once more. Hence they cried "*muungane*".

Negotiations soon started between NAK and the Rainbow Alliance. The late Joab Omino – then Deputy Speaker in the National Assembly – led the Rainbow Alliance team while I led the NAK team in the unity negotiations. It was a protracted process whose history is yet to be written. But by mid-October it was quite clear that we were going places and by mid-November the deal was signed. In a mammoth rally held at the Uhuru Park, the National Rainbow Coalition (NARC) was born with Raila Odinga proclaiming Kibaki as the Standard Bearer of the new opposition alliance, much to the delight of the crowd which numbered almost a million. The only significant opposition party that kept out of the NARC was Simon Nyachae's FORD-People, eventually performing not too impressively in the General Elections.

The shear electrical political fire that went across the nation as a result of the formation of NARC, and its electoral slogan *yawezekana* (all is possible) made it very difficult for the Uhuru candidature to pick up in the areas where Moi did not have purely ethnic support. Uhuru also managed to get support from Kiambu District, his home area. Otherwise NARC went forward to win a clear majority for both the Presidential and Parliamentary elections, thereby undoing the failures of 1992 and 1997.

The 2002 Kenyan elections in a historical perspective

What does the Kenyan electoral victory for the opposition in 2002 tell us about transitions from authoritarianism to democracy — or something else — in Africa? In 1992, Kenya was emerging from over 30 years of what I would want to describe as presidential authoritarianism. It was a one-party state by law. Power was concentrated in the presidency. The party was fused with the state, and state organs were used to run party affairs. Those who comprised the ruling political elite owed their positions to the president who appointed them to both state positions and political positions. Many organisations in society had, over the years, been made subordinate to the state. Civil society, although robust, was given very little room by the state and many state institutions – including the legislature, judiciary and the executive branches of government – had themselves atrophied as the political system became highly personalised around the president.

Kenya had, however, known a tradition of political resistance since colonial times. And the experience of the two World Wars, particularly World War II, had produced a spirit of rebellion against colonial authoritarianism that informed the nationalist struggle beginning with the Mau Mau rebellion, trade union militancy and finally the independence movement of the late fifties. The spirit of resistance and rebellion seeped even into the churches and the education system; the independent education and church movements were not just aspects of the emerging nationalism, they were an expression of self-determination at these other levels of social and spiritual life.

It was not therefore easy for Moi to stamp his absolute authority on society given this heritage of self-determination in Kenyan nationalist past. Before he took over from Kenyatta, the one-party system existed as a matter of fact and not in law. Kenyatta banned opposition political parties in 1969 when his power base was threatened, but he did not legalise the draconian move. Moi, relying on an even narrower political base, found it necessary to prescribe the one-party into law in 1982. From then on, as Mukaru Ng'ang'a, a radical history lecturer at the University of Nairobi put it, "opposition started to go underground."

Between 1982 and 1992, when the opposition finally fought elections after the repeal of Section 2A of the Kenya Constitution Act that had made Kenya a one-party state, there had been intense struggle against the authoritarian regime – underground and above ground. The regime had reacted by extensive repression involving detentions without trial, political assassinations and murders, police

129

harassments, denial of basic freedoms, a state-organised spy system that was extremely intrusive and obtrusive and general fear-mongering and intimidation to usurp strength and determination from the political opposition. In spite of all this, fragments of resistance continued, sometimes finding vocal support from the church and student movements, at other times gaining access to the independent media and underground pamphlets to reach the eager public.

When the Berlin Wall fell in 1989 and the Cold War started to crumble, the regime found it was no longer being protected by its Western supporters as the theme of democracy started to appeal to a North Atlantic alliance ready to export its brand of democracy to the "new democracies" emerging from within the former Soviet Bloc. The Kenyan opposition decided to cash on this. It started making strong and consistent appeals to Western powers to address the political anomalies in Kenya. Shocked at the readiness with which the West was now ready to welcome opposition entreaties, Moi's paranoia increased, now suspecting anybody who questioned anything about his regime – from corruption to the abuse of human rights. It is in the midst of this that he crossed swords with his brilliant Foreign Affairs Minister, Dr. Robert Ouko, over questions of corruption. The latter was murdered under very suspicious circumstances in February 1990.

The murder of Ouko threw the nation into a crisis. Moi's close allies who were not of his ethnic stock increasingly became insecure. Moi, in turn, began to rely more and more on the secret services for his political security. Feeling increasingly vulnerable from within, he could not easily withstand the pressure from the West that increasingly became unsure of him following Ouko's murder. The opposition therefore found a conjuncture in which more pressure on the regime could pay dividend, and hence became more and more emboldened. Rather than wait for a complete showdown with his Western supporters he agreed to abolish the *de jure* one-party state in November 2001 and to plot how he could defeat the opposition at elections, free or rigged.

The opposition immediately registered a broad-based opposition party called the Forum for the Restoration of Democracy (FORD) in Kenya with the doyen of opposition politics, Jaramogi Oginga Odinga, as its chairman. FORD had a loose structure dominated by ethnic and regional potentates called "the six". A solid support and policy making team of "Young Turks" comprising Anyang' Nyong'o, Joe Ager, Gitobu Imanyara, Mukhisa Kituyi, Paul Muite, Raila Odinga and James Orengo gave the party a youthful and vigorous leadership. But the

"Young Turks" were soon to be outwitted by the politics of "the six" in the struggle for ethnic-based political power, and FORD was soon to be divided into ethnic and regional "FORD-lets", losing to KANU in the 1992 General and Presidential Elections.

Lessons learnt in a comparative perspective

The first lesson that we, therefore, learn from the 2002 victory of the opposition in Kenya is that it had a long history of opposition failures to win elections at two previous counts, 1992 and 1997. And that these failures were based on the fact that the opposition was still too weak organisationally to win (division among the parties was just one factor of organisationally weakness) while the authoritarian regime still had the power and institutions of the state on its side, including the power to manipulate and rig elections.

What happened between 1992 and 1997 is that the opposition continued to struggle, in Parliament and outside, for further constitutional reforms that weakened the authoritarian regime further. Joining hands with civil society, the opposition pressed for further constitutional reforms before the 1997 elections. These were finally packaged by a rapprochement in Parliament between the government and the opposition as the Inter-Party Parliamentary Group (IPPG) reforms. The main feature of these reforms is that they allowed the opposition parties to nominate their representatives to the Electoral Commission of Kenya (ECK). The Commission was also given more powers to run the electoral process independent of the normal state apparatus. Stricter rules were to be observed at polling stations and a code of conduct that criminalised certain behaviour as electoral offences was now to be more closely enforced by the ECK. More important, the power to nominate the 12 special Members of Parliament was removed from the President and given to political parties to do so according to their strengths in the National Assembly. What was left intact, however, was the gerrymandering of the electoral boundaries that continued to favour the ruling party KANU, and hence helped it in its victory of 1997 given the divided opposition.

A strong opposition in the 1997 Parliament started to put even more pressure on further constitutional reforms. Realising that he could not stand again for the presidency given the 2-term limit by the 1992 amendments, Moi started to play around with a reform process that could still guarantee KANU victory in 2002. It is because of this that the opposition realised that wresting power from the

131

authoritarian regime would not simply come from constitutional reforms and changes in the rules of the game alone. While a sound political strategy that delivers victory at the polls, however skewed the rules were against the opposition, was necessary, the struggle for constitutional reform was important in opening up the democratic political space. The struggle against the authoritarian regime had to be first and foremost a political struggle for changing the rules of the political game before a winning strategy at the polls would be successful. Opposition unity became a key component of this strategy.

The second lesson that we learn is that it is necessary to weaken the hold of the authoritarian regime on society through constitutional and other reforms so that it can lose its clients and agents through which it controls society and its politics. The constitutional and legal reforms between 1992 and 1997 weakened the Moi regime although they did not lead it to losing power altogether to the opposition. But the opposition gained considerably in Parliament, forcing further reforms between 1997 and 2002. It must also be noted that programmes of privatisation that the regime undertook between 1992 and 2002, though state assets were privatised mainly to Moi's cronies – "crony capitalism"[2] – alienated a wide section of the elite from the regime (the "losers"), and predisposed the latter to sympathy with the opposition. As Moi became more isolated from this estranged elite, so did he rely more and more on his ethnic kinsmen and the few he could trust in the security forces.

With privatisation in the offing, access to funds from state-owned enterprises also started to narrow, leading to the necessity to get funds straight from the Treasury so as to buy support and finance elections. Moi therefore cooked up a plot with one Asian businessman, Kamlesh Pattni, to export fake gold and diamonds from Kenya and receive export compensation from the Treasury. Between 1992 and 2002, it is now estimated that they must have received close to US$ 2 billion from the Treasury – an action that made state bureaucrats who were in the know even have less faith in the viability and sustainability of the authoritarian regime.

The third lesson that we learn from the opposition victory in 2002 is that it came at the tail end of the continued decay of the authoritarian regime and its crumbling from within, not only politically, but also economically. But it could have continued to crumble and yet stay in power had the opposition not come out with a viable political strategy that took advantage of this process of decay in the elections.

---

2   See P. Anyang' Nyong'o, *The Context of Privatisation in Kenya* (Nairobi: Academy Science Publishers, 2000)..

Before the elections of 2002, the ECK came up with electoral rules that made it more difficult for the Moi regime to rig the elections of that year. Key among these was the rule that stipulated that votes be counted at the polling stations at the end of the polling day. Further, these votes were to be counted in full view of the people, making it difficult for the election officials to be compromised in one way or another. In previous elections, votes were usually counted at the divisional or district headquarters, making it possible for ballot boxes to be changed or stuffed with new ballot papers en route to the counting station. This time, once the votes were counted, agents of candidates and parties at each polling station had the figures that were simply tallied at a central point in the constituency.

The fourth lesson that we learn is that how votes are counted is key to victory or failure in a democratic electoral process.[3] The fifth lesson that we need to learn from the election of 2002 is that it was held in the midst of a telecommunications and media revolution in Kenya. Both in 1992 and 1997, the cellular phone was not a popular medium of communication. In 2002 it was. Similarly, in 2002 there were a number of private TV and radio stations; in 1992 and 1997, the Moi regime controlled all radio and TV broadcasting. Thus in 2002, the opposition was able to coordinate the voting process and tally counting across the nation from one monitoring station in Nairobi.[4] This made it even more difficult for KANU to try and manipulate the results. The regime, of course, tried a rearguard action to stay in power even after the results were out but the security forces dissuaded them from that foolishness and they beat a quick retreat.

How did the opposition manage to hold on to a pre-election pact?

It must be understood that politics, in the final analysis, is about power. And power comes with positions of authority in the state. When power is concentrated in the presidency, all political parties that seek to govern will want that position. All ethnic groups that want "a share of the national cake" will also want that position. Indeed, it is because power was concentrated in the presidency that the opposition, between 1992 and 1997, could not win because

3   The people of Florida need to have gone to Kenya in December 2002 to learn how next to prevent the Republicans from stealing the votes from the Democrats in future elections in the United States of America.

4   The Citizen TV and Radio stations went on to announce results as they came from polling stations.

each party – and quite often the party coincided with the ethnic group – wanted that power. Realising eventually that given the rules of the game they could not get it through electoral competition under Moi, the opposition political parties decided on a strategy that would do two things:

1. Win power through an electoral pact that will lead to equitably sharing cabinet and other state positions; and,

2. Initiate constitutional reforms that would do away with the imperial presidency while establishing a democratic polity institutionally protected from any future emergence of an authoritarian system.

Since the National Rainbow Coalition came to power in 2002, these two processes have been going on simultaneously. The process of living up to the electoral pact (the Memorandum of Understanding) of 2002 has not been very easy as the Liberal Democratic Party (LDP) – the child of the Rainbow Alliance – has been dissatisfied with the power dispensation that its partner in the NARC – the National Alliance Party of Kenya – gave it. Negotiations, which have been protracted and inconclusive, explain largely why the coalition has not worked very well. Indeed, in a recent address to the Kenya Private Sector Alliance (KEPSA), I noted that one of our major failures in the NARC government is that we have not learnt how to manage a coalition government. Yet, looking into the future, we need to master the art of governing through coalitions because this is where Kenya's political stability in the future lies.

Secondly, the process of constitutional reform has also gone a long way although agreement has so far not been arrived at regarding the system of devolution and the structure of executive power and the nature of the legislature.

These, however, are issues which could be tackled more easily were the coalition partners to develop a consensus on the management on the constitutional dialogue. My proposal is that the old Parliamentary Select Committee be allowed to pilot the process. That the chair of this committee be agreed on by consensus by Parliament's Business Committee. Further that the PSC should deliberate on the Naivasha Accords on the basis of which the Bomas of Kenya Constitutional Draft should be discussed in Parliament and presented subsequently for a referendum. All contentious issues, if any, should be deliberated upon across political parties with the view of decisions through consensus rather than the vote since the Constitution is a fundamental law that should not be crafted on the basis of winners and losers.

Economic recovery

In the meantime, the economic reform agenda of the new government is being implemented under the *Economic Recovery Strategy for Wealth and Employment Creation* (2003-2007). It is essentially based on a radical rehabilitation and building of the physical infrastructure through public-private partnership, massive investment in the productive sectors of the economy – particularly agriculture and small and medium enterprises, heavy public investment in human resources development – hence priority in free primary education and a comprehensive social health insurance programme, and building sound governance institutions based on the rule of law and respect for human and peoples rights.

But old habits do not die easily. Even within the context of the new political dispensation under NARC, problems of corruption in the state and tribalism among the political elite still bedevil society. These are contradictions in the womb of the people that the reform process must face and deal with. They cannot be resolved overnight, nor can they resolve themselves merely because they are unpopular with progressive change agents. But they do become potent and powerful when the elite feels it is losing and it needs a power base in mass support so as to assert its privileges.

It is hoped that by succeeding to establish a constitution that will enhance a democratic political culture, and by this culture being consciously promoted by a political elite working within national popular organisations that will give people democratic voice, the debilitating politics of tribalism will be reduced. Instead tribe, as peoples with rights within the democratic polity, will claim such rights not in opposition to others, but in complementing them as they also do the same. This, perhaps, is the final lesson that Kenya may share with other African peoples struggling for the new democratic order in our continent.

14

Political Scientists and the "Democratic Experiment" in Africa

Based on Professor Billy Dudley Memorial Lecture, Ibadan University, Nigeria, delivered on 25 June 2004

Introduction

As one of the first political scientists in our continent to enrol for membership in the African Association of Political Science, I am aware of the important role played by Billy Dudley in the founding of our organisation. He was among the first generation of African social scientists who came into the intellectual stage immediately after independence — together with Ali Al'Amin Mazrui in East Africa, Claude Ake in Nigeria, and Martin Kilson in the African diaspora — and made a lasting impact in a professional world hitherto dominated by European expatriates. We owe that generation of African scholars a lot. In their category we must include such luminaries as historians Ade Adjayi, Adu Boahen and B.A. Ogot; anthropologists like Archie Mafeje; and geographers like Simeon Ominde and Akin Mabogunje. We also must acknowledge literary giants such as Ngugi wa Thiongo, Ezekiel Mphalele, Wole Soyinka, Sembene Ousmane, Chinua Achebe, Christopher Okigbo, Okot p'Bitek and many others. In fact, Africa has contributed immensely to the field of literature, and this literature has in turn enhanced our knowledge of African societies and politics. Suffice it to say too that many African political scientists have picked their queue from literary giants. The political imagery in Okello Oculli poetry betrays the influence of Okot p'Bitek; Ali Mazrui wrote a political novel in response to the writings of Christopher Okigbo.

At a time when Africa was full of hope, these African scholars gave African studies and the African academic community an energised and new sense of direction, and what is now called "local ownership". Billy Dudley wrote on a wide range of subjects including political parties in Northern Nigeria, ethnic identity and political conflict in Nigeria, and he was already aware of the dangers of militarisation of politics in Africa before many others. For all these reasons, we deserve to honour him and his generation, whenever we gather for occasions like this one.

The role of African political scientists in the current wave of democratisation in our continent is a subject that has preoccupied my mind for some time, and I welcome the opportunity to give it some thought so as to develop some systematic understanding of the role played by our discipline and by political scientists, qua political scientists, in the efforts of making democracy the governance model of choice in our continent. This opportunity has therefore compelled me to take time to reflect on the role that our discipline, and African scholarship in general, has played in contemporary efforts to democratise politics in Africa, whether that role accords with the normative model expected of scholars in a democracy, and what the African experience accords with the received wisdom on social scientists and the practice of politics as it has been handed down to us by such noted authors as Karl Marx, Antonio Gramsci, Max Weber, Karl Mannheim, Amilcar Cabral and many others.

I do not believe that we are involved in a "democratic experiment in Africa." Life, as it were, is not a dress rehearsal before the main play. What we are engaged in is a *process of democratisation* which can, at times, be rolled back, at other times it may take several leaps into the future while at others it may be stable, smooth and even predictable. It all depends on what we may call "the configuration of social forces" given their interests pursued under very specific circumstances — local and global — that we as social scientists need to discern and interpret. In order, therefore, to understand the nature of this democratisation process and the role of political scientists in it, we need also to appreciate history and how the heritage of the past shapes, or gives context to, the current struggles and experiences. I do believe that, in this regard, our nationalist past is important in our understanding of the process of democratisation in Africa today. Karl Marx could never have put it any better: "people make their own history, but they do not make it under circumstances of their choice; they make it under conditions received from their past."[1] Without being very faithful to Marx's text, I believe my general recollection of what he said is by and large correct. In this regard, our understanding of the processes of democratisation in Africa must, of necessity, be traced from our nationalist past.

---

1   Karl Marx, *Theses on Feurebach* in Quintin Hoare (ed.) *Karl Marx: Early Writings* (London: New Left Books, 1974).

The political scientists and African nationalism

We do not often think of nationalism and self-determination as components of democracy. As a matter of fact they are, to the extent that these are based on the struggle to eliminate unaccountable foreign authoritarian rule and substitute it with one based on the supremacy and inviolability of individual liberty and a government, to quote Locke, "that rests on the consent of the governed".[2]

In his autobiography, Ghana,[3] Kwame Nkrumah states that he drew his early inspiration for self-determination from reading the histories of such people as Cavuor, Garibaldi and Mahatma Gandhi. But Nkrumah had also studied political science at the University of Pennsylvania and at Lincoln University, in addition to history and economics. Nnamdi Azikiwe, "Zik", had also studied political science as one of his subjects at university in the United States. Although they were not formally trained as political scientists, Patrice Lumumba of Congo, Tom Mboya of Kenya, Julius Nyerere of Tanzania, and Milton Obote of Uganda, clearly read the works of leading political philosophers and political scientists. We can tell this from reading their speeches and published work. Indeed, Apollo Milton Obote was given the name "Apollo" as a result of his love for Milton's Paradise Lost,[4] that famous poem where Milton depicts Satan (Lucifer) as a rebel in God's Kingdom who prefers having his own "self-determined freedom" as opposed to the comfort of heaven where nobody but God has a voice. Satan says defiantly: "though heaven be lost all is not lost". The defiant hero in Satan appealed to Apollo the rebel against colonial rule. Further, though fraught with many difficulties during the anti-colonial struggle, Milton Obote—like Lucifer before him—never believed in giving up. He was a politician struggling for independence as well as a student of political philosophy and epic poetry seeking political inspiration from the political philosophers of yester years.

Likewise, Mboya and Nyerere were both inspired by the Fabian Socialism taught at Ruskin College in Oxford under the "matronage" of Dame Margery Perham. I say "inspired" deliberately because they already had that socialist and humanist spirit before they were cross-fertilised by Fabian ideas which they found putting their struggle in an international context.

---

2 John Locke, *Two Treatises of Government*, with an "Introduction" by Peter Laslett, (Cambridge: Cambridge University Press, 1988).

3 Kwame Nkrumah, *Ghana: The Autobiography of Kwame Nkrumah* (London: Thomas Nelson, 1957).

4 Milton, *Paradise Lost* (London: Penguin Classics, 1988). .

Political science and political philosophy were not the only disciplines that fed the intellectual origins of African nationalism. Other disciplines counted too. J.B. Danquah, Jomo Kenyatta and Eduardo Mondlane were trained as anthropologists. Their work sought to demonstrate that far from being "primitive" as colonialists thought, African traditions in governance, law and the use of resources were just as rational and as sophisticated as those of any other people in the world. Nelson Mandela, Obafemi Awolowo and Oliver Tambo were practising lawyers. Julius Nyerere had studied Biology at Makerere College (as it was then) and then English at Edinburgh University in Scotland. Robert Mugabe was trained as a teacher, and then later took up studies in political science, history and economics while in prison. A large number of the early African nationalists were schoolteachers. Yet other African nationalists were schooled in the harsh university of colonial life, where they experienced daily indignities and discrimination at the workplace, and at home. That is what provoked the moral outrage that informed their work and the urge to organise rallies and campaigns against the injustices of colonial rule.

Tom Mboya, in his autobiography *Freedom and After,*[5] recounts an incident at Nairobi City Hall where he worked as a sanitary inspector. A white female farmer came to have her milk approved for sale and, finding Mboya in the office, asked him whether "there was anybody in the office to help her." Characteristic of his growing defiance against white settler racism, Mboya replied: "Madam, perhaps you need to have your spectacles checked rather than your milk." Struggling for democracy and freedom meant struggling against white racism as well, and the African nationalists drew plenty of inspiration from the political philosophy of utilitarian and liberal democratic theories, not to mention the Bible and the Koran.

Yet whatever their intellectual inspiration or disciplinary training, African nationalists articulated concepts that were, and that remain central to our discipline. The memorable African nationalist slogan" One man, one vote" (this remember were days before we discovered women rights!) is one that is central today in the academic discourse on democracy, electoral systems and voting rights. That applies to the principle of self-determination too. Indeed it was invoked in the recent successful negotiations for peace in Sudan that took place in Naivasha, Kenya. The right to self-determination was a fundamental

---

5   Tom Mboya, *Freedom and After* (London: Andre Deutsch, 1963).

demand in African nationalism as Ali Mazrui reminds us in his book *Towards a Pax Africana*,[6] in common with many third world movements that fought to dismantle European empires after World War II. All this makes the case for an intensified rather than diminishing role of political science and political scientists in the evolution of democratic governance in contemporary Africa.

Political scientists in post-independence Africa

In the immediate post- independence era, the dominant concern in our discipline — here in Africa as opposed to Europe and North America — shifted from democracy and self-determination as justification for the liquidation of colonial empires, to nation building and the consolidation of national independence. The question of integrating conflicting ethnic and regional identities into the new nations presented a particular sense of urgency in view of what had happened in Katanga between 1960 and 1964, the problem of bringing the Buganda Kingdom under Uganda national constitutional framework, conflict between Northern and Southern Sudan, the Arab-African differences in Zanzibar, and so on. Not surprisingly, Claude Ake's first book was entitled simply *National Integration*,[7] and the subject never really left him. He was still writing about strategies of resolving the "National question" within Africa's new political dispensation through a more open, participatory role by local communities, when he was tragically taken from us a few years ago.

As we have already seen, Billy Dudley was interested in the subject, as were Ali Mazrui, A.G.G. Gingyera Pincywa and Apollo Nsibambi at Makerere, and John Okumu in Kenya. Among political practitioners of course, Kwame Nkrumah was dead set against any form of "balkanisation" (as he saw it) that would have established a multitude of unviable ethnic African states, that would be preyed on by imperialist ambitions thereby sabotaging the project of continental African Unity. And he wrote about it too in his *Africa Must Unite*.[8] Beneath the ground the fundamental concerns of the African political science community was changing. The series of military coups, which occurred in 1965 (in Benin, then Upper Volta—Bukina Faso, and the Central African Republic, followed by Ghana, Nigeria and Congo the following year), brought an unexpected phenomenon to the fore. The study of military rule and domestic

---

6   Ali A. Mazrui, *Towards a Pax Africana: A Study of Ideology and Ambition* (Chicago: University of Chicago Press, 1967).

7   Claude Ake, *National Integration* (London: Irwin, 1966).

8   Kwame Nkrumah, *Africa Must Unite* (Paris: Presence Africaine, 1974).

political instability gradually took centre stage. Ruth First, an African patriot worth remembering, came out with a landmark study on military rule in Africa at the time entitled *Barrel of the Gun*.[9] We all remember that she died at the forefront to the struggle against apartheid when a parcel bomb exploded at her face in Maputo in 1986.

Ruth First gave the study of a distinct twist from your run-off-the-mill publications in Western journals dealing with military rule in Africa. She brought the class analysis into the African post-colonial political crises and argued that military coups represented intra-class conflict as the new *petit bourgeoisie* fought over national resources and power, ignoring the fate of the peasantry and the working class, who were also fighting back. Other African political scientists also wrote on the military tracing coups, mostly to factional struggles of one kind or another.

Along with the study of military rule in Africa came the study of *democracy, development* and the *party system* in Africa. In many of his writings — but particularly so in *Democracy and the Party System* — Julius Nyerere contended that multiparty democracy was alien to both the African tradition and the African psyche. He likened the Westminster type of democracy to a football match where the two teams do not really differ on anything fundamental; on the contrary, both are united on the necessity of competing in order to score. The politics of development, argued Nyerere, was more serious. Africans could not afford even a minute of their lives competing for the sake of competing. All were agreed that the fight against poverty, ignorance, disease, racism, discrimination of all types and so on were urgent. Nobody needed to form a party defining these problems any different from the others. All that was needed was to define the "how". And even here, African socialism — or *ujamaa* — provided Africa with the way forward.

Many political scientists — Ahmed Mohiddin leading the pack — came to the defence of Nyerere and many other nationalists who thought like him; Milton Obote of Uganda, Ahmed Sekou Toure of Guinea, Tom Mboya of Kenya and Kenneth Kaunda of Zambia. The exchange between Mohiddin and Mboya in *The East African Journal* some time in the mid-sixties elevated the debate on African socialism and development beyond the confines of the mere uniqueness of African tradition as its *raison d'etre*.[10] The debate was now becoming richer, and scholars began wondering whether the one-party regime and the ideology of socialism were not being pushed by the narrow interests of the ruling African elite and even *development*, as defined and practised by this elite, was also *class-based*.

---

9   Ruth First, *Barrel of the Gun* (London: Allen Lane, The Penguin Press, 1970).

10   See, for example, Ahmed Mohiddin, *African Socialism in Two Countries* (London: Groom Helm, 1981).

141

By now you can guess that I am coming to the golden era of "political economy" studies in Africa political science that used, as its point of departure," Marxist theories of the state and in particular the specific conjecture of African societies in a world dominated by international capitalism and the political power behind it. The archetypical study here is Walter Rodney's *How Europe Underdeveloped Africa*,[11] but we might cite (as fast a few examples) Samir Amin's *Capitalism and Underdevelopment in West Africa*[12] and Claude Ake's *Revolutionary Pressures in Africa*.[13] At the time the flagship journal of the Association of African Political Science was called *Journal of African Political Economy*. The political science community in Africa had in general, moved a great distance from the concern of democratic rule and self-determination of the 1960s into looking at politics as *class struggle*. Issa Shivji was the first to throw the spanner into the fireworks when he wrote *Class Struggles in Tanzania* in 1973.[14] I have documented all this in a recent publication entitled, *The Study of African Politics: A Critical Appreciation of a Heritage*,[15] which I am quite willing to give to the Nigerian Political Science Association to have a local version published in Nigeria.

But the African crisis had its own way of bringing back old political subjects. At a meeting organised by the Third World Forum at Arusha, Tanzania, in 1985 a gathering of distinguished African political scientists met to deliberate on "Popular Struggles for Democracy in Africa". The product, a book published under that title which it was my privilege to edit, contain essays from Mahmood Mamdani, Michael Chege, the late Emmanuel Hansen, Taiser Ali, Ibbo Mandaza, Wamba dia Wamba and others.[16] It was the first publication on democracy in Africa by Africans in a long time. The tide was turning and African political scientists never looked back. Contrary to the thinking and writing of *development missionaries* from the West, whether working as consultants or government agents, the African people did not submit willingly to authoritarian rule after independence. If anything, protests and rebellions continued in many forms in the quest for democracy — or, as Ogot and Welborn once called it, *a place to feel at home*.[17]

---

11 Walter Rodney, *How Europe Underdeveloped Africa* (dare s Salaam, Tanzania Publishing House, 1973).

12 Samir Amin *Capitalism and Underdevelopment in West Africa* (New York: Monthly Review Press, 1973).

13 Claude Ake, *Revolutionary Pressures in Africa* (London: Zed Press, 1978).

14 Issa Shivji, *Class Struggles in Tanzania* (Dar es Salaam; Tanzania Publishing House, 1973).

15 P. Anyang Nyong'o, ed. *The Study of African Politics: A Critical Appreciation of a Heritage* (Nairobi: Heinrich Boll Foundation, 2000).

16 P. Anyang Nyong'o (ed.), *Popular Struggles for Democracy in Africa* (London: Zed Press, 1987).

17 Bethwell Ogot and F.B. Welbourn, *A Place to Feel at Home: A Study of Two Independent Churches in Western Kenya,*(London: Oxford University Press, 1966).

142

African political scientists and contemporary experiments in democracy

I will cover this theme in two sections:

(i) The contribution of political scientists in their professional roles to current trends in African democracy, and,

(ii) The contribution that political scientists have made to African democracy as activists, or what Gramsci called "organic intellectuals".[18]

I have already stated that African political scientists were already concerned about the lack of democracy in the African continent in the early 1980s. This is at least one decade before political scientists in the West began writing about democratic governance as a solution to the chronic problems of our continent, the rest of the Third World and the post-communist states. Richard Sklar's seminal article "Developmental Democracy",[19] for example, appeared in 1987, while Samuel Huntington's book *The Third Wave*[20] (now considered the epitome on the beginnings of democratisation in our age) did not appear until 1993. I often think sometimes that we in Africa do not give sufficient credit to our own scholars. More than anyone I know, Thandika Mkandawire has written about that, inviting African social scientists to quote each other; and he has demonstrated that repeatedly by example. As a professional association, I would urge you give some thought to this problem.

I would like to say, without fear of being contradicted, that we were writing about democracy in Africa well before Sklar and Huntington came to the scene. And this is not just in regard to our work that led to the publication of *Popular Struggles for Democracy*, but also in reference to other works before then. The 20th issue of the *Review of African Political Economy* that I edited was devoted to the "Peasant Question in Kenya".[21] In it we not only discussed the political economy of agrarian change in Kenya, but we also posed questions regarding the authoritarian regime and the prospects for democracy. I subsequently got immersed into studying the disintegration of the nationalist coalition in Kenya, and published an article under that title in a 1986 issue of *African Affairs*. All these were precursors to our concern for democratic openings in Africa.

18 Antonio Gramsci, *Prison Notebooks* London: Blackwell Publishers, 1971).

19 Richard Sklar, "Developmental Democracy," *Comparative Studies in Society and History,* Vol. XXIX, No. 4 (Oct. 1987): 686-714.

20 Samuel Huntington, *The Third Wave* (Oklahoma: Oklahoma University Press, 1991).

21 P. Anyang Nyong'o "The Peasant Question in Kenya" *Review of African Political Economy* (1980).

During Thandika Mkandawire's tenure as Executive Secretary of CODESRIA, Africa witnessed perhaps the greatest number of publication by African social scientists on democracy in Africa. These publications, in the form of edited books, the CODESRIA "Green Papers" monographs, and learned articles in the *Journal of Africa Development* are all familiar to you. I say they are familiar to you because it seems to me that Nigerian authors dominate these publications – an accomplishment that your Association ought to be justly proud of. But in addition to the work on democracy in CODESRIA, we witnessed an upsurge on publications on democracy in Africa in overseas professional journals such as *African Affairs, Journal of Modern African Studies, African Studies Review,* and many others. Claude Ake at this time published *Democracy and Development in Africa,*[22] Mahmood Mamdani wrote the book, *Citizen and Subject,* which contains some highly critical conclusions on the state of democracy in post-apartheid South Africa.[23]

Suffice it to say that we now have a substantial collection of journal articles, unpublished papers, authored and edited books on the contemporary democratic experiments in Africa, written by many African political scientists either working on the continent or the Diaspora. Some, if not a substantial part of the writings on democratic struggles in Africa, in fact comes from the ladies and gentlemen present at this conference. I wish to state for the record that future generations of Africa will appreciate the work you have done in recording the historic political transformation of our continent from the early 1990s, as African peoples struggled to rid themselves of military and civilian dictatorships and to take the destiny of their respective countries in their own hands.

But professional African political scientists have done more than that. The most objective and learned publications have given those of us in government much information on where our parties and state officials have gone wrong. They have given us opinion surveys on what African peoples think. That picture is needed by us in order to move forward. The beauty of democracy lies in that mistakes are corrected by successes. Success in establishing a truly free press, for example, acts as a check on the executive branch and on the judiciary as well. Both cannot afford to trample on justice without being called to account for their actions by a free press. The press, in turn, must use this freedom responsibly else an alert civil society will denounce its lack of professionalism and cost it some

---

22 Claude Ake, *Democracy and Development in Africa* (Washington: Brookings Institution, 1996).

23 Mahmood Mamdani, *Citizen and Subject* (Princeton N.J.: Princeton University Press, 1996).

readership or a listening audience. A vocal and informed legislature acts as a counter balance to excesses in the executive branch, corruption in the judiciary and so on. Ultimately an empowered people act as a check on their government, as we saw recently in India. As George Bernard Shaw once said in his play *The Apple Cart*, "we need to be governed, and yet to control our governors."[24]

Democracy is about the governing gaining control over their governors; authoritarianism is about the governors solidifying control over those they govern. That in fact is what happened in Kenya in 2002; the people were driving the agenda of unity in the opposition while shaking off three decades of cemented control by the discredited authoritarian Moi regime. The people compelled the opposition to unite in order to drive the agenda of the people — that of democratisation and the opening up of the democratic space.

There has of late been a cascade of learned publications (especially from France and the United States) that dote exclusively on what has gone wrong with democracy in Africa: the violence, witchcraft and the occult, the big-man syndrome, HIV/AIDS, etc. It is a school called *Afro-Pessimism*. Please make them understand, that despite many problems, Africa is more than the sum total of its miseries. Studies on democracy by African political scientists that I have read bear testimony to that. This debate clearly needs to be joined, and I hope that many of your members are deeply engaged in it.

When democratic gains are made they do not instantly destroy the political economy that sustained the authoritarian society of yesterday. Instead, the gains seek to change or transform this political economy and this process of change is quite often fraught with uncertainty. The period of uncertainty — of trial and error politics — can be prolonged and frustrating. If the old order succeeds in sabotaging it or the change agents cannot successfully insert their hegemony and give confidence to an over expectant citizenry, regression into the politics of the past may easily restore the old order. In that regard retrogression, not change, will itself shrink the democratic space into an order qualitatively different from that expected from a democratic or open society. Like V.I. Lenin once wrote, and I cannot now remember where he did it: "a revolution may be ripe, but when there are not enough revolutionaries to carry it out, a society may slide back into social and political decay, and this process of decay can go on for decades and decades."[25]

---

24 George Bernard Shaw, *The Apple Cart* (London: Constable and Co. Ltd., 1930).
25 V.I. Lenin, "Two Steps Forwards One Step Backwards," *Collected Works* (Moscow: Progress Publishers, 1978).

Perhaps that is what happened to the Congo after the assassination of Patrice Lumumba. Perhaps that is what happened to Haiti more than two hundred years ago. I hope it does not happen to Kenya under the National Rainbow Coalition.

The transition period is a trying one. Its success does not depend on those who easily transgress into romantic cynicism when the going is tough; it is, on the contrary, enhanced by the dogged determination of the change agents, those who are determined not to allow social and political decay to set in and recruit its active reactionary missionaries.

The political scientist as a political actor

As I stated in my introductory remarks, there has never been a shortage of political scientists (and other social scientists) in the practice of African politics. In the struggle for democracy in Africa over the past two decades numerous political scientists have felt the calling to be personally engaged in the campaign for change, mobilising people for a noble cause, running for office, and making life difficult for authoritarian regimes by peaceful means.

The late Claude Ake ran for the highest political office in Nigeria in the 1983 elections. Professor Nzongola Ntalaja was the foreign affairs envoy for the Union Sacre', the anti-Mobutu coalition of the 1990s. Mahmood Mamdani was a key player in the canvassing public opinion on the proposed democratic constitution for Uganda in the early 1990s, and what he found among the people did not please the incumbent government. The late Emmanuel Hansen worked with the Rawlings government in early 1980s before falling out with it to join the early opposition parties in Ghana. Issa Shivji has long been involved in shaping land policies in Tanzania. Taissir Ali Mohamed is still with the Democratic Alliance in Sudan seeking the democratic resolution to the conflicts in that African nation. Okello Oculli has led a crusade for African unity working with the youth for the last three decades. Wamba dia Wamba is still at the forefront in Congolese politics struggling for democratic change in the context of his time. A number of scholars have perished in Algeria fighting for democracy. Amos Sawyer became an interim president of Liberia at a crucial time in that nation's dodged transition to democracy.

In Kenya our struggle against the authoritarian tendencies of both the Kenyatta and Moi governments began in the late 1970s. Political scientists at the University of Nairobi, once it was fully Africanised, began to question the fate of Kenya since independence. In particular they were concerned about

146

arbitrary rule, oppressing and inequality especially in rural Kenya. And while the Kenyatta regime was content to treat the university as a mere nuisance, Moi began his rule in 1978 with an all-out war against academic freedom before his final assault on all our liberties after 1982. We made that clear to the people of Kenya through unscrupulous scholarship. But the people needed very little persuasion to join the democratic opposition.

Unfortunately, divisions among opposition parties, and electoral fraud on the part of the Moi government, denied us victory until the elections of December 2002. In all these struggles the intellectuals in active political opposition paid dearly for their stand. Many and especially students lost their lives.

Yet while some of us were busy making personal sacrifice against African authoritarian regimes, some of our academic colleagues went over the opposite side to give succour to despotic rule whether for financial consideration, political position or prestige. I do not need to give you specific names. The Nigerians witnessed this shameful spectacle throughout the Babangida and Abacha years. We see it today in Zimbabwe, where some social scientists are defending brazen and open authoritarian politics and intolerance. Even as we fought for academic freedom, the Moi regime went out of its way to recruit intellectual retainers to serve its propaganda war against the opposition. Among them were some political scientists though, fortunately, not very bright ones. Mobutu had a large contingent of *soi dissant* political scientists who rationalised his rule in the names of *authenticite*. However, nowhere have intellectuals degenerated to a lower level than Rwanda during the 1994 genocide. The reaction of some Hutu scholars to a proposed democratic constitution based on power sharing was to join in the propaganda war justifying all-out killings. As you know, some of them have been already convicted and sentenced by the international tribunal on Rwanda sitting in Arusha.

Of late the Afro-pessimist school has written a lot on unprofessional behaviour among African intellectuals citing academics who behave in this fashion; that is, brains for hire in the service of dictators. This is unfair to those, perhaps a majority, of African scholars who took a stand in favour of democracy and who paid a price higher than any that their Afro-pessimist detractors in the West have paid.

I have always wondered why some scholars choose to conform to the status quo of authoritarian rule while others rebel; why some sit on the fence while others jump into the tumult world of politics seeking change even when the odds look so bad. This is not a particularly African phenomenon; it is a historical phenomenon that has been studied by historians, political scientists, philosophers and even theologians. Now that we have a rich history from nationalism to the present, we should be able to do a comparative study of African intellectuals faced with democratisation, and intellectuals in other histories and other societies. Without undertaking this comprehensive task myself, I have a hunch that, in general, the African intellectual's involvement in shaping the democratic future of this continent stands to be appreciated.

Conclusion

I began my lecture with a brief survey on the role of African political scientists and other social scientists in the struggle for African independence advisedly. To the extent that it was an anti-imperialist struggle, the campaign for African independence was part of a wider struggle in the Third World to democratise global governance – to give ordinary Africans a right to determine who should govern them, and to give African governments in turn the right to participate in how the world should be run. *If that history teaches us anything at all, it is that political ideas count.* The first generation of African leaders wrote political literature in justification of their strategies that is wholly alien to the despots who succeeded them. As we move deeper into the new phase of democracy that ought to change, political leadership needs to specify what direction it is leading the people, in speech and in writing. Organic African intellectuals have a vital role to play in this. Those political scientists who confine their work to research and publication have a significant contribution to make, in providing data and analysis on where we are in the democratic process all over Africa.

There has never been an academic consensus on the role of intellectuals in politics. In *The German Ideology*, Marx states that the dominant intellectual ideas of an epoch represent – though not directly – the dominant political orientation of the class that owns and dominates material production.[26] Gramsci, as we stated earlier, struck a blow in favour of organic intellectuals, while Max Weber had argued for a clear separation between "science as a vocation" and intellectual engagement in political life.

You all have your take on this debate. That is as it should be. What I believe is that political scientists have a great role to play in the current wave of democratisation of our continent, in any of the above categories. As I have tried to show, African political scientists played a major expository role as our continent went through the vicissitudes of disappointment after independence,

---

26 Karl Marx, *The German Ideology*, (London: Prometheus Books, 1998).

the rise of authoritarianism, the oppression by military rule, underdevelopment and falling incomes, and now democratisation. Our scholars do not often get the credit they deserve. I can assure you that African political scientists have done a better job in explaining and guiding political change than many imagine. This is true whether they were engaged in professional work as political scientists (as Weber recommends) or as organic intellectuals engaged in undermining a hegemonic culture of authoritarianism (as Gramsci recommends). As for what we should do with those who have chosen to mortgage their conscience to African dictatorial regimes, I will leave that to the profession. The fortunate thing is that with the opening of democratic space their role has become more exposed, just as the positive role of those who took a stand against tyranny begins to shine. In the final analysis, democracy will surely progress in Africa if *we make a thousand cows graze and a million thoughts contend.*

15

Political Parties in East Africa

*Speech given at the IDEA/DPMF conference on Political Parties,
Mombasa, Kenya, 15-16 December 2005*

Introduction

In my study of political science, I realised in the 1970s, theoretically at least, that Lenin was right in his arguments on the importance of organisation in the running of political parties. One of the things that I did as a graduate student was to write my Option Two Paper on what I called "Lenin's Theory of Revolution and its Application to Political Change in Africa".[1] I will subsequently refer to some of the ideas that I developed more than 30 years ago

I would like to see us discuss political parties in Africa not simply as a way of engineering them – because the academic discussion of political parties of late has concentrated on how to engineer political parties – the financing of political parties, passing laws about political parties, how to get membership of political parties, all those things have to do with engineering political parties and they have very little to do with conceptualising political parties and understanding what political parties are all about.

The origin of political parties

If there was anyone who was a student of political parties and wrote extensively about them, it was Lenin. We may disagree about his own ideas of what a political party should be, but if you want to know about political parties, and how to conceptualise a political party, you cannot be a student of political parties without studying Lenin.

---

1   P. Anyang' Nyong'o "Lenin's Theory of Revolution and Its Critics," University of Chicago, Department of Political Science, 1973.

I have been involved in founding political parties, both in theory and in practice. One of them being the original of FORD, then FORD-Kenya, then the Social Democratic Party, and then the National Rainbow Coalition, and of course, of late, the Orange Democratic Movement.

If we are to begin thinking of political parties historically, we will find that they, properly so-called, are the outcome of the Industrial Revolution. It was as a result of the decline of feudalism and the division of society into social classes under capitalism, that political parties emerged as major actors on the political scene. Whether you are looking at Germany or France or Britain or even China, and later on in the post-colonial societies, political parties emerged as organisations for aggregating social forces in the struggle for state power, after the industrial revolution and the period of capitalism. Roberto Michel, in his study of political parties, discussed them as elite organisations dominated by a small group of people, trying to organise for the purposes of gaining political power and competing for that power.[2] In certain cases where certain political parties with very narrow interests gain state power, and tend to be exclusivist while stopping any competition for this power by other rival elites, the phenomenon of *fascism* has been witnessed. In that regard, those are leaders of political parties that are very good at championing populist causes which they argue can only be realised by the total exclusion of some races, ethnic groups, religious groups or regions from access to the arena of political competition or access to state power.

Towards the end of the nineteenth century, with the rise of Marxism and the publication of the *Communist Manifesto* and other documents, political parties emerged as well-organised, professional organisations in the hands of the left for capturing state power and putting it in the hands of the working class. Lenin, in actual fact, said that proletarian democracy is a thousand times more democratic than bourgeois democracy. By this he meant that in the struggle for state power, if you leave it at the level of bourgeois democracy, power will still be in the hands of the propertied classes, to the exclusion of the masses. It is only the workers who can expand this power to a larger section of society, and hence make a more democratic state, in terms of the rule by the majority.

So that background of the study of political parties is very important for us to understand, firstly, how to conceptualise political parties; second, the kind

---

2   Roberto Michel, *Political Parties: A Sociological Study of the Oligarchical Tendencies of Modern Democracy* (Glencoe Ill.: The Free Press, 1949).

151

A LEAP INTO THE FUTURE

of organisation that goes into forming political parties; and third, the social aspect of it. We cannot really understand political parties in our times, unless we appreciate that history.

Even in colonial societies, for example if you read the history of Kenya, when the first settlers came here in the early twentieth century, the first Legislative Council that was established in Nairobi in 1907 was by settlers who organised as political parties. As Winston Churchill once said when he visited Kenya, he had never seen a society where there are as many political parties as there are politicians! Even in colonial Kenya we had a plethora of political parties, just as we have now. So, that historical background of the phenomenon of political parties, we need to appreciate.

In the context of Africa, if you read David Apter's "The Gold Coast in Transition",[3] political parties emerged as a result of the struggle against colonialism. At first, they were based on other social movements, like cooperatives, burial societies or social welfare societies; eventually as district societies, depending on the specific history of the colony. But soon after World War II, when the British colonialists were now resigned to having to negotiate with emerging nationalists, political parties started taking the form of what they had been in Europe after the Industrial Revolution. Again, the specific history of how these parties were formed differs from one colony to the other, and is important. If you look at Portuguese Africa, there is a bit of a difference on the historical origin of political parties and how they were formed.

In Portuguese Africa, there was a delayed process of decolonisation, and emergent political parties took much more of the form that they had taken in the Soviet Bloc; revolutionary political parties, very tightly organised, ideologically much more rigorous than elsewhere in colonial Africa. There was a different consequence of the impact of political parties and political mobilisation in these former Portuguese colonies.

But much more important, I think, in our context of Eastern Africa, was Nyerere's perception of political parties (which was very akin to Nkrumah's), and really formed the ideological foundation for the one-party political system in Africa. Nyerere's argument was that, in Africa, you could not afford the luxury of multiparty politics, because the issues around which parties organise are the same everywhere. The issues facing Africa are not really class issues: they are issues to do with the building of the nation; the doing away of colonial

---

3   David Apter, *The Gold Coast in Transition* (Princeton, N.J.: Princeton University Press, 1955).

oppression; the liberation of the common man and the making of the state accessible to all the ordinary Africans. And therefore all people, organised as one, should come together as one mammoth political party, based on the masses – internally democratic and therefore identified as one. So the one party democracy, which dominated Africa in the 1960s and 1970s, was based on the fact that the kind of contradictions that led to multiparty democracy in the Western world never found their counterparts in Africa.

The political party in Africa

The above philosophy of the political party system in Africa is very clearly outlined in Nyerere's essay, "Democracy and the Party System in Africa",[4] as well as his other essay on democracy and socialism in Africa. If you look at his other much more lengthy essay on "Ujamaa: The Basis of African Socialism",[5] that argument is again elaborated upon. I think Nyerere's sentiments were not really different from Kwame Nkrumah's, and eventually picked up by people like Obote, whereby in order to consolidate and institutionalise democracy in Africa, multiparty competition was not necessary. What really happened is that, although in the case of Tanzania, that institutionalisation of the one-party system was very different from the institutionalisation of the one-party system in both Ghana and Kenya, in the sense that there was much more internal competition in the one-party system in Tanzania, and because of the personality of Nyerere, there was less authoritarian presence in Tanzania. Elsewhere, the building of the one-party system logically led to what I have called the presidential authoritarian regime.[6]

The essay that I wrote in 1986 on the disintegration of the nationalist coalition and the rise of the authoritarian presidential regime in Kenya is an analysis of this phenomenon in Africa; how the ideology of the one-party system eventually led to the rationalisation of presidential authoritarian regimes in most African countries. The essence of the presidential authoritarian regime really, was to make political competition irrelevant in post-colonial Africa, organised under the aegis of the party system. While fascism deliberately excludes whole sections

---

4 Julius Nyerere, "Democracy and the Party System in Africa" in *Freedom and Unity: A Selection of Writings and Speeches, 1952-1965* (Oxford: Oxford University Press, 1966).

5 Julius Nyerere, *Ujamaa: The Basis of African Socialism* (Oxford: Oxford University Press, 1966).

6 See my essay, P. Anyang Nyong'o, "State and Society in Kenya: The Disintegration of the Nationalist Coalition and the Rise of Presidential Authoritarianism," *African Affairs* (April, 1989):229-251.

of society from the arena of political competition, the one-party presidential authoritarian system simply limits political competition to a few around the residential palace, with the president always having the last say, and even anointing people to positions of authority.

And to reduce politics to the domination of the presidency within the state, whereby, given the dominance of presidential authority in politics, all other political actors had to pander to the president, and hence the elite involved in politics, more or less became the clients of the president, organised either along ethnic lines, regional lines, religious lines and so on, depending on the particular society we are dealing with, His Excellency the President more or less became a god on earth! The essence of this is that, the presidential authoritarian regimes rarely leaned to the kind of development that Nyerere had talked about. If anything, the consequence of the consolidation of the presidential authoritarian regime was political decay, economic backwardness, and quite often the emergence of very fractious internal conflicts in Africa; expressing themselves quite often in military regimes, like in Uganda, and a breakdown of society, again like in Uganda. But that history is repeated, very much, in many other African countries.

Those who have studied military rule in Africa, whether in Nigeria or Ghana or Uganda, or wherever, again find one commonality in the emergence of military rule– the fact that, with the emergence of presidential authoritarian regimes and the elite finding that they have no avenues for competing against state power, where you cannot compete politically, you often resort to competing clandestinely, using guns and conspiracies, and overthrowing the others, through the use of force. Whether it is in Burkina Faso or in Zaire or Congo-Brazzaville, or Ethiopia, for that matter, this history is repeated; in some cases as a farce, in others as a tragedy. One wonders why, given that history of political parties and competition in Africa in the 1970s and 1980s, how come multiparty politics re-emerged in Africa in the 1990s?

I think there is a false analysis here: many people have said that multiparty politics re-emerged in Africa because of the fall of the Berlin Wall and the pressure exerted by donors. Nothing could be further from the truth!

When we did our study, and Michael Chege was involved in it, in the mid-1980s, in the book that was eventually published, our finding (and this was a study based on many countries such as Rwanda, Kenya, Cote d'Ivoire, Nigeria, Zaire, Uganda, Swaziland, Liberia)[7] was that there had always

---

7   P. Anyang Nyong'o (ed.), *Popular Struggles for Democracy in Africa* (London: Zed Press, 1987).

been intense resistance to authoritarian rule in Africa all through the post-colonial period. When few talked about democracy in those days, there were clandestine popular organisations that struggled for democracy. We began by asking ourselves the question: "Is it really true that after the emergence of so many various types of presidential authoritarian regimes in Africa there are no struggles for democracy in Africa? That people are just sitting there being sat upon by these powerful presidents?"

And we discovered that the struggle for democracy from below, had actually been going on all this while, since independence. They had taken the form of trade unions or youth movements, or peasant rebellions. We decided to look very carefully, with a fine-tooth comb as it were, to see what types of resistance were going on in various African countries and how people were resisting oppression, and our final thesis was that there were popular struggles for democracy in Africa. Sooner rather than later, some of these movements and organisations would overthrow these authoritarian regimes, or would succeed in opening up what we call democratic political space. The term 'open political space' that NGOs are now using is not their own!

Secondly, even in those days, the term 'democracy' was not popular with international NGOs, let alone the World Bank. The term generally used in the late 1980s was what was called 'good governance'. And we should really interrogate this concept of good governance, because good governance was originally a euphemism for democracy by institutions such as the World Bank. If you read the Berg Report of 1981, *Accelerated Development in Sub-Saharan Africa: An Agenda for Action*,[8] there is no such word as democracy used in the analysis of what ailed the body politic in Africa then.

But we thought really that the real contradiction at that point in time, was between the repressive state and the people. And the form of rebellion against this repressive state took the form of what we called 'popular struggles' for democracy in Africa. Given the confluence of these popular struggles, including the rebellion in the Portuguese colonies and the gains being made by the ANC in South Africa then, the Berlin Wall fell at a very opportune time. The African societies were, as it were, pregnant with change, and they simply needed a midwife to accelerate the birth of this change and this arrived in the form of the transformation of global politics through the collapse of the Soviet Bloc. The

---

8   E.Berg, *Accelerated Development in Sub-Saharan Africa: An Agenda for Action* (Washington: World Bank, 1981).

imperialist powers had no contradiction now, to keep on propping their client states in Africa, such as Zaire, against communism. And of course, the client states were expensive to sustain; clearly Mobutu and his coterie of women, and organising to take all this money to Belgium, was not an easy task for the Americans and British, and the Belgians.

All of a sudden the programme of defending democracy in Africa by Western powers became possible, historically. It was very opportunistic, but nonetheless, that opportunism helped us as agents of change in Africa, because we also wanted democracy. It was now possible to get people to come to Nairobi or Cape Town, to talk about democracy, as we are doing now, in the post-1989 period.

The idea of forming political parties and the discourse on political parties had three very important outside influences:

1. What I call the German influence. The Germans after World War II had to re-engineer democracy, given the collapse of fascism and given the threat of fascism. So German Foundations came up aligned with various political parties in Germany – Frederick Ebert Foundation, Friedrich Neumann Foundation, Hans Seidel Foundation, etc. If you look at these foundations, their mission is to engineer democracy and fight fascism, and they believe that if you support political parties with training, with teaching democracy, etc. you can promote democracy and keep fascism and all other anti-democratic forces at bay. Germans are teaching democracy 40 or 50 years after the fall of fascism; yet we think that democracy can be taught for 2 weeks before a referendum in a place like Kenya; that is not possible! The Germans have been doing it for years and continue to do it at home and abroad because the building of democracy is a continuing process and not an event.

2. The other streak is the English tradition. The tradition believes that political parties are the responsibility of the various social classes and interest groups that support them. The state has nothing to do with the formation of political parties. The idea of engineering political parties is very alien to the British, and the only organisation involved in such activity is the Westminster Foundation, which is a very recent invention in British politics. And for the British it is very clear: the Westminster Foundation is an institution focused on selected interventions with regard to elections, seminars and conferences in the developing world, or the so-called "emerging democracies."

3. Then there is the American influence. This influence is primarily through the Republican Institute and the National Democratic Institute, which again think that political parties can be engineered if you influence the ideas of the elite in those political parties, and you show them the goodness of democracy, and so on.

Now we in Africa must be very clear about these brands of engineering democracy and political parties in our systems. What are the problems of political parties in Africa? Our problems are:

1. Our limited understanding of the sociology of political parties and how they come about and are formed. Quite often we think that political parties can be engineered from nowhere, and quite often we discuss political parties without understanding their history in our own societies. In Kenya, you cannot say that parties are useless, that is a very simplistic notion. The parties, even if they come and go, like those that have come and gone, have some thread that connects them.

2. The second thing is that we should really begin analysing, in a very traditional political science way, the various interest groups and pressure groups that could be the pegs on which the political parties stand, or the foundations, which they lack. In other words, political parties may come up and, ignoring the pressure groups that they should be representing, become irrelevant to these pressure groups and interest groups in that society.

3. We do not seem to understand our political parties very well in terms of identity. How do African peoples, in the process of political struggle, identify politically? It is often assumed that people in Africa identify politically in terms of ethnic groups or races.

4. How do people identify politically? What is the basis of political identity in our society? Unfortunately, this issue of political identity is quite often discussed as a "by-the-way". But it cannot really be discussed meaningful without reference to the issue of ideology. What is the role of ideology in political parties? I am saying it is a by-the way because some people begin by saying, rather simplistically, that you cannot build a political party without an ideology. On the other hand some people say that ideology is not necessary in African political systems, because African political parties are ethnic-based and so on, but ethnicity itself is an ideology! So what do we understand by ideology, and what is the role of ideology in the building of political parties in Africa?

157

5. Let us consider the forms of identity that influence political parties in Africa. And which, I am afraid the manner in which they are analysed is sometimes quite simplistic too. These forms of identity are race, colour, tribe, ethnicity, religion, region, gender, etc. These are forms of identity – cultural identity, philosophical identity, etc – but how do these impact on, and relate to, political processes in Africa, especially political party building?

6. Then there is 'political engineering'. Spend a lot of time discussing political engineering – how you get political membership, whether they have cards, some might be paying for membership, who is the president, how many committees there are, how often should we meet in the political parties; what are the bargaining positions, what are the inter-relationships between political parties, etc.; these are what I call issues of engineering, which are important, but I do not think they should form 95 per cent of the discussion.

'The model political party in Africa'

We should not belittle the literature by those of a conservative point of view, who specified the format and structure of political parties. The trainers for any type of organisation always talk of the vision and mission – they have a point. In modern society, we should not begin an organisation if we do not have a vision and mission!

1. *Vision* and *mission*. This has a lot to do with ideology, one's perception of the world, where are you going and why should others follow you? For example, a company that has a vision of achieving 7 per cent growth will obviously inspire people to invest in it since it will stand shoulder high among other companies in terms of potential to make profits.

2. A party must have some *core support*. There must be a group of people who believe that this is work worth doing. You cannot build a party without a cadre, a group of people willing to sacrifice their lives for that party. These 'disciples' must be carefully chosen, as Jesus chose his 12 disciples!

3. *Party militants* or *missionaries*. These are people who will do the work required, even if they are not remunerated, purely because they perceive other rewards for their labour other than monetary gain.

4. *Rules of the game.* There is need to explain to people how the system works and what keeps it efficient and effective.

5. *Followers.* If your mission and vision are taking you somewhere, who should your followers ideally be (more like your target market)?

6. *Winning and keeping state power.* This is important. Political parties are not neighbourhood women organisations for making cookies, nor are they Boy Scout associations for attending mountain climbing courses. They are founded to get state power and keep it through democratic political competition.

16

The Explosion of Freedoms After an Election
The Challenges of Consolidating Democratic Governance

Address to the Members of the National Assembly of the Republic of Rwanda, Kigali, 8 April 2003

When a democratic coalition won

On the 27th of December 2003, Kenya held its general elections, the third after the advent of multiparty politics in the early 1990s. Unlike the previous two elections – one in 1992 and the second in 1997 – the opposition political parties that formed one grand coalition called the National Rainbow Coalition (NARC) won this election and proceeded to form the government.

The manifesto of the NARC was entitled *Democracy and Empowerment*. The Coalition argued that, after more than three decades of being ruled by an authoritarian regime, the Kenyan people needed some substantial amount of political freedoms to appreciate their new government as legitimate. They also wanted to put into power a government that would not be arbitrary in the way it ruled but would respect the Rule of Law. By this they simply meant that if a policeman found you walking on the streets, he would not simply pick you and lock you up for doing nothing; you needed to have broken some law for your freedom to be interfered with by the state. Further, were you to buy some property from someone, you would expect the state to help bind your contract together through some well-known mechanism independent of the two of you as buyer and seller of some property.

Authoritarian regimes do not only mess people up by arbitrarily interfering with their lives and making them serve the powers that be through political

160

coercion, they also make life generally unpredictable. If and when they do good things, it is always with a heavy dose of benevolent dictatorship that in turn thrives on the gratitude of slaves and not the spontaneous approval of free persons.

The explosion of freedoms and election dividends

That Kenyans were happy to see political authoritarianism thrown off their back through the democratic process of voting in a general election has been praised nationally and internationally. But the NARC knew that, soon after obtaining this newly found freedom, Kenyans would want economic satisfaction as well. Democracy, therefore, had to go hand in hand with *economic empowerment as an election dividend*. A hungry man, it has always been said, knows no law. A hungry person can also express his or her newly found freedom in ways that can easily undermine the capability of the state to safeguard such freedoms. And this very often happens in periods soon after the overthrow of authoritarian regimes.

The high expectation of election dividends in economies that are usually in decline becomes dangerous in consolidating democratic gains soon after elections are won. It has often been observed that, as various groups enjoy newly-found political freedoms following the overthrow of an authoritarian regime, there is always the danger of assuming that laws, regulations and various forms of behavioural restraints are no longer that binding. Further, that the assertion of previously repressed demands requires redress by the state over and above any other demands by other competing, and equally legitimate, groups or interests. Such situations can lead to an explosion or implosion of demands expressed in various forms such as wildcat strikes by workers demanding increased wages, demonstrations by university students demanding better bursaries, public petitions by agitated civil society groups and even attempted coups within the army demanding better equipment and salaries.

The extent to which such explosion of demands are met or contained will depend on the extent to which the newly-elected government is reviewed as legitimate and can enforce its authority to rule using state power. More fundamentally, however, the success will depend on how far the people see the new economic dispensation as empowering and the government capable of delivering given its composition and its demonstrated capacity and sincerity to fulfil its economic agenda in the not too distant future.

161

Objective and subjective conditions

While *capability* is largely an objective issue, *capacity* and *sincerity* are both subjective. In other words, the former is largely a function of received institutions, processes and resources. The latter, however, can be created and generated by the regime itself in terms of the persons running such a regime, the ideology they promote, the resources they generate, and the commitment to what they do.

If the objective condition is very constraining, however capable and sincere leaders are, their ability to institutionalise democratic gains may likewise be constrained. For example, objectively, we live in a globalised world economy where certain structures are imposed on us; we have very little option in operating within these structures and living by their rules. We may seek to influence and change some of these rules, but quite often our room for manoeuvre is very small. We may not like globalisation and the mind-set of those who run global institutions such as the WTO and the IMF, but very often all we can do is to seek some reforms within these institutions that can be beneficial to us.

Likewise, objectively, we are constrained by the natural resource base in our economies, how they have been used by previous regimes, the messes that have been created and the options thereby received by us. Objectively, too, the extent to which the economy is indebted, the level of development of human resources, the attitudes of the people and the received political culture all provide the *context* in which we must operate not out of our choice but out of the heritage of history.

When the NARC came into power, it inherited an international economic context in which Kenya had become a pariah nation in the eyes of the IMF and the World Bank. International credit lines had dried up. The government had relied on heavy domestic borrowing to finance its operations as well as service foreign debts. A huge domestic debt had grown facilitating and subsequently facilitated by escalating borrowing interest rates that simply crowded out the private sector in the credit market. The downward economic decline had therefore been structurally embedded into the political economy of the authoritarian regime. This is an objective condition that would prove very constraining in NARC's attempt to kick-start economic growth so as to empower the people economically.

But the explosion in freedoms could not be constrained by the limits put on NARC by this objective condition. Workers in the Export Processing Zones (EPZs) went on strike, plant after plant, demanding higher wages in the months of January, February and March. Although the Minister of Trade and Industry explained to them that their salaries were actually much better than those paid to their counterparts in Asia, they would not budge. What was important to them was not the salary itself, but what the salary could buy; in other words, the cost of living. Teachers, likewise, immediately pressed for their pay to be increased – a move for a long time promised by the previous regime but never honoured. University students went on the rampage, demanding that their lot be equally improved with corrupt university officials dismissed and bursaries promptly paid.

Barely three months in existence, the Executive Director of the Federation of Kenya Employers (FKE) was asking the NARC government: "Where are the 500,000 jobs you had promised Kenyans? I don't see any signs of such jobs on the ground?" The Director had forgotten the nature of the liberalised market economy for long advocated to him by the IMF. In this kind of market, the government does not create jobs, it is the employer who does. The government's function is to create the *enabling environment* for private sector investment. This enabling environment includes good governance, the rule of law, upholding human rights and property rights, and maintaining a viable infrastructure. The NARC government had embarked its work by aggressively delivering on its promises on these governance issues. But when freedoms explode, even the private sector forgets the rules of the game and begins to demand of the government deliveries that the very objective conditions make difficult for the private sector itself to deliver on in the short run when governance conditions are improving.

Fulfilling the social contract with the people

Explosion of freedoms soon after the overthrow of an authoritarian regime can make it very difficult for a democratically elected government to fulfil its social contract with the people, especially with regard to economic empowerment. As workers in the EPZs go on strike, production also stops and hence exports of garments to the USA under the AGOA arrangement are likely to be adversely affected. This may also threaten the attraction of more investors to the EPZ, which in turn make it difficult to kick-start economic growth and create job opportunities.

As high profiles in the private sector make demands that do not seem to be met – or cannot possibly be met in the short run – negative interpretation of what the new regime is doing in fulfilling its electoral pledges can themselves scare potential investors from abroad when they read such categorical statements out of context in the internet. This, likewise, may make it difficult for investors from abroad to make critical decisions to relocate their capital from Eastern Europe to Kenya, for example.

Yet, when a democratic regime succeeds an authoritarian one, it cannot afford to stop the explosion in the exercise of freedoms however harmful they may prove in promoting the agenda of empowerment through economic recovery and renewed growth. The success with which this is done depends largely on the subjective factors.

One, the regime must be able to convince those making demands that cannot be fulfilled that postponing such demands is in the long run in their interest. In order to do this successfully, the regime needs to have a *plan* or strategy that is viable and achievable, and that can address such demands within a time framework acceptable to the "demanders."

Two, the leaders of the regime need to be convincing in their sincerity to carry out the social contract with the people. This is a subjective element that is vital. When people begin to perceive those in power as first and foremost using state power for personal interests then the confidence can wane and the explosion of demands can undermine the ability of the state to generate the social and community capital that cements legitimacy.

Three, the explosion of demands can also come from the subjective feeling of international actors such as the World Bank and the IMF that a new democratic regime should deliver on its social contract with them much faster than is objectively possible. In this regard, the regime itself should have people strong enough to state the facts as they are and not mislead so as to gain easy access to credit that may not be sustained in the short or medium term. In the case of Russia, Yeltsin's official actually lied to the IMF in order to obtain lines of credit which Russia was ill equipped to repay under the terms negotiated then. Russia, unlike Kenya, is a huge economy with resources that the major shareholders in the IMF need. Hence such lies, though taken seriously, may be easily overlooked by the IMF. Smaller African economies cannot enjoy such luxuries.

Four, the consolidation of new democracies in Africa may also depend on the subjective nature of African politics at the continental level. Although substantial cynicism has been poured on NEPAD and its intention to jump-start African economies by deepening democratisation and initiating programs of economic growth, the cynicism must be seen as a function of the perception that people have of African political leadership. It is often assumed that the *visionary* nature of African leadership of the nationalist period was long buried under the heavy weight of military autocrats and single-party *"lootocrats"*. Anything to the contrary after the advent of "new democracies" since the 1990s is seen as impossible.

Yet the NEPAD leadership must prove these cynics wrong by ensuring that the Peer Review Mechanism works; that regional integration initiatives produce results, and that cross-border infrastructure projects stimulate economic growth and strengthen domestic markets. All this is not going to be easy. But one thin is certain: as the NEPAD leadership begins to persist in their plans and demonstrate successes, the doubting Thomases will begin to have renewed faith in Africa, and with this renewed faith, renewed risks by investing in African economies. But first and foremost, African leadership needs to keep faith with its people by unfalteringly promoting democracy because democracy is good in and of itself, but also because it is good for development and the African renaissance.

In his address at the conference on "Elections, Democracy and Governance" yesterday, President Thabo Mbeki warned against being too dogmatic about the *democratic "musts"* drawn from political science textbooks. For us to pass judgement on our democratic processes and democratic performance, these "musts" include:

- We must have multiparty political systems;

- We must have regular elections;

- We must limit the number of times anybody can be elected head of state or government;

- We must have independent electoral commissions;

- We must allow international observers to observe and make judgements on our elections;

- We must have a strong civil society; and

- We must have an Independent Human Rights Commission.

While we would not like to advance any argument for some kind of African "exception" in the practice of democracy as some "core value and practice" for good governance, the form it takes need not necessarily be guided by all the "musts" if the democratic political culture is totally lacking or cannot be promoted even when the "musts" exist in plentitude. As President Thabo Mbeki pointed out, Great Britain does not limit the number of times a party leader can be the Prime Minister. Her head of state, the Monarch, actually rules for life. International observers have never gone to Britain to pass judgement on her democracy when she holds her elections. Instead, people troop to Britain to observe how democratic elections are held.

Now that Kenya has just held a violent free multiparty election, we hope India will send observers to Kenya next time we hold elections to see how democratic elections are held. We also hope that the State of Florida in the USA will send her observers to Kenya to see how the Presidency can be won without rigging.

What President Thabo Mbeki was trying to point out was that we need not legitimise our democracies simply by blindly going through textbook prescriptions. What we need to do is to establish the rules of the game, *in the context of our time* – and without necessarily being opportunistic given the real demands of the people and the objectives of developing our societies – that seek to promote democratic governance whose key contents include the following.

One: Governing by the rule of law

Two: Promoting, upholding and defending human rights

Three: Ensuring that the principle of citizenship is sacrosanct

Four: Promoting the wellbeing of all citizens by guaranteeing access to basic needs and a society in which all citizens feel at home.

No government can be more democratic than one in which the above four things are met. That is why a democratic state in Africa must, by its very nature, be a *developmental state*. It cannot be democratic without being developmental; it cannot also be sincerely developmental if it is not, at the same time, democratic.

IV

DEVELOPMENT WITHIN PAN-AFRICAN AND GLOBAL PARTNERSHIPS

17

Democracy and Political Leadership in Africa in the Context of NEPAD

Paper presented at the World Summit on Sustainable Development,
session organised by the Japan Institute for International Affairs,
Johannesburg, RSA, 31 August 2002

What is NEPAD?

The New Partnership for African Development (NEPAD) is a product of the initiative taken by four African President: General Olusegun Obasanjo of Nigeria; Thabo Mbeki of the Republic of South Africa; Abdoulaye Wade of Senegal; and, Abdelaziz Bouteflika of Algeria. It reflects the view that the continent's leadership needs to take an accommodative approach to world politics, and to adjust to the realities of neo-liberal globalisation that seems to have become triumphant after the fall of the Berlin Wall in the late 1980s. It also acknowledges that this process of accommodation must involve internal political and economic reforms that will be in line with liberal democracy and neo-liberal globalisation that seems to have become triumphant after the fall of the Berlin Wall. It also acknowledges that this process of accommodation must involve internal political and economic reforms that will be in line with liberal democracy and neo-liberal economics. In other words, it concurs with Francis Fukuyama when he states that, as mankind approached the end of the millennium, the twin crises of authoritarianism and socialist central planning left only one competitor standing in the ring as an ideology of potentially universal validity: liberal democracy, *the doctrine of individual freedom and popular sovereignty*.[1] For Africa to make it into the twenty- first century, it must be part and parcel of this universalism, otherwise called *neo-liberal globalisation*.

---

1   F. Fukuyama, *The End of History and the Last Man* (New York: Avon Books, 1992), p. 42.

The dilemma in Africa is that it has not been liberal, and even the proponents of NEPAD and their ardent followers may not be culturally liberal. Individual freedoms have been severely curtailed by the state, and the market has not been free to grow because of a hostile political and cultural environment in which the state has played a mischievous role. Access to external markets so as to earn the revenue needed to support the growth of the home market has been confined to lowly priced raw materials for export. The OECD community of nations has not been very liberal in exporting capital goods and means of production to Africa. Little has been made of comparative advantages, even where they exist in this very illiberal international environment. Technology, manufactured goods and technical know-how have, however, been imported at prices way above those earned from exports, creating a situation of tremendous unequal exchange between Africa and the world market, indebtedness and *structural underdevelopment*.

Taking this historical backdrop into account, NEPAD now seeks to offer a recipe for a quantum leap from underdevelopment to capitalist prosperity in which there is a *partnership* between two key players:

1. A competent and liberal democratic state in Africa, and

2. A friendly and "capital providing" world market in which public and private investors will have interests in creating wealth in Africa and eradicating poverty.

In league with the fight against poverty is a target of 7 per cent GDP growth rate that will see improvement in infrastructure, human resources development and a focussed fight against the HIV/AIDS pandemic. The end result is a self-reliant and sustainable process of development that effectively fulfils the basic human needs.

Is this a tall order or can it be realised in our lifetime? What has been the experience of other forms of "partnerships" that Africa has had with the West and how do the new perimeters stated in NEPAD – giving primacy to democratisation – provide an alternative framework for greater payoffs to Africa?

Fukuyama distinguishes between liberalism and democracy. *Political liberalism* has to do with the rule of law: the recognition that certain individual rights and freedoms should lie outside government control. These are the civil, religious and associational rights normally contained in the Bill of Rights. *Democracy*, on the other hand, is the right held universally by all citizens to have a share in political power by participating on the same footing in the making of a government that exercises this power on behalf of the citizens. There are, therefore, certain procedures and "rules of the game" that make it possible for citizens to make democratic governments. These rules, usually founded on democratic constitutions, are as important as the governments they create.

In its economic manifestation, liberalism has been associated with the right of free economic activity and economic exchange based on private property and markets. In essence, economic liberalism is the idea that the market should operate freely, allocating values and resources in an atmosphere of competition. In the final analysis, the fittest may be the ones who survive in this competition, but this is usually good for innovation in production, capital accumulation and wealth creation in the interest of all.[2]

But the capital accumulation and wealth creation that led to the foundation of colonies in Africa and the exploitation of the colonial peoples could not possibly be seen as a process that created wealth in the interest of Africans. Walter Rodney, Basil Davidson and many other chroniclers of colonial history have spoken in detail of how Europe – or the West for that matter – underdeveloped Africa.[3] The colonial experience was seen as a tragedy, and the wars of national liberation and the rebellions that were waged against colonialism, from the times of Shaka the Zulu to the fall of the *apartheid* regime to the African National Congress in 1994, produced heroes of African freedom who could not possibly associate any benevolence of the free market with the malevolence of colonial accumulation.

Independence was won, not with the belief that capitalist prosperity would be brought by the free market and political liberalism, but with the faith that nationalists in political power, using the state, would bring development and prosperity for the people. Liberal freedoms, enjoyed in a sea of poverty, would do the people no good. In many of his speeches and writing, Julius Nyerere expressed this view in justifying the one-party state in Africa. He even referred to Westminster type of democracy pejoratively as "football democracy,"[4] and did not then receive much disapproval from the people of Tanzania.

The experience in many African countries during the first decade of independence is that the nationalist state performed the task of development pretty well. Standards of living rose as the state provided more education and health facilities, and as the frontiers of employment as well as private property were opened to more and more

---

2   Ibid, p. 44.

3   W. Rodney, *How Europe Underdeveloped Africa* (Dar es Salaam: Tanzania Publishing House, 1973); B. Davidson, *The African Genius* (Boston: Atlantic Monthly Press, 1969).

4   J.K. Nyerere, *Freedom and Socialism* (1968); *Freedom and Unity* (Dar es Salaam: Oxford University Press, 1966).

people by the policies of indigenisation or Africanisation. As part of the expansion of the frontiers of private property, the informal sector grew and challenged the dominance and privileges enjoyed by foreign and comprador capital in Africa's neo-colonies. But the two frontiers, given the nature of the dependent economies whose structures were hardly changed by independence, could not expand for much longer. Samir Amin analysed these economies as "blocked economies",[5] going nowhere in terms of development, but extremely exploited by multinational capital and the "chain of foreign indebtedness."

By the beginning of the second decade, records of good performance by the state started to wane. State power, in the hands of the military or civilian elite, began to be seen as an instrument of the personal enrichment of a few to the detriment of the majority. What Issa Shivji called the *bureaucratic bourgeoisie* had emerged within the state to subvert its developmental role, and to use state power for personal consumption and accumulation of property.[6] Corruption and misuse of power, in ascendance almost everywhere, led to erosion of legitimacy and the increasing militarisation of politics, culminating in chronic political instability.[7]

Having been justified on the ground that it would bring development or prosperity for the many, the balance sheet of the one-party system, or political authoritarianism, proved dismal in Africa. Unlike in South East Asia where authoritarianism could be said to have led to development, in Africa authoritarianism had proved the opposite; it had presided over underdevelopment, conflicts and the growth of misery for the many. By the end of the seventies, the one-party state was largely discredited in many African countries as popular demands for democracy and more open societies increased.[8]

Perhaps there were key elements missing in the presidential authoritarian systems in Africa which were present in their Singaporean counterpart to explain why the latter presided over tremendous economic growth in a short period of time while the former failed in their development enterprise. It is not the so-called "Asian values" that explains this. Victor Mallet, in his book, *The Trouble with the Tigers*,[9] has ably put to rest the myth of the Asian values

5   S. Amin, *L'Afrique de L'Quest Bloquee* (Paris: Les Editions de Minuit, 1971).

6   I. Shivji, *Class Struggles in Tanzania* (New York: Monthly Review Press, 1973).

7   R. First, *The Barrel of A Gun: Political Power and the Coup d'Etat* (London: Allan Lane, 1970); P. Anyang' Nyong'o, "Political Instability and the Prospects for Democracy in Africa," *Africa Development*, 8 No.1(1988): 71-86.

8   P. Anyang' Nyong'o, *Popular Struggles for Democracy in Africa* (London: Zed Press, 1987).

9   V. Mallet, *The Trouble with the Tigers: The Rise and Fall of South-East Asia* (London: Harper Collins Publishers, 1999).

hypothesis. Lee Kwan Yew gives a much more convincing explanation of why and how Singaporean authoritarian rule laid the necessary political and cultural framework for rapid social transformation and economic growth. Without the *enlightened leadership* of Lee Kwan Yew himself, and the team of committed and honest people he mobilised and put in charge of the rule of law, the Singaporean leap into modernity would not have taken place.

Our greatest asset was the trust and confidence of the people...We were careful not to squander this newly gained trust by misgovernment and corruption. We needed this political strength to maximise what we could make of our few assets, a natural world-class harbour sited in a strategic location astride one of the busiest sea-lanes of the world...The other valuable asset we had was our people: hardworking, thrifty, eager to learn. Although divided into several races, we believed a fair and even-handed policy would get them to live peacefully together, especially if such hardships as unemployment were shared equally and not carried mainly by the minority groups. Singapore had no natural resources for MNCs to exploit. All it had were hard-working people, good basic infrastructure, and a government that was determined to be honest and competent. Our duty was to create a livelihood for 2 million Singaporeans. If MNCs could give our workers employment and teach them technical skills and management know-how, we should bring in the MNCs.

The second part of my strategy was to create a First World oasis in a Third World Region. This was something Israel could not do because it was at war with its neighbours. If Singapore could establish First World standards in public and personal security, health, education, telecommunications, transportation, and services, it would become a base camp for entrepreneurs, engineers, managers, and other professionals who had business to do in the region. This meant we had to train our people and equip them to provide First World standards of service. I believed this was possible, that we could re-educate and reorient our people with the help of schools, trade unions, community centres, and social organisations.[10]

In other words, the Singaporean success did not simply require a strong state, but a strong, legitimate and performing state, with a political leadership that had the confidence of the people because it had a vision, was honest, hard-working

10 Lee Kuan Yew, *From Third World to First: The Singapore Story, 1965-2000* (New York: Harper Collins Publishers, 2000), 7-8 and 58.

and paid economic dividends in terms of the improvement in the standards of living of the people. It dealt with corruption by not only upholding high moral standards itself, but also "determined enough to deal with all transgressors, and without exception."[11] Singapore did not look for aid from outside as a necessary condition for its take-off; the state created an atmosphere for an investment boom for both domestic and foreign investors. In other words, the answer to bad governance is not to shift the responsibility away from the state to civil society organisations and NGOs; the answer is to build and sustain a strong, responsible, legitimate, accountable and performing state. Will this state be found in Africa in the era of NEPAD?

Africa: Confronting the dilemmas of progress since 1990

Since 1990, African states have been going through diverse political changes. The most dramatic was the collapse of the *apartheid* regime in the Republic of South Africa, resulting in the election of the African National Congress (ANC) government led by Nelson Mandela in 1994. Much earlier, Kenneth Kaunda of Zambia saw his 27 years in power as President and leader of the United National Independence Party come to an end as the multiparty elections of October 1991 ushered into power the Movement for Multiparty Democracy (MMD) led by Fredrick Chiluba, a trade unionist turned preacher, turned politician and finally turned president with an insatiable appetite for authoritarian rule. Further north, the long-awaited political changes in Kenya were thwarted as the one-party regime of Daniel arap Moi managed to maintain power in a controversial multiparty elections of December 1992, with a repeat performance five years later.

In French West Africa, Benin led the way in 1990 with a national conference of what were called *popular living forces* to put aside the Mathew Kerekou Marxist regime through elections won by Neciphor Soglo's democratic alliance. But five years later Kerekou was back in power, a beneficiary of a reasonably competitive electoral process which he had denied his people the many decades he ruled his country with doctrinaire Marxism. In Senegal, Leopold Sedar Senghor had long given way to his Prime Minister, Amadou Diouf, in the early eighties, such that the changes of the early 1990s did not much rock the Senegalese political boat. Abdoulaye Wade, the doyen of African opposition politics, capitalised on the changes of electoral laws initiated by Diouf towards the end of the nineties to finally win the presidency after 26 years of struggle.

---

11 Lee Kuan Yew, *From Third World to First: The Singapore Story, 1965-2000* (New York: Harper Collins Publishers, 2000), 163.

What seems to be common in almost all African countries that changed from being ruled predominantly by one-party regimes to having elections which put in power new political parties — or reconfirmed the old regimes under a new 'semi-competitive' electoral system — is that these regimes had to confront, and adjust to tremendous pressures for democratic political dispensation. The question to be asked is whether these pressures led to the establishment of democratic regimes or not. If not, why not? The other set of questions to be asked is whether these adjustments to democratic political dispensation have led to any difference in the performance of government in terms of social and economic policies and development. If not, why not?

The answers to these questions are important because the success of the NEPAD initiative presupposes good, capable, responsible and democratic governance in various African countries as a necessary condition for this success. Hence we need to examine the extent to which there is potential for this in Africa, and how obstacles to processes of democratisation in Africa can be removed.

The resilience of authoritarian regimes

It has always been argued that it is difficult for authoritarian regimes to give in to pressures for political openings of a democratic nature. Being more or less "closed regimes", pressures for political openings threaten their staying power and tend to undermine the privileges that political, military and business elite enjoy under such regimes. This may well explain the intransigence of the rulers in Africa to give in to pressures for democratic change, or their cunningness to wear the robes of democrats and reinvent themselves into power even after so-called multiparty elections.

But what, in the first place, do we mean by an *authoritarian regime?* The authoritarian regimes have been heavily studied in Latin America. Guillermo O'Donnell, James Petras, Philippe Schmitter, Peter Evans, Torcuato de Tella and many others [12] have written profusely on Latin American authoritarian regimes, characterising them mainly as *bureaucratic authoritarian regimes.* Such regimes

---

12 Guillermo O'Donnell, P. Schmitter, and L. Whitehead (eds.), *Transitions from Authoritarian Rule: Comparative Perspectives* (Baltimore: Johns Hopkins University Press, 1986). See also books edited by the three scholars in the series by the same publishing firm, Transitions from Authoritarian Rule: Latin America, and Transitions from Authoritarian Rule: Tentative Conclusions About Uncertain "Democracies". Other examples are: Torcuato Di Tella, *Latin American Politics: A Theoretical Framework* (Austin: University of Texas Press, 1990); James Petras, *Politics and Social Forces in Chilean Development* (Berkeley and Los Angeles: University of California Press, 1969)..

depend on heavy use of political power at the centre of the state where a civilian or military bureaucracy dominates policy as well as decision-making. The state, in this regard, allows very little "voice"[13] in the manner in which it runs public affairs, and it justifies its existence on the ground that it is "developmental", or is a "provider of peace and security" or is a "protector of the common man" and works in the national interest. In other words, being a do-gooder for society, it needs very little legitimacy except what it does. It is, by and large, accountable to itself first and to the people second.

A bureaucratic authoritarian regime may therefore be populist or technocratic. The Peron regime in Argentina was populist while the successive military regimes in Brazil were technocratic. But while most authoritarian regimes in Latin America have been *bureaucratic,* their counterparts in Africa have largely been *presidential.*[14]

Presidential authoritarian regimes

A *presidential authoritarian regime* is one in which the president is the central entity in the wielding of political power. He wields this power through appointments to the civil service, nominations of candidates for competitive or semi-competitive elections in the one-party or no-party state, control of the armed forces, police and the secret services, dispensation of rewards and punishments, award of national honours and artefacts of privilege, determination of national symbols, distribution of economic, social and other "developmental" goods, and disposal of public assets.

While there may be institutions within the state that are charged with some or all of these responsibilities, they are quite often ignored by the president, or they have to seek the "presidential nod" in fulfilling their functions. In the process of privatisation in Kenya, for example, presidential powers have been used to ensure that public assets are disposed of in a manner that favours "the politically correct". In other words, those close to the presidential palace or those who are part of the circuit of presidential prebendal politics. Laws and procedures have been *fudged* to enable the process of looting public assets

---

13 For the concept of "voice", see Albert Hirchman, *Exit, Voice and Loyalty* (New Haven: Yale University Press, 1967).

14 See, for example, P. Anyang' Nyong'o, "State and Society in Kenya: The Disintegration of the Nationalist Coalition and the Rise of Presidential Authoritarianism, 1963- 1978", *African Affairs* (April 1989):229-251.

through privatisation to appear *legal*. Hence we have spoken of the process as institutionalising a *lootocracy* rather than a democracy.[15]

Presidential authoritarian regimes have to be distinguished from civilian or military dictatorships. The Idi Amin regime in Uganda (1971-1979) functioned with little regard to any form of legitimacy, abused human rights wantonly and relied on naked force to keep itself in power. Presidential authoritarian regimes do not behave that way. They tend to invoke popular causes and seek to renew their legitimacy through elections that are quite often non-competitive or semi-competitive. The elections in Zimbabwe in early 2002 were obviously non-competitive as state power was used to ensure that President Mugabe enjoyed enormous advantage over his opponent Morgan Tzvangirai of the Movement for Democratic Change. But Mugabe was championing an issue very popular with the poor and landless of Zimbabwe; that is, land to the landless. Acquiring land by force from those who were using it productively did not make sense to right-thinking people, but Mugabe knew it would win him political support, and he did it through an election and not a presidential decree as a military dictator would.

Likewise, the Sani Abacha regime in Nigeria, Emperor Bokasa's regime in the Central African Republic, and Tombalbaye's rule in Chad were all various forms of dictatorships and not presidential authoritarian regimes. Here the presidents ruled by decrees and beheaded those who opposed them with little regard for the rule of law.

Presidential authoritarian regimes do not rule by decrees; dictatorships do. Presidential authoritarian regimes also have more respect for public institutions. They use them, and they may destroy them over time, but they do not wantonly raze them to the ground as dictatorships tend to do when such institutions stand on their way to power, or challenge what they see as their bases of legitimacy. Presidential authoritarian regimes tend to seek to transform social processes and organisations into "tools of presidential legitimacy" within the state.

Since many states in developing countries in Africa are in reality "state-nations" and not "nation-states", the corporate power of the state tends to dominate society, and the discipline of citizens is enforced through various cultural and material means that seek to ensure their loyalty directly to the state rather than through "intermediating civil society organisations." That is why both presidential authoritarian regimes as well as the dictatorships in Africa find civil society organisations uneasy bedfellows in the contest for political power. And that is why, even though NEPAD pays homage to

---

15   See Anyang' Nyong'o, *The Context of Privatisation in Kenya* (Nairobi: Academy Science Publishers, 2000).

civil society, the very nature of presidential authoritarian political processes may not envisage the involvement of civil society in the conceptualisation of NEPAD, let alone its implementation.

Both presidential authoritarian regimes and dictatorships in Africa are averse to dissent, and only suffer political pluralism to the extent that actors run their affairs within the bounds of the "one-party prerequisites" or "presidential pleasure". For example, while civil society organisations may be very sympathetic in supporting some land reform policy in Zimbabwe, and may not necessarily share Robert Mugabe's approach to the issue, the latter would hardly be ready to listen to their alternative views, albeit such views may help Mugabe design a more acceptable policy to the Zimbabwe people. In other words, in presidential authoritarian regimes, the limit to diversity of opinion in public policy making may quite often prepare the ground for demagogic approach to public policy by presidential power.

While African intellectuals and civil society organisations do share NEPAD's genuine concern to leap-frog Africa into modernity through a process of rapid socio-economic transformation, they do not share the faith in and reliance on the benevolence of the NEPAD leadership, the dependence on external financing, and the hurry to implement the programme without proper institutional arrangements owned by the African people. Enlightened or benevolent leadership may only be found in a few African countries; the majority of the leaders may care less about the NEPAD proposals. The proposals may, in fact, even threaten their stay in power. The four presidents currently leading the NEPAD crusade are also the ones most likely to respect their constitutional mandate to be in power for a specified period of time. Hence the institutionalisation of the NEPAD needs to be guaranteed while they are still in power if NEPAD is to outlive them. On the other hand, they may have put in place a closely-knit system, which will only allow "a circulation of elites" within the leadership, making the departure of the incumbent president inconsequential to the fate of the NEPAD. To what extent is this the case?

In the Singapore case, although Lee Kwan Yew acknowledged that they tended to formulate policies within a tightly knit group around his leadership, they were always careful to endure that their ideas were tested within certain circles of leadership and within the business community and civil society. "Debate and criticism would not take place in public, but among members of the government behind closed doors".[16]

---

16 Mallet, op.cit., 29.

While dictatorships tend to survive in power through force or the threat of use of force, presidential authoritarian regimes tend to seek the mandate of the people through regular elections and the pronouncement of popular policies. Such elections are almost always non-competitive or semi-competitive. They are, as it were, "*choiceless*" *elections*. Very often they are organised in a corrupt way, with voters being bribed for their votes and those elected deriving their legitimacy from being *loyal* to the president. The so-called *patron-client relationship* tends to dominate the chain of relationship and loyalty of voters, campaigners, candidates and the government. The policies, further, may not necessarily be implemented, but they remain in the public domain and may enjoy enormous public discourse for purposes of winning, or even manufacturing legitimacy.

In this regard, NEPAD could be such a policy that a club of presidents may espouse for purposes of legitimacy, locally and internationally. This might appear a cynical view, but it is a view that the leaders themselves need to negate in terms of the concrete actions they take from now on in implementing the NEPAD proposals and not simply in speaking about them or popularising them for purposes of winning legitimacy.

If presidential authoritarian regimes seem so well knit in terms of "power ownership" and "power control", how did they begin to unravel in Africa? How was their social bases eroded or somehow dislocated in certain African countries to allow for multiparty elections which have overthrown presidents, brought into the centre of power previously excluded elites and somehow promised the people "a new dawn"? Is NEPAD a continental ideological response to these changed political circumstances, or can it actually evoke pressures from below that may compel African leaders to implement it?

Presidential authoritarianism: Resistance and adjustments

Many years before the fall of the Berlin Wall in 1989 — a factor that now seems to "periodise" the age of authoritarianism from the age of various forms of liberal democratic "openings" — there were diverse forms of popular struggles for democracy, and resistance to authoritarianism in Africa.[17] The struggles took various forms in different places, depending on different social and economic contexts and historical antecedents.

---

17 See, for example, Anyang' Nyong'o (ed.), *Popular Struggles for Democracy in Africa* (London: Zed Books, 1987), also published as *La Longue Marche Ver La Democratie en Afrique* (Paris: Edition Published, 1988).

In former *settler* (or *plantation*) regimes like Kenya, South Africa, Zimbabwe, and Cote d'Ivoire, transition from authoritarianism has been more difficult to accomplish without the active and proactive cooperation of the incumbent president. This only happened in the case of South Africa where it can be argued that *enlightened leadership* saw the writing on the wall and pre-empted long drawn political paralysis by accommodating democratic political opening at the expense of losing presidential authoritarian power.[18] With the absence of enlightened political leadership in Kenya, Zimbabwe and Cote d'Ivoire, this transition has been protracted and detrimental to economic growth, as the regimes have continued to inspire little confidence in investors and have, by and large, ruled in antagonism to popular pressures for democratisation. In Cote d'Ivoire, the apparent accession to power by the Popular Front Party has been accomplished through an election, which was *non-competitive* in a typical presidential authoritarian regime.

Enlightened leadership has played an important role in adjusting authoritarian presidential rule to democratic openings in other *peasant-based economies* like Senegal and Tanzania. In Senegal, there was really no significant popular pressure for democratisation to force Leopold Sedar Senghor to leave the presidency to Abdou Diouf in 1980, and to begin a slow process of accommodating pluralist politics that eventually saw Diouf out of power through elections almost two decades later. In Tanzania, Julius Nyerere voluntarily accepted his own failures at economic development through his *ujamaa* policies and accepted to bow out of the presidency, allowing multiparty elections to be held even without the popular approval of the Tanzanian people. In both cases, it was the element of enlightened political leadership, no doubt by Africa's leading *intellectual presidents* that prepared the way for political pluralism.

In the former settler or plantation regimes, however, the active voice of civil society organisations makes the staying in power of the authoritarian presidents' tenors. Sooner or later they must cave in to external pressures for political opening, and the regimes tend to renew themselves through the old elites within the president's party, re-inventing themselves as democrats as has happened in the case of Malawi under Bakili Muluzi.

In the *military dictatorships* such as the Democratic Republic of the Congo (DRC), Somalia, Ethiopia, Rwanda, Uganda and Burundi societies have

---

18 See, for example, the account of this by Nelson Mandela, *Long Walk to Freedom: The Autobiography of Nelson Mandela* (London: Abacus, 1994); Henrik de Klerk, *The last Trek – A New Beginning: The Autobiography of F. W. de Klerk* (Basingstoke: Macmillan, 1988).

suffered, for a long period of time, political instability, internal conflicts and displacement of people. In these societies, civil society has either not developed or, where it was developing as in Uganda military rule, scattered and destroyed its economic and social sinews, rendering "new benevolent authoritarianism" desirable for reconstituting civil society itself. The Yoweri Museveni regime that has now been in power for sixteen years is benevolently authoritarian and NEPAD is right in placing premium on conflict resolution as a necessary condition for economic take-off in Africa.

Certain African state-nations have also been of strategic importance to Western powers, particularly former colonial powers. This has meant that political changes in these countries have been of particular interest to these powers, quite often making the *alliances* developed over time with sitting presidents the determinant factors on the nature and character of change from authoritarianism to democracy. Kenya, Cameroon, Togo, Congo Brazaville and Gabon seem to fall in this category. In Kenya, it is now known that forces within the conservative and liberal parties in Great Britain have been very protective of Daniel arap Moi and have in the past been doubtful of the ability of the opposition to handle state power competently in 1992. Hence, the British High Commissioner in Kenya in 1992 made it very clear to the opposition politicians, well before the multiparty elections in December that year, that Britain would be quite happy to see Moi continue in power while the opposition was well represented in Parliament and "learning how government works" so as to use that knowledge in the future "and not now", he emphasised.[19]

The demands for good democratic governance as a condition for implementing the partnership proposals in NEPAD could easily be overlooked by Western governments when it comes to countries regarded as strategic. For example, as long as the Khartoum government continues waging a war against its own people in Southern Sudan, it is doubtful how this government can be a partner to any member of the OECD, let alone belong to the African Union in accordance with the provisions of NEPAD as well as of the Constitutive Act of the African Union. Yet Western governments are now falling over each other scrambling to have relations with Khartoum as a result of the oil resources discovered in the south. Canada, in particular, should be ashamed of allowing her companies to do oil business with Khartoum, thus providing it with the revenue it uses to kill the Southern Sudanese in a war that has claimed close to 3 million lives over

---

19   The author was present at the discussion in the High Commission in April 1992.

the last forty years. But Canada is not alone in this. Apart from the Canadian firm, Talisman Energy, other Western oil companies like Total, FinaElf of France, Lundin Oil from Sweden and British engineering firms have direct interests in providing the oil blood money to Khartoum.

It must also be noted that *globalisation* has greatly influenced the timing, speed and nature of political changes in Africa. In the early 1990s, economic liberalisation was held to go hand-in-hand with political democratisation, and the World Bank and the IMF gave both as conditions for financial support for African governments. Governments that were successfully implementing *structural adjustment programmes*, like Jerry Rawlings government in Ghana, were actually given resources, time and space to democratise. Thus Rawlings was able to reinvent himself as a democrat and stand for elections, which he won very much with the support and approval of the West. In Uganda, Yoweri Museveni's no-party regime has held two non-competitive elections without any voice of disapproval from the OECD due to the fact that Uganda has been one of the most celebrated implementers of structural adjustment programmes in Africa. But in both cases, income inequalities have grown and corruption has re-emerged with a vengeance, making unsustainable the economic growth gains that have been attributed to the SAPs, and underscoring the role of the rule of law as a necessity for social equity and government integrity.

African perceptions of democracy and the rule of law

How have Africans, however, perceived democracy and the rule of law? What is the idea of democracy by those who have waged tremendous pressure for it? What has been the perception of democracy by those who rule? What is the role of elections in the clamour for democracy? If good governance or the rule of law is a necessary condition for realising the NEPAD objectives, is democracy part of this good governance the way Africans perceive it?

Under authoritarian regimes and the military or civilian dictatorships, those who wage the war against authoritarianism and political repression see democracy as getting rid of "closed power". Closed power has negated the aspirations of independence. Independence promised a better world; a world of education, health, employment and freedom. Closed power only gives these "developments" to those in power and their supporters.

Democracy, therefore, means *entering political power* by those who have been left out and oppressed for so long. The politics of those who want to enter political power can therefore be called the *politics of entrism*. It is state power that they are after, because it is state power that they have been denied so that those within the presidential authoritarian regime can enjoy the good that comes with state power. The *politics of exclusion* is the politics of the presidential authoritarian regime; it is also the politics of the military dictator. The *politics of inclusion* is the politics of democracy.

People get excluded on the basis of tribe, clan, region, religion or colour. The politics of entrism and the politics of inclusion as forms of democratic struggle can also lead to those who were formerly excluded starting to exclude the previous political insiders once an election is won and they become the new insiders. Fredrick Chiluba, then leader of the Movement of Multiparty Democracy (MMD) in Zambia, won the election in 1991 and removed Kenneth Kaunda of the United National Independence Party (UNIP) from the presidency, a position Kaunda had held for 26 years. Chiluba immediately started to harass Kaunda's people, going to the extent of declaring Kaunda not to be a Zambian citizen since one of his parents had apparently been a Malawian. Chiluba's fear was that Kaunda would possibly stand against him the following elections and, like Kerekou was to do in Benin, perhaps stage a popular comeback to power. Chiluba started to change the rules of the game to make it impossible for Kaunda to contest any future elections for his re-entry into political power.

When faced with popular pressure for political opening, those who wield power in presidential authoritarian regimes tend to view democracy mainly as adjustments to the rules of the game so as to allow an organised entry into the political arena by those formerly excluded. In the case of Nigeria, this was done by the military rulers writing a constitution that allowed for only two political parties: one conservative and the other liberal. Nigerians were expected to organise themselves and make political choices *prescribed* by the political insiders. In the case of Zaire under Mobutu, the president organised a *national conference* to which the people were invited to deliberate on a new constitution under terms set by the military rulers. Even the national conferences initiated by *popular living forces* in Benin, Togo and Cameroon were successfully co-opted by the insiders, leading only to one success – Benin – but where the ancient regime managed to re-capture power five years after the conference was over.

Thus, from the ruling presidential authoritarian regimes, adjusting to pressures for democracy has largely been an issue of *political engineering* ensuring that political opening, in terms of new entrants into the political arena, goes hand-in-hand with maintaining the same political economy. Hence, as I have argued elsewhere,[20] *electoralism* is not a sufficient condition for either expanding the democratic space or enhancing democracy in an authoritarian regime. It does help to create an atmosphere for expanded political discourse, but left as such, the discourse may only help to legitimise authoritarianism and not undermine its staying in power. NEPAD now goes beyond mere political inclusion as an aspect of democratisation and gives an economic and social programme for democratisation. NEPAD assumes thereby, that conservative authoritarianism will give way to democracy through competitive electoral politics.

The persistence of authoritarianism in Africa

But why does authoritarianism find it so easy to re-invent itself in the different African countries in spite of a plethora of multiparty elections? To answer this question, we need to go back to Franz Fanon's arguments in *The Wretched of the Earth* and Rene Dumont's arguments in *False Start in Africa*.[21] While Fanon deals with the *subjective factors* that influence the actions of African nationalists when they assume political power, Rene Dumont looks at the *objective conditions* that were going to inhibit social and political changes in Africa after independence. In both cases, we realise that the subjective and material bases for democracy in Africa were bound to be very problematic.

Subjectively, the *rising middle classes* in Africa were very much attuned to be *conveyor belts* for external interests in the continent in terms of their material tastes, cultural inclinations, intellectual perceptions and identity with their fledgling nations. Objectively, even those elements of the middle class who tried to *be national* – like Nkrumah – would soon find out that the ties that bound the independent states with their former colonial masters could not easily allow another road of development except a neo-colonial one. In external trade, the multinational companies continued to dominate the export economy, reducing the former colonies to continue being providers of raw materials with very little value addition to what was exported. This kind of economy, producing very little surplus, could not generate sufficient revenue to invest in productive sectors that could expand employment opportunities, and hence increase incomes. Subjectively, the ruling elites did not develop a passion for

---

20 See Anyang' Nyong'o, *The Study of African Politics: A Critical Appreciation of a Heritage* (Nairobi: Bookprint Creative Services, 2002).

21 See Frantz Fanon, *The Wretched of the Earth* (Harmondsworth: Penguin, 1964), and Rene Dumont, *False Start in Africa* (Harmondsworth: Penguin, 1967). Both titles were originally published in Paris by Francois Maspero under the titles *Les dames de la terre* (1961) and *Afrique Noire est Mal Parti*.

relying on their own human resources; they preferred the use of the expert from abroad. Hence, even where there is a high development of human resources as in Kenya, the expert from abroad – World Bank and IMF included – takes the place of the native, and the native votes with his feet as he seeks employment abroad. Singapore developed by exploiting its own human resources; Kenya has failed to develop by misusing or ignoring its own human resources.

It is this vicious cycle that Rene Dumont described and analysed in his book, leading to the conclusion that, short of a complete restructuring of the African economies, poverty would increase and governments – faced with tremendous economic problems – would tend to be more repressive as they continued only to satisfy the interests of the ruling elites tied to metropolitan capital.

This, perhaps, is why NEPAD seems to be first and foremost a "dialogue between the donors and the African leaders" before it becomes a dialogue between the African leaders and the African people they lead. This does not, however, mean that it is wrong in its diagnosis on what needs to be done to kick-start economic growth in Africa. It is, however, not quite explicit on what needs to be done by the leadership and the African people in their involvement together in this process of leap-frogging Africa from the Third to the First World the way Singapore did it. NEPAD proposes the "peer review" mechanism as a way of ensuring that leaders and governments pass the test of good governance from time to time. But the targets and objectives to be met, especially in terms of economic performance, remain general and difficult to apply for strict accountability.

It becomes therefore rather difficult to see how democratic space can be expanded in Africa without, at the same time, initiating rapid economic growth and economic prosperity as necessary conditions for democracy. Rapid economic growth and the expansion of democratic space must somehow go together. Nonetheless, as Kenichi Ohmae, writing on China in an issue of the magazine *Strategy and Business* observes, there is always the tendency to argue, in a rather linear manner, that it might be necessary to win the war against poverty first before paying attention to issues of democracy. He writes:

> I do not believe China should be forced to hold democratic elections, even if that were possible. Its population would vote for leaders who distribute wealth to the poor. But there are still 900 million farmers in China with an average annual income of $500; distribution of wealth would simply be synonym, as it is in India, for the distribution of poverty.[22]

---

22 Kenichi Ohmae, "How to Profit in China, Inc" *Strategy and Business*, First Quarter (2002).

In Africa, likewise, elections have led to the distribution of poverty as elites who "buy their votes to power" seek, once in office, to profit by looting public coffers and implementing policies that are least attuned to fight the war against poverty. The graph of public and private consumption rises so much faster than the graph of public and private savings that there can hardly be a time when domestic savings will provide a firm basis for capital formation in the service of development. *Structural corruption* – corruption in which the people also seem to benefit from the elites through intricate webs of dependence – may legitimise presidential authoritarianism, which in turn seeks to present itself in this setting as *popular authoritarianism*. The late Hastings Banda of Malawi once admitted to a journalist when asked whether people rightly or wrongly accused him of being a dictator: "Yes," he concurred, "But I am a dictator that the people choose to put up with."

What then should be done to enhance democracy in Africa?

First, democracy should not be understood simply as the *politics of entrism*. Entrism can easily entrench political opening within the terrain of authoritarian politics. Democracy, however, should be understood first and foremost in terms of a process of enhancing *political participation*. Participation of the citizens in the process of government in terms of policy making, decision-making, share and distribution of responsibility as well as scarce values. If the level of citizenship is low, participation is not likely to enhance further democratic values of fairness, justice, social solidarity, and the rule of law.

Secondly, the *rule of law* is a cardinal aspect of democracy. In other words, participation should be based on rules of conduct, behaviour and decision-making that are not personal, traditional, particularistic or parochial. The rules should be universal and applicable to individuals as citizens and not any other essential categories unless such categories are also arrived at on the basis of certain universal norms. For example, all those who achieve undergraduate degrees are entitled to compete for jobs in the civil service.

Third, democracy is much more than *good governance*. While good governance may be looked at in terms of the efficiency and effectiveness with which government manages public affairs, democracy is about how this management is done through the participation and consent of the people as citizens. *Social democracy* goes further; it demands that democratic governance promotes human dignity, encourages social solidarity and ensures the realisation of basic needs as citizens seek to improve their lives under an actually existing democratic regime. Thus, good governance that creates permanent conditions for inequalities, however effective such a government is, falls short of seeking the ideals of democracy and the demands of social democracy. In NEPAD, there is a desire to go beyond good governance for a new democratic dispensation that will enhance possibilities for the state to achieve social democratic goals under a partnership with the outside world. But can this be done while authoritarian regimes still dot the political map of Africa?

Conclusion

Transitions from authoritarian regimes to democratic ones have not always been easy, nor do they take place in short periods of time. The ease with which they take place depends on diverse circumstances, some historical, others cultural and others economic and political.

The length of time that the transition goes through depends largely on how the old regime is capable of resisting change and adapting to changing circumstances. It also depends on the political strength and mobilising capacity of the democratic challengers.

In Mexico, the transition from the authoritarian Institutionalised Revolutionary Party (shortened as "PRI" for *Partido Revolucionario Institucinado*) regime started in 1968 with the student riots that were ruthlessly put down by Louis Echeverria, then interior minister, as the students demanded democratic reforms. A few years later, Echeverria could only stay in power as the President of the Republic by appeasing the restless masses with populist policies. The authoritarian PRI regime, however, remained unchanged as Echeverria's populism bought it some more time in power.

It took almost three decades for the Mexicans to be able to elect a president from one of the opposition parties. This was Vicente Fox of the National Alliance Party (NAP) elected by a broad-based movement that wanted to see PRI out of power. But Fox could not have been elected had his predecessor, Ernesto Zedillo, not have disobeyed the PRI political power barons in changing the electoral laws to ensure that an open and democratic election was possible. Zedillo did three things:

1. He made the National Electoral Commission independent of the executive and the ruling PRI party;

187

2. He ensured that the laws would prevent vote rigging and that vote counting would be free of any bias; and,

3. He ascertained that political representation would be fair and nobody would become president with a minority of the popular vote.

In other words, Zedillo made the opposition win the battle over the rules of the electoral game first before they won the votes cast by the people. He established a political culture of fair competition by putting into force rules and laws that would enforce this culture before the people started to enjoy the electoral outcome of this culture.

It is the struggle to build such a culture that authoritarian regimes always resist. It can be seen in the behaviour of Robert Mugabe in Zimbabwe. It can also be seen in the behaviour of Daniel arap Moi in Kenya. Both have resisted any changes in the rules of the game that would make it difficult for the presidential authoritarian system to be relegated to the museum of bad and non-development political culture. It all shows that the struggle for democratic rules of the game is as important as the struggle for a democratic political system itself. As long as the rules favour presidential authoritarianism, election after election will be held in one African country after the other, but *plus ca change plus ca rest le meme chose.*

For NEPAD to be embraced by the African people, it must involve internal democratic changes in each African country that makes people have confidence in the leaders implementing NEPAD, and hence own the process itself. It must also be a partnership with the international environment that leads to wealth creation in Africa as a basis for development.

So far all past arrangements in terms of trade, access to foreign markets, foreign aid and foreign investments have not served Africa's need for internal wealth creation and the growth of domestic home markets. That, perhaps, is why the war against poverty has been so difficult to win and why authoritarian regimes have demagogically painted the outside world as the enemy in shifting the responsibility for the people's misery away from themselves.

While bad governance may, indeed, account for Africa's continued underdevelopment, these *domestic problems* – as Dani Nabudere calls them – have intensified rather than caused the negative developmental experience. Africa's present-day problems can be traced to five hundred years of slave trade and colonisation, a hundred years of unequal exchange with the developed world in trade, and fifty years of undemocratic imposition of development models by multilateral institutions such as the World Bank and the IMF.[23] In making an argument for a new partnership to reverse this past negative experience, an argument for reparations also needs to be made as a redress for these past injustices.

Even under the Lome Conventions and the Cotonou Agreements, ACP-EU partnership presupposed equity in trade relations, improvement in good governance in Africa and development payoffs for the people. In the 25 years between the signature of Lome I in 1975 and the expiry of Lome IV in 1990, the share of ACP exports in European markets fell by half, from nearly 8 to about 3 per cent. The main beneficiaries were other developing countries such as South East Asia, which enjoy a level of preferential access to the EU (the Generalised System of Preferences) that is less favourable than under Lome. In other words, "supply constraints" within the ACP countries themselves made them not take full advantage of the preferential agreements for their exports to the EU markets.

Even supposing that ACP countries were to succeed in improving considerably the performance of their economies, it is now very late to hope to reverse the trend of preference erosion. First, there are the WTO rules, which make preferences outdated. But second, there are the "veterinary and quality standards" that national governments in Europe use to keep out agricultural and livestock imports from the ACP to Europe purely to protect European farmers.

NEPAD is now proposing to go beyond "preferences" as a framework for providing partnership in development with the OECD, and arguing for a more comprehensive Marshall Plan for Africa. As Adebayo Adedeji recently reminded us, unlike NEPAD — which has been initiated and prepared by the African countries — the Marshall Plan was a joint endeavour of the war-devastated European countries (the recipients) and the United States (the donor) for a period of four to five years. Europe was an industrialised and developed market economy before the war; Africa is still largely agricultural and peripherally industrial. Europe was to rehabilitate what it already had in terms of production capacity, infrastructure and human resources; Africa still needs to build production capacity, infrastructure and to develop human resources through massive public investments in education and health.[24]

---

23 D. Nabudere, "Africa's Development Experience Under the Lome Conventions", in P. Anyang' Nyong'o (ed.), 30 *Years of Independence in Africa: The Lost Decades?* (Nairobi: Academy Science Publishers, 1992).

24 Adebayo Adedeji, "From the Lagos Plan of Action to the New Partnership for African Development and the Final Act of Lagos to the Constitutive Act: Whither Africa?" Keynote Address to the African Forum for Envisioning Africa, *Focus on NEPAD* (Nairobi: African Academy of Sciences, Heinrich Boell Foundation, and Mazingira Institute, 2002).

Mere global economic integration will not do this, hence NEPAD is right in calling for a more deliberate initiative that focuses on the need to eradicate poverty and leap-frog Africa into modernity through another version of a Marshall Plan under very different historical circumstances. The only trouble, however, is that NEPAD's Marshall Plan does not seem to have any time frame, nor does it seek to create institutions for its implementation such as the Organisation of European Economic Cooperation (OEEC) that were so central to the success of the US-European Marshall Plan.

Are the parties to this partnership serious and committed to the endeavour they have assigned themselves? On the one hand are the proposers of the new Marshall Plan, the African leaders. They argue that they are now committed to good democratic governance, and that those who deviate will be called upon to account for themselves through a *peer review mechanism*. What are the institutional guarantees? They are currently not clear. On the other hand are the OECD partners who have, in the past, insisted on the need for this democratic governance as a condition for economic partnership, but have quite often created exceptions where their national interests are at stake.

Whatever uncertainties and problems we have pointed out, we want to believe, first and foremost, that the proponents of NEPAD are serious about their intentions. Secondly, that the difficulties we have pointed out in the political and economic environment should indicate obstacles to be overcome and not necessarily roadblocks that make the initiative futile from the word go. Thirdly, in the final analysis, the success of NEPAD will depend on the following:

- The dismantling of presidential authoritarian regimes as enlightened political leadership and democratic social movements win more democratic political dispensation locally and internationally, and institutionalising the rule of law and citizenship rights.

- The elimination of political conflicts that dissipate human resources, allow natural resources to be plundered and create the opportunity for wasteful military expenditure in defence of so called *national security*.

- The ability of the state, therefore, to create an attractive environment for investment and capital accumulation, by investing heavily in social and physical infrastructure, and enhancing regional economic and political integration as intended in the African Union.

- The pursuit of global social democracy as the only viable ideological basis for the new partnership proposed, away from the old models of cooperation such as the ACP-EU relationship, or even the WTO arrangements.

18

NEPAD

A Timely and Useful Institution for Africa

Paper presented at the conference on "Regional Security Issues in the Age of Globalisation", organised by the Heinrich Boll Foundation, the National Defence College and the Diplomacy Studies Institute, Nairobi Safari Club, Lilian Towers, 16-18 March 2004

In recent discussions on the New Partnership for Africa's Development (NEPAD) some observations were made by some critics that need to be clarified. Some key ones are:

- That nothing is new about NEPAD; African leaders have come up with such lofty ideas before;

- That NEPAD was really the initiative of the OECD countries wanting to impose their own version of globalisation on Africa;

- That NEPAD is the cowardly acceptance of neo-liberal economics by African leaders in a world in which the powerful countries are strengthening their states while aggressively using neo-liberalism to search for and penetrate foreign markets;

- That in Africa, the Republic of South Africa is the client state for this creeping neo-liberalism, hence President Thabo Mbeki's strong championing of NEPAD; and,

- That, therefore, as a top-down approach to African development, civil society was duty bound to reject it and look for more people-based approaches to African economic integration and exit from poverty.

There could have been many other derivatives of the above arguments, but they could all fit in neatly within the above arguments.

In our book, *NEPAD: A New Path?*,[1] while discussing the grounds on which these arguments emerged, various contributors sought to respond to them and to give a more "internal reading" of NEPAD than some of these critiques had been prepared to have. The weakest argument of course, was that NEPAD was a top-down idea. While accepting that it was, indeed, a top-down idea, this we saw as inherently useful, if not essentially necessary. Few good ideas ever come from crowds, committees or commissions. If anything, most ideas that have inspired mass movements and changed societies — for the better or for the worse — have come from individual persons.

The Christian movement was born out of the missionary work and the theology of one man: Jesus Christ. Saint Paul carried this further, and at great personal risk to his own reputation and life, toured the whole of the Middle East writing and preaching to both the converted as well as the diabolical cynics. Likewise, the Islamic faith was inspired by the theology and ideas of Prophet Mohammed. Much later, the political, philosophical and economic analyses and treatises of Karl Marx and Friedrich Engels changed the history of many countries in the world.

None of these prophets, theologians and political economists convened "stake holders" discussions first before they espoused their theologies, theories and philosophies that they then sought to influence minds and hearts so as to change the world. Hence there was nothing inherently wrong in Thabo Mbeki, Abdoulaye Wade, Olusegun Obasanjo and Bouteflika coming up with the NEPAD agenda and seeking to influence the course of Africa's history hopefully for the better. A much more interesting discourse should, therefore, be carried more on the message than the bearers of the message, hence the usefulness of an "internal reading" of NEPAD.

Scholars and civil society activists have extensively discussed the key issues raised above since our book was published, thereby raising the level of participation in the process of internal reading. Of greater importance has been the issue of the relevance and usefulness of "neo-liberalism" as a viable framework for shaping African economic and social policies in the context of globalisation.

NEPAD accepts globalisation as a reality but, unlike Francis Fukuyama,[2] does not see it as the end of history. If anything, globalisation is something to

---

1   Anyang' Nyong'o, A. Ghirmazion and D. Lamba (eds.), *NEPAD: A New Path?* (Nairobi: Heinrich Boll Foundation, 2001).

2   F. Fukuyama, *The End of History and the Last Man,* (New York: Free Press, 1992).

engage and challenge with innovative ideas and processes that will reshape the flows of world trade, undo global inequalities, democratise political and social systems and institutionalise global social democracy. It is not socialism that is on the political agenda of the oppressed and exploited of the Third World; it is the building of a democratic developmental state at the national level while pursuing global social democracy at the international level.

The collapse of the Cancun WTO talks has revealed quite clearly this contradiction between the pursuit of global social democracy by the developing countries regarding trade and development (the Doha Agenda) and global trade hegemony of the OECD-led economies (the Singapore Agenda). NEPAD cannot therefore be simplified and reduced as a mere agenda of the West; it would be difficult thereby to explain a phenomenon like that which occurred in Cancun. Even the issue of being a cowardly acceptance of a Western agenda also falls on its face at this juncture, and we must therefore proceed to an internal reading that will get us beyond this populist discourse.

In calling upon the need for a developmental national state that promotes pan-African economic relations in the context of globalisation, NEPAD puts emphasis on *private-public partnership* in filling the "resource gaps" and "resource needs" in investing for economic growth. These "gaps" and "needs" were estimated to amount to at least US$ 64 billion annually if Africa is to achieve a rate of economic growth that will drastically eradicate poverty and set the continent on the highway towards modernity in the next two decades.

Cynics interpreted this to mean that Africa was going on a begging spree to the G8 to look for this money as aid to finance development. There is a big difference between holding a discourse with the G8 on how they will support private sector investment flows from the developed countries to Africa and begging them to give "free money" to Africa to finance development, whatever form of development one is talking about.

It is to be noted that in the area of infrastructure—roads, railways, telecommunications, airways transport, maritime transport, energy—the public sector, alone or in partnership with the private sector (local and foreign), will be vital in Africa's economic recovery and development. Whichever form the investment takes, good corporate governance is important for successful operations. NEPAD has more than emphasised this, hence the proposal for the Peer Review Mechanism (meant to compel the state to set good examples of governance and best practices so as to percolate in the rest of society. It ought to be remembered that the private sector is not, by its very nature, prone to probity and integrity; laws, values and regulations, enforced by the state and other public, corporate and professional bodies will make the private sector observe probity and integrity.

At the recent meeting of the Eastern African region member states of NEPAD, private-public partnership was emphasised in fast-tracking projects that enhance regional integration, increase connectivity, stimulate cross-border trade, lead to greater national harmony, create wealth and thereby reduce poverty.[3] A dozen key projects in the area of infrastructure and agriculture were approved, a good number of them already underway with substantial private sector input. For example, the Indian Ocean Submarine Fiber Optic Cable network that will increase telecommunications connectivity with the island states and the inland landlocked states with the rest of the region already has substantial private sector investment.

It was further agreed that an office be set up in Nairobi for coordination and networking. This office is thus coming into being as a *demand-driven initiative* and not a supply-side NGO. Its first item on the agenda, in line with the nature of the NEPAD Steering Committee in Kenya, will be to concretise the private-public partnership at the regional level. In all this, *increased connectivity* is the key factor, for on connectivity comes economic integration and the growth of the home market.

Nonetheless, without *peace* and *security* everything else comes to naught. Thus, it was emphasised, at the same summit, that primacy must be given to establishing permanent peace and security in the region if development is to be given a chance. The *rapprochement* between the Sudanese People's Liberation Movement/Army and the Khartoum government is well advanced at the Naivasha Peace Talks here in Kenya. The Peace Agreement was supposed to have been signed before Christmas last year, and then the development and reconstruction work was to start in earnest in Southern Sudan this year. It would be a complete disappointment to the people of Southern Sudan, and to Africa as a whole, were that peace process to remain protracted longer than it has already been. Likewise, the Somalia peace process must not be left to the dictates of the privileged, and quite often handpicked warlords. Member states within the region need to give a strict timetable for the peace process. The Somalia leaders need to realise that negotiations do not necessarily get better

---

3 NEPAD Eastern African Regional Summit on Private-Public Partnership in Development, Nairobi, 25-29 October 2003.

the longer they take, especially when the objectives are not clearly appreciated and when private agenda take the place of national goals.

The African Peer Review Mechanism (APRM) recognises the political problems that will, of necessity, make the process of peace building problematic, especially when internal conflicts within states have gone on for a long time. It is therefore necessary that peace and security be taken as paramount in establishing the environment for development.

One can already see that, in the developed world, the Peer Review process is not that easy. When Chancellor Schroeder of Germany and President Jacque Chirac of France recently tried to "peer review" President Bush and Prime Minister Tony Blair over the Iraq war, they did not go very far. If anything, the relationship among these four NATO partners soured considerably. The difficulties in using the peer review process in creating a continent safe for democracy and development must not be allowed to provide a vote of no confidence in the viability of the process.

Priority must also be given to infrastructure connectivity between Southern Sudan and Ethiopia, Kenya, Uganda and the rest of the region. Thus the roads, railways and telecommunications construction already approved at the recent Nairobi summit must be fast-tracked. A special Sudan Reconstruction Conference is therefore a priority, and the Nairobi-based African Research and Resource Forum (ARRF) has been making proposals to this effect and has had extensive discussions with the New Sudan Council of Churches as a working partner.

Discussions aimed at a Somali Peace Agreement have been bogged down by demands at the peace talks that are, to say the least, uncompromising. It is even doubtful whether the majority of those at the talks represent bona fide social forces in the Somalia conflict. It would be necessary for Kenya, Ethiopia and Djibouti to establish a *modus operandi* for the negotiations cognisant of the real conflicting forces prior to accepting the individuals in Nairobi at the moment as the real negotiators.

In the final analysis, NEPAD's usefulness is that it brings together African governments to discuss development matters without the excessive bureaucracy that often bogged down discussions at the OAU as well as the ECA. Whereas the latter had reasonably good technocrats that proposed good programmes, it rarely had substantial political power to implement its proposals. While the former had political legitimacy, its political power was dispersed among its members none of whom was prepared to sacrifice sovereignty for the common good.

NEPAD has come at a time when the African elite as well as people are anxious for results rather than mere palaver if concrete change is to be realised. It is therefore time to urge for action rather than celebrate cynicism. In the corridors that civil society activists exchange ideas, it is quite often easier to sit on the comfort zone of cynicism and not to plunge into the deep end of trying to change Africa through concrete political action by engaging political power. Unfortunately, under authoritarian regimes, political power is so badly misused that its destruction becomes, in itself, a necessary action to lay the ground for development discourse and praxis.

When a society enters the transition from authoritarianism to democracy, civil society activists may take long to engage political power in the transition, themselves not quite clear whether the transition is real or is a chimera. This period of uncertainty and procrastinating can undermine the synergy that needs to be built between progressive forces in government as well as civil society.

It would look as if in South Africa the building of this synergy is much more advanced than in Kenya and other African countries where the NEPAD idea is taking root. The challenge is therefore for more discourse to take place so that time is not wasted in the urgent task of giving development a chance in Africa after so many years of authoritarian misrule.

19

Re-thinking Euro-African Relationship
The Blair Commission on Africa

Speech delivered at the Blair Commission Dialogue, AMREF, Nairobi,
5-7 December 2004

Allow me to dispense with one major preliminary issue in this dialogue. Whether or not the Blair Commission should have been established is now not a very relevant issue. What is more important is to ask and answer the question: having been established, what difference will it make to what the European Union does under the Chairmanship of Prime Minister Blair?

First, Prime Minister Blair has, by establishing this Commission, signalled the fact that he would like to have a creative dialogue on Euro-African relationships and interactions. The terms of discourse and the discourse itself, between Africa and Europe today are therefore seen as either leaving some key issues out or not addressing some key issues adequately.

Second, having established proper and relevant terms of discourse and the important issues themselves, Prime Minister Blair hopes to receive informed African opinion on these issues. Some of the issues directly touch on the MDGs themselves; for example, to meet MDGs of halving hunger by 2015 growth rate of a least 7 per cent per annum. With only a decade to 2015 many of our countries have not made marked progress in this area. To shift from low to higher growth path requires both decisions like the one on Commission for Africa.

We need to redefine what we mean by stable macroeconomic framework when poverty is rising right in our face. Some areas where the commission can focus on are:

(a) Designing strategies for financing development beyond the traditional ways;

(b) Formulating how to actively engage the private sector as the engine of economic growth and expanding the space for more rapid economic growth; and,

(c) Supporting the institutional capacity development to support such growth.

The commission can and should help in designing and implementing anti poverty programmes as well as checking the illegal transfer of capital from Africa estimated at 37 per cent in 1998 compared to only 3 and 17 per cent for Asia and Latin America respectively.

Third and finally, Prime Minister Blair will, during his tenure as Chairperson of the EU, act on these issues so as to make a difference on Euro-African relationships and interactions.

On creative dialogue with Africa

Europe's current major concern with Africa is to be involved in the debate on *good governance, democracy* and *aid*. Almost every ambassador and high commissioner's discourse begins with the sentence: "My government would like to increase our aid but this will depend on the seriousness with which your government promotes democracy, fights corruption and demonstrates that it is committed to good government." While democracy and good governance are important to all reform governments in Africa today and key to progressive social change, they should not be on sale, nor should they be used as the purchasing price for aid. If aid comes as the reward for democracy and good governance, then aid itself is a wrong commodity for Africa.

The creative dialogue with Africa today must begin by honestly recognising the long chain of historical causation to the problems and opportunities that exist between our two continents. Without an honest appreciation of this history, the terms of our discourse today will not lead us to a creative dialogue.

We must recognise that Africa's relationship with Europe changed significantly with slavery and the slave trade, empire building and colonialism. This history is recent and it still affects our relationships today, dominating the character of trade, debt, aid, the discourses on economic partnership agreements and even this present discourse. This history forms the bedrock of *Europe's underdevelopment of Africa*, something that still goes on in the open pillaging of the Congo and the massive transfer of values from Africa to Europe through debt servicing and tied aid.

If the terms of discourse are to fundamentally change, then we must begin by creating a discourse that will turn underdevelopment on its head in favour of real development. I want to submit that Prime Minister Blair will make a difference to Euro-African relationships and interactions if they are for the first time based on really developing Africa and continuing to underdevelop Africa. How will this be done?

On an informed African opinion

Informed African opinion will begin by saying that we first and foremost need to change the objective conditions under which we interact. Our first arena of interaction with Europe is through *trade*. We must change the structure of trade. What we produce to trade with Europe must change away from raw materials and unfinished goods to value added goods and manufactures. This means priority must be given to investments and intra-African trade. This further means greater emphasis on infrastructure development to promote economic and regional integration in Africa. This process has been going on in Asia with or without democratisation. The nature of our trade with Europe will only change in accordance with the changes on the objective conditions under which we produce and trade.

That is why, during the *Big Table* meeting in Addis Ababa recently, we urged our OECD partners that it is necessary for the World Bank to ensure that there is a special IDA facility for financing infrastructure development that involves two or more African governments, i.e. cross-national infrastructure development. I hope the European Investment Bank will provide leadership in this regard.

Second, informed African opinion, while giving priority to trade and investment in the context of infrastructure development and regional integration, also holds that the contentious issues of debt and aid should finally be put to rest during Prime Minister Blair's chairmanship of the European Union. Aid provided in the midst of heavy debt servicing makes no sense, hence the division between HIPC and non-HIPC countries is a divide-and-rule tactic, which punishes those who service aid while only releasing marginal resources to those designate as HIPC. This division also militates against regional integration by creating lines of favouritism that politically divide Africa in Euro-African discourses. What exists today as aid and debt continues the chain of underdevelopment. Blair should break this chain by a more development-oriented "Blair Plan."

Third, we are today confronted by some new-generation global threats such as AIDS/HIV and poverty. Although poverty has been known in human history before, earlier poverty was the result of the primitive development of productive forces. The present poverty occurs in spite of some very high development of productive forces and misuse of human resources. Unlike AIDS/HIV humankind knows the cure for poverty but refuses to use it due to selfishness, national barriers, imperialism etc. Blair's Europe has this cure.

Prime Minister Blair must do two things. Put Europe on a firm path towards dealing with poverty eradication in Africa in a manner that makes sense. In this regard, NEPAD has made very practical and do-able proposals. The G8 Action Plan for Africa is therefore the initial response designed to encourage the imaginative effort that underlies the NEPAD and to lay strong foundation for action to achieve the Millennium Development Goals (MDGs). The Plan emphasises promotion of peace and security; strengthening institutions and governance; fostering trade, investment, economic and sustainable development; improvement in the promotion of education and health; expansion of the digital space; confronting HIV/AIDS and communicable diseases; increasing agriculture productivity; and improving water and environmental management. If the massive resources that Washington and London have used in Iraq were used for the fight against HIV/AIDS in Africa, there would be a major difference to winning the war. And most of these resources would go towards the fight against poverty, a major cause of HIV/AIDS.

The challenge for the Commission on Africa is to develop a set of comprehensive, coherent and practical proposal for action by the international community, which together with African leaders, will help to accelerate sustainable growth of the continent.

In conclusion, let me say that what we say here will only make a difference if, as I said earlier, they lead to action by Prime Minister Blair when he takes the chair of the EU. Let us hope that this will be the case, and that future chairs of the EU will continue to build on the long lasting changes that Mr. Blair is committed to bring about.

20

African Peer Review Mechanism
The Kenyan Experience

*A speech to the Royal Africa Society at the School of Oriental African
Studies (SOAS), London, 11 November 2004*

The New Partnership for Africa's Development (NEPAD), as we all know, was conceived against the backdrop of an overweening pessimism about the prospects of Africa to redeem herself. This pessimism was predominantly the view of many looking forward in from outside. We who live in Africa think otherwise. In a recent BBC survey 90 per cent of Africans interviewed said they were proud to be Africans. As African leaders, therefore, we read with consternation reputed international newspaper headlines pronouncing "Africa: The Hopeless Continent" as *The Economist* did two years ago. Others wrote us off because of the high prevalence of HIV/AIDS. Learned people are now writing that there was too much witchcraft in Africa and this hinders development. A prominent American economist at New York University (NYU), William Easterly, called Africa as a whole "a tragedy," while another based at Columbia University, Sala-I Martin, wrote that Africa's poor economic performance since the 1970s was the twentieth century's greatest catastrophe.

Let me make this clear. There are monumental problems in Africa. It is true that sub-Saharan Africa accounts for 60 per cent of the reported HIV/ AIDS cases in the world. But that is not all there is. After some hesitation in the 1980s, African countries have generally responded to this unprecedented pandemic with vigour. Uganda and Senegal have set the pace for the rest of us by lowering infection rates to single digits. And while it is true that African economic growth rates per capita fell for most of the 1980s, evidence in the last three years reflects a turnaround, as a result of reform measures adopted in the 1990s and good weather. Progress in democratic governance in Africa, weighted by national population, has been more impressive than in some other regions. Armed conflicts have been wound down in Angola, Liberia and Sierra Leone. Peace making and stable national governance are on the way to Sudan and Somalia. All this owes a lot to African initiatives, as does the multinational effort to stabilise the complex conflicts in the Great Lakes region with South Africa at the helm. Again, Africa has its multiple problems, but helplessness and fatalism implied by her detractors is not one of them. Progress is being made. Progress will be made.

Kenya is a case in point. We have lived under poor governance in the last 41 years, but the last 24 of them were unnecessarily harsh. The country was exposed to economic plunder to a scale not known in our history. Those of you who are familiar with the ongoing inquiry on the Goldenberg scandal know that something in the order of US$ 800,000,000 disappeared into private bank accounts between 1990 and 1994, under a scheme to export non-existence diamonds and gold. Human rights abuses became rampant. I know because I was on a number of accessions held in brutal prison conditions simply for expressing myself as a scholar. State land and public forest were casually handed out to political cronies. Our civil service, once the best in the developing world, was severely weakened by nepotism, sycophants and ethnic appointments.

When the opposition parties failed to unite in the 1992 and 1997, and thus handed victory by default to the ruling party, KANU, which had a minority vote of 36 and 39 per cent respectively in these elections, we (the Kenyan opposition) became the despair of many of our friends abroad, including here in the United Kingdom. But in 2002, we redeemed ourselves and did Kenya proud. The opposition parties united in abroad mass movement — the National Alliance Rainbow Coalition (NARC) — which took 62 per cent of the votes. Kenya celebrated and the democratic world rejoiced at the exit of one of the Africa's most reviled dictatorships. In an international poll done in December 2002 Kenyans were judged the most optimistic people in the world. There was not a hint of African hopelessness here. Kenyans had redeemed themselves.

When I speak about our experience in implementing the African Peer Review Mechanism (APRM), therefore, it is necessary to take our recent political history into perspective. For even the poorest of Kenyans in the remote countryside is determined never to go back to the dark days of the dictatorship. Kenyans are expressing themselves, in speech, the press, talk radio, and on the street, an extent never seen since independence. Those of us in the Cabinet have learnt to live with an assertive Parliament and a muck raking press. After a clean-up exercise in the judiciary, our system is much better than it was two years ago. The economy is making a gradual turnaround, but we must accelerate our rate of growth. The world hears less about the progress we are making in Kenya than it does about corruption in the new administration. But I can assure you that we have made real progress and we are determined never to go back. This is where the APRM comes in.

The African Peer Review Mechanism is first and foremost an exercise in internal self-assessment. We as a government felt that Kenyans deserved to do just that. The African Peer Review Mechanism is also an event in which we invite our peers in the region to join in our self-assessment, provide some advice and when the process is over, to give us some constructive suggestions on how we could strengthen democracy and the rule of law in Kenya. For as Kenyans we have our eyes set on perfecting our newly won freedom. Any help from African friends in a similar position is therefore welcome. But when all is said and done, we chose peer review because of our past experience, which had taught us that political transparency is the best guarantee for individual freedom.

Therefore, Kenya, under NARC acceded to the APRM because it was already sold to the idea of transparency in the national governance when it came to power. Our citizens would not hear of anything less. On 15 March 2004, Kenya formally offered herself for peer review under NEPAD thereby honouring an announcement to that effect by myself on behalf of the Kenya Government at the NEPAD heads of state and Government summit in Kigali, Rwanda, the previous month. The Kenya review process had commenced. Before proceeding to narrate our experience with the APRM since that time, it might be useful (for the benefit of anyone unfamiliar with APRM) to give a bare-bones outline of what the APRM involves.

As I have stated, the APRM begins with an in-house country assessment, involving as wide popular representation as possible, on how well the government has discharged its obligation to the public in the following areas.

1. *Political governance and democracy*: This section of the review deals specifically with political and constitutional reform goals of the government, the status of human rights, electoral fairness, respect for the Bill of Rights, etc.

2. *Economic governance*: This part of the evaluation concentrates on how far the state has met its macroeconomic targets on growth, low inflation, corruption, employment generation, and adequate foreign services.

3. *Socio-economic goals*: The substantive commitment under evaluation here includes poverty reduction, under-five and maternal mortality, health standards, literacy, gender parity and equity issues across classes and geographic regions. In other words, what progress has been made to meet the MDGs?

4. *Corporate governance*: The key indices that should be generated here include the extent of transparency in corporate procurement, perception of corruption, fairness in recruitment, and degree of social responsibility in the private sector.

Once the country formally accedes to the review process it begins in-house preparations of the roadmap to a highly consultative and independent internal review of government in those four key areas. This is done in collaboration with the NEPAD Secretariat and its Group of Eminent Persons.

Provided the groundwork meets the mark, it is followed by the survey of domestic opinion on how the public evaluates the incumbent government in these four broad areas. The survey methods should (in our case) include polling, discussion with local leaders, and focus groups involving ordinary citizens, as well as consultation of existing research and published evaluation of government programmes. It should be carried out by independent technical experts answerable to a non-governmental council (or commission). This evaluation should produce a four sector comprehensive report. After comments from civil society, the public and professional associations, the report is then submitted to the government for its own comments, which could appear as an appendix to the final document.

This is where external review kicks in. The report is subsequently transmitted to the NEPAD Secretariat and upon technical review being done, it is handed over with remarks to the NEPAD Eminent Persons Group. "Provided the government concerned accepts" the APRM Group of Eminent persons should engage it "in constructive dialogue...offering technical and other appropriate assistance" to resolve problems arising from the report. If the reviewed country government is not amendable to reform "appropriate measures within a given time frame will be taken". The Group of Eminent Persons presents its recommendations to the APRM Forum for participating Heads of State and Government.

After six months the report is tabled publicly in international organisations, starting with local ones like COMESA, the AU, and UNECOSOC. It all sounds complicated but as I propose to show, the process could work reasonably well.

The APRM process from start to finish should take 6-9 months, a deadline that could prove difficult to meet even with all the political goodwill that you need.

In Kenya right now, we have just inaugurated our independent APRM Governing Council of 30 well-regarded Kenyan men and women to preside over the APRM process. Only 20 of them, however, have a right to vote. If I were to go by the APRM Guidelines, which detail the stages of the APRM, we are at stage three; that is, survey and preparation of report – out of five stages. We have yet to complete the report and subject it to the structures of review – domestic and external – that I mentioned earlier.

What problems have we encountered along the way? What lessons could other states and those interested in the welfare of Africa learn from our experience so far?

First, we should not give in to the Afro-pessimists and the cynics who wrote off NEPAD and APRM as soon as the ink on the documents was dry. They thought African governments would not and could not subject themselves to a domestic evaluation of their achievements, much less criticism from their peers. Southern Africa's reaction to Zimbabwe was given as an example. But this ignores the cases where the review process is already in progress in good faith, and where African citizens for the first time are speaking their minds in presence of local government officials and, in our case, NEPAD country support missions too.

The first step that we took after we had formally notified the Chairman of the NEPAD Heads of State and Government Implementation Committee, our decision to undertake the APRM was to constitute an inter-ministerial task force based in the Ministry of Planning and National Development, the ministry responsible for NEPAD projects in Kenya. The task force was intended to map out the guidelines and to work out a programme of action and a cost estimate of the entire exercise. Chaired by the PS Planning, Mr. David S.O. Nalo, the task force was made up of officials from the Kenya Ministries of Justice and Constitutional Affairs, Finance, Foreign Affairs, Office of the President, Trade and Industry, and Agriculture, and the Central Bureau of Statistics. Assembling the task force was completed in March 2004.

After the first three meetings, the taskforce decided to bring in distinguished representatives from the following areas: the private sector, civil society groups, universities and independent research institutes, and faith-based organisations. The four representatives sat in the task force in an advisory capacity, and we found their practical suggestions on what line of action to take, well informed and useful. Their selection was based on the level of their activism in society and was biased towards leaders of "umbrella" organisations like Kenya Federation of Employers, Central Organisation of Trade Unions (COTU), National Christian Council of Kenya (NCCK), etc. The first duty of the expanded task force was to examine the regulations of the APRM and to prepare a preliminary programme for the fist two stages: the assembling of background documents and material on Kenya's commitment to its people, in consultation with the NEPAD Secretariat, with the intention of generating the APRM agenda; and the preparation for wide consultative forum to discuss the agenda and formulate the institutional structures for realising it.

The result of these deliberations was the first Kenya national consultative forum on the implementation of the APRM, which took place on 14 July at the Kenya School of Monetary Studies, just outside of Nairobi. Participants had been drawn from a long list of relevant organisations prepared by the APRM task force. The over five hundred delegates who took part in this forum came from the NGOs, charity groups, the disabled, women organisations, professional bodies, trade unions, farmers organisations, business executives, students, political leaders from all political parties, members of parliament and government officials. A considerable part of the deliberations was taken by detailed explanations on what APRM was about in the context of NEPAD, how specifically it applies to Kenya, what Kenya expects to gain from the process, and the five stages of the review. But the meeting also discussed at length the appropriate modalities for selection a genuinely independent and representative governing council, which after being sworn in would preside over the implementation of the rest of the APRM process. At this assembly delegates agreed on which of the four APRM thematic areas they would fall.

A week latter, the four broad groups classified under political governance, corporate governance, social-economic development, and economic governance, met at the Kenyatta International Conference Centre in downtown Nairobi. Each of the four groups was expected to generate a list of two names of nomination into the Kenya APRM Governing Council. At the end of the day eight names of noted independent-minded Kenyans were presented to me as Minister for Planning and National Development to be considered for membership as of the APRM Governing Council. The rules drawn by the APRM task recommended three additional nominees to be made at the discretion of the Minister in order to compensate for under-representation by region, gender, religious faith, or whatever criteria be deemed fit. With that, the state was set for the first external visit – the Country Review Mission which would examine our programme so far, meet as many groups as it could and suggest any amendments before the process moves into the political survey and report writing phase.

Before the first consultative forum in mid-July, I had in my capacity as the minister responsible for NEPAD in Kenya, consulted with NEPAD Secretariat in Johannesburg about the composition of the first country review mission. It was agreed that Dr. Graca Machel, one of NEPAD Group of African Eminent Persons, would lead the mission to Kenya. Accordingly she arrived in Nairobi on 25 July 2004 for a four-day visit, accompanied by a contingent from the NEPAD Secretariat, and four African experts, in the APRM thematic areas.

The experts went through the background documents and the opinion evaluation strategy adopted by the consultative forum and discussed these with their Kenya counterparts. Out of those negotiations came some constructive suggestions on the proposed survey instruments, national coverage of the survey by thematic area, and the shape of the final report.

The most eventful and lasting changes to our programme were in fact made in open forums, which were led by Dr. Machel. She galvanised the country around the idea of self-assessment followed by peer review, in a manner only she could have done. In a series of open meetings, which were extensively covered by the press, she met with students, youth groups, women associations, the captains of industry, Members of Parliament from all parties, trade unionists, journalists, and the APRM Task Force. Kenyans who met Dr. Machel and her party expressed their opinions freely on the progress made by APRM process so far and what direction it should take henceforth. She persuaded the sceptical that APRM was worth the while if African governance was to be redeemed the spirit of African nationalism in the 1960's rekindled. She urged inclusiveness and reproached any groups which threatened to boycott the process because they felt excluded, or underrepresented.

One result of these consultations was the expansion of the Governing Council. The Kenyan NGO sector complained that it was underrepresented and had not been consulted sufficiently. After discussions with the APRM Task Force and Kenya NGO Council it was agreed that the council would be expanded by eight members (two for each of the four APRM sections) from the NGOs and voluntary groups, to bring the total representative membership to sixteen. This process took a whole month and slowed our progress considerably as no survey could be done before constituting

207

the council. Remember, it is the Council that should be responsible for the overall domestic evaluation of our government's performance in the four designated areas. In addition, in order to follow the government's statutes in constituting the Council, it was necessary to make a public announcement of the council's existence in the *Kenya Gazette* (the official bulletin of the Kenya Government). In the end, the Kenya National Governing Council of the APRM was sworn in at a public ceremony on 25 October 2004. It had thus taken us seven months to cover the first two stages of the APRM process.

The composition of the Council of 30, which has now assumed full ownership of the APRM process in Kenya is as follows:

(i) 8 members nominated by the four thematic groups constituted at the July consultative forum;

(ii) 8 members nominated by the Kenya NGO Council representing registered civil society groups, NGOs and voluntary bodies affiliated to it;

(iii) 2 members from registered civil society groups NGOs and professional associations nominated by the Minister;

(iv) 4 (ex-officio) Kenyan civil servants responsible for APRM managerial and financial services;

(v) 4 convenors (ex-officio); one each for an APRM thematic area; and

(vi) 4 experts (ex-officio) representing the four lead technical agencies.

The four technical agencies selected by the APRM Task Force in consultation with members of the incoming Governing Council are the following:

1. African Centre for Economic Growth (ACEG) based in Nairobi will be responsible for the survey on Political Governance and Democracy. ACEG has an established and internationally recognised track in evaluating governance reforms in Kenya under the annual UNECA African Governance Report. It is staffed by Kenyan scholars.

2. Kenya Institute of Public Policy Research and Analysis (KIPPRA). KIPPRA is a quasi-public economic policy research institute headed by an independent board. Its publications on macro-economic and sectoral issues are of the highest professional calibre. It provides professional policy advice to the Ministry of Planning and the Government.

3. Institute for Development Studies (IDS) at the University of Nairobi has been charged with the task of evaluating the government's performance in meeting the socio-economic indicators it is committed to under the Economic Recovery Strategy Paper for Wealth and Employment Creation, and also under the MDGs. IDS has published the *Kenya Human Development Report* annually since 1999 in collaboration with the UNDP. We in Government think highly of their work.

4. The Centre for Corporate Governance (in Nairobi) will be conducting the assessment the status of corporate governance in Kenya since 2002. Over the years, this Centre has produced a series of well-informed reports on corporate behaviour in Kenya

The four research directors of these institutions are ex-officio members of the Governing Council, as we saw. They should work closely with theme "convenors" to access the most critical individuals, social groups and organisations in their areas of inquiry. The convenors were selected by the consultative forums to sit on the council because of their in-depth knowledge of the diversity of opinion in the thematic area of their specialisation. They play a mediating role between researchers and civil society.

The Council is in the process of consulting with the lead technical agencies responsible for evaluating overall Kenyan perceptions on the best research strategy how our government has met popular expectations. This will lead to the writing of the report in conformity with the APRM guidelines from the NEPAD Secretariat.

This is where we are as regards the APRM in Kenya today. As I have already stated we have three critical stages to cover: (i) Data gathering and report writing; (ii) Internal reaction to it from the Kenyan and the Kenya Government; and (iii) finally external peer review.

Lessons from APRM

Now, what lessons have we learnt from our experience with the APRM so far? First, the deadlines envisaged in the original APRM template may prove difficult to meet even with the best of intentions. We are now in our seventh month and, with the Christmas holidays looming, after the second week of December, it is unlikely that we shall complete our APRM process in the nine months suggested by the NEPAD Secretariat. One year or slightly more might be the right duration. Remember that as long as APRM is done in an open and democratic manner, dissent, debate, consensus building, and compromise will always be an essential part of it. I mentioned how the compromise will always be an essential part of it. I mentioned how the composition of our governing council was challenged by the NGOs during the first external country visit, and the extra time it took to accommodate the new demands. We expect similar challenges to arise as we embark on the home-stretch to complete the surveys and to compose the report and debate it with government.

Secondly, the financial cost of APRM is an issue that calls for careful consideration. The NEPAD Heads of State and Government Committee of Participating States of the APRM has indicated that African governments should try to be as self-reliant as possible in financing the APRM. There has always been fear that excessive donor dependence and reliance on foreign technical advisors may influence the outcome, or, at any rate make the management of the process unduly cumbersome. In all cases, Africa needed to develop her own technical capability for inter and peer review. But when, as in our case, the total cost of the APRM process is estimated at close to US$ 1 million, what option do we really have? The Kenya Government has until now been the principal benefactor of the APRM process. The UNDP Office in Nairobi has been the only external donor to the APRM process so far, having extended a grant to my Ministry for the APRM Project – some $100,000 so far. This is 10 per cent of our needs. I am keen to learn how our colleagues in Ghana, Rwanda and Mauritius are handling the financial aspect of the APRM. This issue should be subjected to greater debate and analysis than it has been so far. Good peer review does not come cheap.

The third lesson I wish to discuss with you this afternoon concerns the extent of popular consultative meetings, which APRM calls for. We are enjoined by NEPAD and APRM protocols to rely as much as we can on open consultative forums in formulating policies and structures, and in collecting data on public opinion. Yet all this has costs in time and money. Consultative meeting are now the standard requirement of development policy making in Africa. They are part and parcel of the formulation of the poverty reduction strategy papers, educational reform programmes, constitutional review commissions, electoral reform programmes, law reform commission, economic reforms, etc. It is not easy to explain to a peasant how the popular consultative forum on poverty differs from the one on the APRM in MDG evaluation, and the one on the APRM from that on constitutional reform. The situation is made worse by the fact that the committees and experts involved in these activities follow each other in and out of villages. If our government fail to deliver, should we be surprised when our rural people become cynical about experts and leaders arriving in four wheel drives to ask their opinions and then speed off to the city never to be heard from again? We are heading towards consultative fatigue in Africa unless we show results to the people.

Should it come to that, let us not fool ourselves that we are doing good governance and economic development in Africa any service. The test of our work lies in how much we better the lives of the poor majorities in our societies.

As I stated in the beginning there are some people outside of our continent, who despair about Africa's capacity to perform. We who live and work there think otherwise.

Some pronounced NEPAD and APRM a failure no sooner than they had been announced. Kenya and three of her peers, as I have informed you, are already quite advanced in the APRM. There are 23 African states waiting to sign up for APRM. We have done this largely with our own resources because we believe it is the right option for our countries. We will forge ahead no matter what the nay-sayers think. As Kwame Nkrumah and CPP in Ghana used to say: "Forward Ever, Backward Never."

V

THEY BUILT FOR THE FUTURE

21

Thomas Joseph Mboya
A Visionary and Idealist

The Tom Mboya Memorial Lecture delivered at Taifa Hall, University of Nairobi, 5 July 2003

On the fifth of July 1969, at about one o'clock in the City of Nairobi on what was then known as Government Road, Thomas Joseph Mboya, Kenya's second Minister for Economic Planning and Development, was gunned down by an assassin's bullet. It was a warm afternoon. Tom had just left his office on Harambee Avenue. Apart from his bodyguard, he was all by himself, confidently driving his white Mercedes Benz to pick up some drugs in a pharmacy on Victoria Road – the present Tom Mboya Street.

That single bullet altered Kenya's history in a major way. Not only was a young family of six left without a father, but Kenya, Africa and indeed the whole world was deprived of a visionary and an idealist, a man whose charisma and ideas had won the attention of humankind with ease. He fitted comfortably in the team of such world leaders like Martin Luther King, John and Bobby Kennedy, Kwame Nkrumah and Nelson Mandela. Much closer home he was one of the prime movers of our independence with Jomo Kenyatta, Jaramogi Oginga Odinga, Ramogi Achieng' Oneko and C.M.G. Argwings Kodhek – leading luminaries in Kenyan politics then. Our own President, Mwai Kibaki was Tom Mboya's Assistant Minister in the Ministry of Economic Planning and Development; and between the two of them, they masterminded the production of *Sessional Paper No. 10 of 1965 on African Socialism and Its Application to Planning in Kenya.*

Pamela Mboya, later to serve as a distinguished ambassador for Kenya in the UN system, was the lady who was widowed with their children Rosemary,

Maureen, Peter, Susan and Lucas. In the "Postscript" to Tom's book, *The Challenge of Nationhood* — published after his death — Pamela had this to say:

> This volume is proof that while a man's life can be tragically and wastefully cut short, the ideals and principles for which he stood can live on. For me and my children and our family as a whole, Tom's love is a permanent inspiration. It is my sincere hope, therefore, that what Tom stood for, as seen in this book and his other writings, will continue to inspire the future generations in Kenya, Africa, and the whole world.[1]

We are gathered here today, 34 years since TJ left us, with a whole generation of Kenyans born after him for whom he is a mere legend. But those of us who knew him those who danced on the floor of this hall with him, those who were here when he debated the 17 economists from the University of Nairobi on the 1967-72 Development Plan, will vividly remember his brilliance, eloquence, wit and ability to inspire.

But Saturday 5 July 2003 is important in another sense. It marks one of the few Saturdays that fall on 5 July the exact day of TJ's assassination. It also marks the last Saturday of the formal existence of the Organisation of African Unity and the birth of the African Union next week in Maputo, Mozambique, as African Heads of State meet at the first Heads of State meeting of the African Union. Mwai Kibaki, once Mboya's Assistant Minister, later Minister holding the same portfolio, will be sitting in Maputo as Kenya's Head of State. TJ, as he himself recalls in his autobiography, *Freedom and After*, was the first chairman of the All-African Peoples Conference held in Accra, Ghana, in December 1958.[2] This was the precursor of the OAU, now the AU.

One of the longest essays in TJ's book — *The Challenge of Nationhood* — is his speech in Parliament on the fourth of May 1965, when he was moving the motion on "Sessional Paper No. 10".[3] Always cool and collected at such moments, TJ dismissed those who argued that the initiative was devoid of originality and went straight to present the content of the paper and its relevance to Kenya's development agenda. It came out very clearly that the challenge facing Kenya then was that of clearly defining a vision for the future, and a clear roadmap along which development would have to travel if this vision was to be arrived at.

---

1   Tom Mboya, *The Challenge of Nationhood* (London and Nairobi: Heinemann Educational Books, 1970).

2   See Tom Mboya, *Freedom and After* (London: Andre Deutsch, 1963), 13.

3   See the speech on "African Socialism" in Tom Mboya, *The Challenge of Nationhood*, op cit.

Yes, it was true, most African leaders had contended that *socialism* would guide Africa's development process. This socialism, they contended—from Nyerere to Nkrumah and Sekou Toure—would have to be *African socialism*. But the name, contended TJ, was not the most important thing. What the name contained, the actions it inspired, and the changes it brought about through this inspiration were the most important things to look into. For that matter, he contended, African socialism, in the context of Kenya's development agenda then, meant essentially the following:

- Ownership and operations by the state, the private sector, individuals and cooperatives of the means of production in such a way that overall efficiency productivity is raised while national wealth is accumulated in such a way that the economy grows while social inequalities are minimised.

- Distribution of the national wealth in such a way that entrepreneurship is rewarded while those who are better off bear their respective roles in promoting social solidarity and mutual social responsibility through the aegis of the state.

- Planning the use of resources to ensure that needs are fully recognised in the allocation of resources, and, in particular, that the volume of saving and investment is large enough to promote rapid growth and rising standards of living for all.

- Control of the distribution of incomes to avoid excessive concentrations in the hands of a few and to share the benefits of society equitably among all its members.

It is on the basis of these principles that various programmes and projects were proposed in *Sessional Paper No. 10* dealing with the Africanisation of the economy, settlement of the landless, establishment of the national social security system, establishment of the National Hospital Insurance Fund, foreign exchange allocation systems, etc. In other words, within the Sessional Paper was to be found both a *philosophy* and a *programme of development*, clearly stated, articulated and projected into the future.

Thirty-four years later, we are more or less back to where TJ left us. After his death, the imperatives of the Sessional Paper were more or less thrown to the winds. With the Ndegwa Commission Report of 1972, a process of growing social inequalities started with a national income distribution regime that did the opposite of what the Sessional Paper had aspired towards. The *ILO Report on Employment, Incomes and Inequality in Kenya,* published more or less when the Ndegwa Commission was doing its work, confirmed the fact that the model of development that was emerging in Kenya was obviously betraying the aspirations of Sessional Paper No. 10.

Colin Leys, in his book *Neo-Colonialism in Kenya: The Political Economy of Underdevelopment* went further to critically analyse this structure of growing poverty and inequality in Kenya by the mid-seventies.[4] It is no wonder that the prime concern for development economists and aid agencies subsequently became centred on the issue of *poverty reduction,* and not development, thereby more or less turning on its head the main aim of Sessional Paper No. 10 which was "wealth creation as a means of eradicating socio-economic underdevelopment".

Twenty-five years of Moi's authoritarian rule thoroughly undermined the confidence of Kenyans in such a way that the philosophy of "reducing poverty" as the highest aspiration of the people came to be docilely accepted as a noble goal. Authoritarianism makes people doubt the possibility of taking their own destiny in their own hands, and the search for messiahs as a solution to their earthly problems becomes a daily occupation. These messiahs may appear in terms of ethnic demagogues like Jonas Savimbi, religious fanatics of the Alice Lakwena hew or mere fortune-tellers on the streets who preach to while away the lunch breaks in towns that the poor would find boring were it not for these self-styled messiahs.

When we were campaigning for votes to win political power for the National Rainbow Coalition (NARC), we realised that to lead the crusade for democracy was not enough in Kenya; we needed to empower our people as well. We needed to tell our people that they can take their own destiny in their own hands; that they can bring positive changes to their lives; that they can be governed and yet control their governors, and that they were not destined to live with poverty forever.

A man without a job in the rural areas is not totally a poor man. He or she is definitely deprived, denied opportunities, marginalised in society and made to feel unwanted. What he or she needs is not political paternalism and economic babysitting. What she or he needs is the challenge to make use of new opportunities through the politics of inclusion and the economics of social solidarity. Given the opportunity to work, this person can utilise his physical

---

4   Colin Leys, *Neo-Colonialism in Kenya: The Political Economy of Underdevelopment* (London: Heinemann, 1975).

energy and use his or her brain for social invention. That is why those denied the opportunity and not socially included can put their mental might to such destructive — but highly imaginative — activities such as bank robberies, impersonation, and so on. To deflect them from such destructive tendencies we must not only ensure that law and order works for all, but that societal values and practice encourage the positive exploitation of individual endowments for both personal and societal gains.

That is why our manifesto was entitled *Democracy and Empowerment*. While expanding the democratic space and institutionalising a democratic culture in our society, we must empower our people to make full use of this democracy, develop and expand it, and domesticate it in their daily lives.

A poor person cannot do that. Persons without education will be denied the opportunity to develop their personal capacities even in a democratic society. An individual afflicted by sicknesses and with no means or knowledge to prevent or cure such sicknesses is rendered powerless. Yet diseases are not personal but social problems. Mosquitoes that breed in stagnant waters, quite often created by the rich when they scoop sand to build their houses in rural areas, carry the malaria parasite that attack both the rich and the poor. Why should the poor then be held personally responsible for curing the malaria when they fall sick? The disease is a societal phenomenon and not an individual phenomenon.

There is, therefore, a sense in which we cannot really empower our people unless, in our development paradigm, we have concepts of social solidarity that include access to basic needs such as education, health, food, shelter, clothing, security and intellectual development. We in the NARC government decided therefore to implement *free primary education* as a principal aspect of this paradigm. We are also currently working on a comprehensive *national health insurance scheme*. We do believe, too, that our people — in rural and urban areas alike — should be adequately and decently housed.

It is a shame that the National Housing Corporation collapsed under the weight of corruption and mismanagement during the Moi era. This corporation, under proper management in the sixties and seventies, had helped to develop medium and lower income housing in rural and urban areas alike. With a careful arrangement with the private sector and user-friendly mortgage arrangements, we intend to go beyond where the NHC has arrived before Moi — the Wrecker — took over political power in this country.

Let us recall that, when TJ was Minister for Economic Planning and Development, this country enjoyed a very high rate of economic growth. The

219

seven per cent annual rate of growth we are yearning for today was taken for granted in those days. By making wealth through rapid economic growth the government could afford to plan for ambitious social welfare projects. We believe we can recapture this lost ground, hence our focus on Economic Recovery for Wealth and Employment Creation. This strategy is based on *four* pillars:

1. High rate of economic growth while maintaining macro-economic stability

2. Strengthening institutions of good governance while deepening democracy

3. Rehabilitation and expansion of the physical and the social infrastructure

4. Investment in the productive sectors of the economy and in human capital, particularly the poor.

These pillars will hold the edifice in which will be found relevant projects in the productive sectors of the economy: agriculture, manufacturing, industry, trade, tourism and the financial sector. We intend, for example, to invest heavily in arid and semi arid areas (ASALs) so as to expand agricultural production with marginal investment of capital. This will boost food production, increase rural incomes and integrate these areas more effectively into the national economy. We intend also to strengthen and expand micro-financing institutions so that small and medium enterprises in all sectors of the economy can have expanded and easy access to credit. This will help finance production, increase productivity and create more wealth in our economy.

Let me hasten to add that one of our most pressing concerns is to reduce the cost of doing business in Kenya. It is too high. We pay too much for electricity, water, petroleum products and telecommunication. Comparative figures from Mauritius, South Africa, Uganda and Ghana — in all these areas — show that we are a high cost economy that investors are not likely to be attracted to.

Most of the costs are the result of poor economic and political governance in the past. With the changes we are instituting, the cost of doing business will come down. We are working on the energy sector. We shall privatise Telkom Kenya Limited in such a way that its social aspects in rural areas will not be sacrificed at the alter of profit making. Likewise, the availability of affordable energy to rural producers will also be ensured in the face of increased competition and deregulation.

Recently, the Minister of Finance, in the budget speech, announced certain measures affecting taxes with regard to VAT and excise duty. Many have commented in praise or in protest. Our long-term policy, which these measures are meant to lead towards in the long run, is to widen the tax base while reducing the rate of taxation in our economy. This will lead to more compliance in tax payment than what has been experienced heretofore.

We do realise, too, that the previous government was very poor at collecting taxes. Big businesses and the politically correct elite were known more by their tax evasion and avoidance than their compliance. The KRA, as I have always said in Parliament—and I will still repeat it in my capacity as a minister—has been grossly under-performing in the amount of revenue it collects every year. With tighter measures and better governance, we are bound to do better in the coming years.

The secret lies in our becoming "A Working Nation", as the President said on Madaraka Day: a nation of people who work for their livelihood and of systems of government, which perform efficiently and productively within a democratic culture. This means we must be faithful to the rule of law and defend jealously the dignity and rights of our citizens while expecting them to defend and promote our nationhood and be proud of Kenya as a place to feel at home.

I want to end by quoting from TJ's last article that he did for the *New York Times* on "Africa and Afro America" a few days before he was assassinated:

Freedom involves the realisation of our full identities and potential. It is in this sense that the objective of the African must be the development of his nation and the preservation of his heritage.[5]

For TJ, therefore, there was no contradiction between his being a Kenyan of Luo heritage and being a Luo of Kenyan nationality. He was that ideologically clear in his mind and conceptually focused in his discourses. This challenge lives with us to this very day. We must rise up as Kenyans and become equally unbwogable on both fronts as TJ was. As we commemorate his 34th anniversary, let us rise up with one accord and build the new Kenya into a First World nation by the year 2025.

---

5 Tom Mboya, "The Negro Cannot Look to Africa for an Escape," *New York Times Magazine*, (July 13, 1969, p. 30. This essay was published after TJ had been assassinated. It was perhaps one of the last things he wrote before the assassin cut short his very productive life.

22

Tom Mboya and Politics as a Vocation

Tom Mboya Memorial Lecture, delivered at the University of Nairobi, 17 November 2004

The last public position that Thomas Joseph Mboya held was that of the Minister for Economic Planning and Development of the Republic of Kenya. As the current holder of that portfolio in the last twenty-three months, I stand in awe at the accomplishments of the founding father of my ministry. I am sure that I speak on behalf of all the officers in my Ministry when I state that he set some standard of professional excellence in my Ministry that remains a challenge to all of us in Kenya to this day.

Tom Mboya distinguished himself as a leading thinker of development planning in Africa and the rest of the developing world. He published articles and books on development problems facing Africa that are still relevant today. He defended the development policies that Kenya adopted after independence with intellectual logic and an eloquence that is hard to match. His was always going to be a difficult act to follow.

Upon reflection, I thought the term "ultimate politician" as opposed to the "ultimate statesman" had the ring of a hard-driven political self-interest that was alien to Tom Mboya's career as an African nationalist and Kenyan statesman. Ultimate politicians are just that; political power is their ultimate ambition. To them politics is the end all. I therefore chose the title "Tom J Mboya and Politics as a Vocation" in the sense that Max Weber uses vocation in a famous essay entitled "Politics as a Vocation". In this context, vocation refers to a *personal calling* to serve a cause, a greater cause than oneself; a call that is driven less by what we normally call politics, and by a noble social goal.

This is what I see in the public life of Tom Mboya: a person with a sense of vocation which motivated him to serve a cause because it was the right thing to do, irrespective of the personal risks involved. This sense of public service on the basis of moral principle is now sadly alien to a large section of Kenya's political class. It is sad for our country that we now have a young generation to whom this idea is foreign, to whom public service without personal profit sounds outlandish even cynical.

Mboya had the calling to do everything he could to restore African dignity at a time when colonialists, racists and imperialist – for that is what he called them – had doubts about an African's entitlement to full human dignity, to the political rights that were enshrined in the constitutions of our colonial rulers, and that Africans knew before colonial rule. Before and after independence, Mboya told us that tribalism stood in the way of this mission. For that he paid with his life. That is the ultimate price for any leader who believes in a vocation. Abraham Lincoln paid that same ultimate price. So did Mboya's close friends, the late President John F. Kennedy of the US, and the late Dr Martin Luther King.

Tom Mboya in the world stage

In *Julius Caesar* the conspirators who would assassinate Caesar express their envy of him and their frustration in the following words:

"Why, Man, He doth bestride the narrow world like a Colossus
And we petty men walk under his huge legs and peep about
To find ourselves dishonoured graves"[1]

In their personal insecurities, petty men and underlings think that eliminating a political colossus will solve their problems by elevating their stature in world stage. It never works that way. Brutus was not to rule Rome. He perished in desolation, in a dishonoured grave, hounded by the ghost of the Roman emperor he had murdered. But to describe Tom Mboya as an African colossus, a statesman who stands above his peers in African history, would be just another cliché and it would do a great injustice to the finer details of his legacy.

When the world looks at the history of post-independence Africa, it will pay tribute to Tom Mboya for the role he played in making that history. Tom Mboya was the most polished and most articulate spokesman of African nationalism to the rest of the world in the 1950s and 1960s. He explained to the sceptical and the

---

1   William Shakespeare, *Julius Caesar, Act I, Scene II:* lines 134-138, p.1021. The Alexander Text, *Complete Works of Shakespeare* (Glasgow: Harper Collins Publishers, 1994). These were the words of Cassius speaking about Caesar to Brutus.

cynical in the West, that the dramatic events unfolding in colonial Kenya under the Emergency, the Algerian war of independence, and the struggle against *apartheid* were one of a kind. Colonial oppression based on white supremacy had pushed Africans to a corner, he said. When African voices were silenced and racial oppression increased, any violent resistance that arose should be attributed to the oppressor not the oppressed. By and by the world came to rely on his clarity of thought in interpreting the new Africa to it. All this before he was thirty years old!

Take the victims of torture in the Mau Mau detention camps here in Kenya. From about 1957 onwards, he used his position as a member of the Legislative Council to forward evidence from detainees to sympathetic Labour MPs like Barbara Castle and William Bottomley. A bond based on trust developed between his activism for nationalism in Kenya, Labour Party and the anti-colonial movement in the United Kingdom. The colonial authorities in Kenya privately complained that the opposition "Labour Party in Britain will say nothing in Kenya unless they have consulted Tom Mboya". So they tried as best as they could to destroy his personal integrity and standing with the Labour Party. But they failed.

It was not only colonial brutality in Kenya that concerned him. When the Sharpeville Massacre of 1961 took place, Tom Mboya was among the first African leaders to call for the immediate expulsion of *apartheid* South Africa from the Commonwealth. He and other African leaders prevailed. South Africa was booted out of the Commonwealth that year.

In considering the Tom Mboya's performance at the international stage in the cause of African nationalism, however, nothing stands out in those early days as his election as chairman of the All-Africa Peoples Conference in Accra, Ghana, at the age of only 28. This conference had been called by the first president of independent Ghana, the late Osagyefo Dr. Kwame Nkrumah, to adopt a strategy to accelerate decolonisation in Africa, and to chart the way towards the unity of the new independent African states. This meeting was the precursor to that of the Organisation of African Unity, which was born five years later at Addis Ababa, Ethiopia. It was attended by the "who is who" in African nationalism at the time – Frantz Fanon representing FLN from Algeria, Gamal Abdel Nasser from Egypt, Joshua Nkomo from the then Southern Rhodesia, Patrice Lumumba who was to become the first Prime Minister of independent Congo, Holden Roberto of Angola, and many others. At a very young age, Tom Mboya was already presiding over African nationalist history in the making. Books are still being written on what that conference meant for Africa.

Colin Legum, the dean of the African press corps at the time, made acquaintance with Mboya and respected his opinions for all time. Mboya had come to the notice of the world. It was after this event that one of Africa's premier journalists in Britain Alan Rake wrote his short biography of Mboya entitled, *Tom Mboya: Young Man of Africa*.[2] Notice that fame came to him. He did not go out to publicise himself, or to demand adoration from sycophants and praise-singers, which later came to be the norm in Kenya.

Every subject that concerned African people whether in Africa or the Diaspora became an issue of personal concern to him. He made contacts with the late Dr. Martin Luther King when he was waging his campaign to register African-American trade unionist A. Philip Randolph and Jackie Robinson as the first black Americans to play for a national baseball club in that country. He was a friend of Harry Belafonte and dozens of others. All of them played major roles in the Kenya Student Airlift programme starting in 1958. In laying the foundation of the trade unions movement in Kenya as we know it today, he linked it to the world's labour movement in the International Confederation of Free Trade Unions (ICFTU) in Brussels and the AFL-CIO in the United States.

He exposed the shenanigans of the colonialists in Kenya to the international press, much to the ire of these rather intolerant breed of the white race who came to fortune hunt in the attractive climate they called the White Highlands of Kenya. He wrote for *The New York Times* and *The Washington Post* and also gave interviews to countless regional newspapers in the United States of America. In the political arena, his debating skills in the colonial Legislative Council and in the Parliament of independent Kenya were widely acknowledged as among the world's best – even by his opponents. He had a rare intellect – as a writer on Kenyan and African nationhood, African socialism, the problems of economic development and poverty, non-alignment and the international economic relations between ex-colonial territories like Kenya, and the developed world. He was at home in the quietness of his family, nation building in Kenya, the politics of Africa, or as the first African guest on American television in the NBC programme, "Meet the Press". As Cicero would have it, he was neither a Kenyan Luo nor an African politician, but a citizen of the world.

All the activities Tom was involved with at the international activity were for a cause he believed in – not for money. Again this comes as a big surprise to a generation of Africans who have witnessed politicians fighting the most vicious wars to make money on the backs of poor Africans, at times even stealing money intended for starving refugees.

Such people have missed their vocation. And Africa is the poorer for it. What a contrast to the vision Tom Mboya fought for in the 1950s and 1960s.

---

2   Alan Rake, *Tom Mboya: Young Man of Africa* (New York: Doubleday and Co. Inc., 1962).

The genesis of personal commitment

After his studies at Mang'u High School, Mboya went in 1948 to study for the job of a sanitary inspector at the then Jeans School, now Kenya Institute of Administration. The certificate for the course was awarded by the Royal Sanitary Institute and he had no problems completing and passing the course.

But there is a story in his autobiography *Freedom and After* that I believe, explains his life-long commitment to fight for African freedom and human dignity. At one point, as Mboya tells it, he was left by his European boss at the counter to inspect milk from the farmers coming into Nairobi. Seeing a black man in charge of the station, a white farmer who had brought her milk for inspection asked in anger "Is there nobody here?" meaning that Mboya was nobody, while the European boss was somebody.[3] Fanon once wrote that in colonial societies white colonialists looked at Africans as hard as they could but could not see a human being in them. Here is some evidence of this.

With such humiliation, should we be surprised that Mboya took it upon himself to organise the first City Council of Nairobi African Staff Association? In later years his enemies were to accuse him of accepting Western support. If anything, he was offering his time and money free. Here and in later life, nobody paid him to unionise African workers. It came from an inner passion that abhorred colonial indignities African workers suffered in colonial Kenya. This is the difference between him and your regular power-seeking politician which I spoke about earlier. The same applies to his personal sacrifice in founding work in the Kenya Local Government Workers Union (which caused him to be fired by the City Council), and the Kenya Federation of Labour.

Into nationalist politics

If we understand why Africans were pained by the "Is there nobody here?" colonial attitudes, then we can understand why in the case of Tom Mboya, politics of unionisation led to politics of liberation from colonial rule.[4] Again in *Freedom and After*, he narrates how during Operation Anvil in April 1954, he and other Africans were required to squat on the street (Victoria Street then), their hands above their heads for hours, while the police picked up the Agikuyu for detention.

I have already mentioned his work for the sake of those detainees. Giving the Mau Mau Emergency as an excuse, the colonial government did not allow the

3   Tom Mboya, *Freedom and After* (London: Andre Deutsch, 1963), 29.
4   Ibid, 37.

formation of African political parties until 1955. Even then these were restricted to district rather than national level.

Upon returning from a year at Ruskin College, Oxford in 1956, Mboya went flat out to organise the Nairobi Peoples Convention Party. Notice that its title echoed that of Nkrumah's Convention Peoples Party (CPP). From the start it was strategically organised on a national basis, to make it easier to form a nationalist party when the right time came. In the following year, Mboya won the Nairobi African seat for the Legislative Council.

As we reflect on the political achievements of Tom Mboya let us recall two significant observations that have never received as much public attention as I have always thought they should. First, throughout his political life, Tom Mboya was elected to our national legislature, by voters who did not come from his ethnic group – the Luo. Secondly he worked hardest not for his social class which was the new African middle class that arose after World War II, but rather for those less privileged than he was – the working class and those who for some reason or other were unable to complete high school or university education. This is the sense of vocation I mentioned earlier. Again, there was no money for him in any of these thankless tasks. No "*kitu kidogo*" that was to corrupt our country later. How many of our leaders today can boast of a record of public service like this?

Tom had that rare trait in Kenya politics today – the capacity to appeal to all Kenyans regardless of ethnicity or race. On the eve of our independence from Britain in 1963, KANU (which was a very different party from what it is today) decided to field Tom for the Nairobi Central seat – as it was then. This was to be the last constituency he represented in Parliament.

Why did KANU leaders – Kenyatta, Odinga, Gichuru and Chokwe – want Mboya to stand in Nairobi Central? It is because, as they judged rightly, he was the only African politician who could appeal to the Kenya Asian voters. As it turned out, they were right. He won the seat by a wide margin.

Mboya's capacity to win the confidence of voters from racial and ethnic groups other than his own was already evident in the 1957 and 1961 elections when he won the Nairobi East seat (as it was then) even though the voters were predominantly Agikuyu. In 1960, Kenyan nationalists brought from Lancaster House the MacLeod Constitution. It provided for the first election, which brought Kenya an African majority parliament the following year. His opponents in Nairobi East tried to use tribalism to campaign against him. It backfired. Campaigning with the symbol of "Ndege" (aeroplane) to symbolise his achievements in sending

Kenya student airlift, he won the election with a landslide – 29,000 votes against his opponents 3,000. This landslide came from those Kikuyu ex-detainees he had defended in the 1950s, and the "*mama mboga*" of Eastlands, the Luo, Kamba, Luhya and Mijikenda labourers who knew the record of his work from the days of the Local Government Workers Union, and the KFL.

In view of the ugly tribal conflicts that arose after his assassination in 1969, it is worth remembering that the ordinary wananchi in Kariakor, Majengo, Hamza, Bahati, Ofafa Kunguni, Mbotela, and Kariobangi had no problem at all voting for him. As always, we see that tribalism was a disease that started from the top of the political ladder. It still is. As we try to rebuild our country from the ashes of decades of dictatorship and tribal conflict, we should never forget this. We as leaders have the capability to unite or divide our people – be they Africans, Asians or whites, Christian, Hindu or Moslem. Tom chose unity and he showed us the way in word and deed.

Having found it impossible to continue into university education after Mang'u, Tom was determined to do as much as he could to ensure that those in similar social circumstances did not suffer his fate. Not that he stopped his education when he left school. After Jeans School and Oxford he read prodigiously. He could hold his own in debates with the best of scholars. His withering on-stage demolition of the anti-Africanisation report by 18 economists at the University College, Nairobi, in 1968 is still remembered as one of the finest intellectual debates in Kenyan academic history.

He did not have the insecurity that some politicians have of people better educated than they are. He was not part of the PhD (i.e. Pull Him Down) brigade – that is those who treat their intellectual betters with fear and who always try to pull them down to the lowest common factor.

That is why he went to great lengths to ensure that Kenyans who lacked university education at home could get it abroad, and especially in the US where he had friends like the Kennedy Foundation and African-American Association. Today, Kenyans seem to respect anyone with money no matter how he or she earned it. Let us never forget that under our best nationalist leaders like Tom Mboya what you knew mattered more than what you owned. Knowledge not money is what pushes a country forward. The sooner we retrace our steps to what Tom taught us the better for Kenya.

I do not want to leave you with the impression that as a politician, Mboya had no faults. All great statesmen do. For all his greatness, Churchill was compulsive and he meddled unnecessarily with the armed forces. Saint that

228

he was, Gandhi would not hear of partition in India even when it was a reality. Mboya had very little patience with ill-informed, ill-read politicians who loved empty slogans with no substance behind them. He was such a sharp debater that he often left his opponents licking their wounds and made no apologies for it. Yet in spite of all that, he served his country well.

When Tom was shot, the sound rang around the world. Radio stations in the US broke the news with shock and disbelief. He had just returned from a US tour. The following morning his assassination was front page news in *The New York Times*, *The Times of London*, *Washington Post*, *Le Monde* and the *Times of India* – to mention but a few. It was extensively covered by television stations around the world. The British Broadcasting Corporation (BBC) lead item in its international news that day was the following: "One of Africa's youngest and most brilliant politicians, Mr Tom Mboya of Kenya has been assassinated." And the BBC has never been accused of hyperbole.

The world mourned his passing. And all those who loved him wept with his young family.

Upholding the dignity of Africans in the world
Nationalism and nation building
Public service without discrimination
Fighting tribalism and racism at once
Cultivating one's intellect as a virtue in its own right
African development and African socialism
Recognising the benefits of a mixed economy.

These were the watchwords of a world statesman who took politics as a calling, not as a business.

"Here was a man take him all in all
"We shall not look upon his like again"[5]

---

5   William Shakespeare, *Hamlet, the Prince of Denmark, Act One, Scene Two, lines 186-187*, p. 1085. The Alexander Text, *Complete Works of Shakespeare*, (Glasgow: Harper Collins Publishers, 1994). These were the words of Hamlet speaking to Horatio about the King, his father, who has been slain by his brother so that the latter could re-marry the Queen, his wife, and inherit the thron as well. The whole play is about Hamlet's rage about this murder and his consumate determination to avenge the murder of his father.

23

Dr. Apollo Milton Obote
The President I Knew[1]

Essay written in memory Dr. Apollo Milton Obote and published in the
Sunday Nation, *20 October 2005*

I first heard of the name of Milton Obote when I joined the Alliance High School in 1962. I must have got it from the radio, the newspapers or class discussions. Uganda was then just about to get her independence, and Milton Obote, Kabaka Mutesa, Ibingira, Adoko Nekyon, Sir William Wilberforce Nadiope and many others were becoming familiar names for us in the columns of the *Daily Nation* and the *East African Standard*. The radio also boomed with them at the one o'clock news in the recreation room as we played table tennis after lunch.

We also heard of the jostling among political parties and politicians in Uganda, just as we were amazed by the same in Kenya. There was the Democratic Party, the Kabaka Yekka (Kabaka only) and the Uganda People's Congress (UPC). During the holidays, as the Luo students at Makerere came home and displayed their smart suits at their annual "League" dance in Kisumu, we heard them talk endlessly about UPC and Obote. The man began to fascinate me as a young boy.

Whether it is true or not, I believe I first saw Obote at the Kenya independence celebrations in December 1963. I was in the joint choir from the Alliance High School and the Alliance Girls High School with people like Victor Ongewe, Richard Baraza, Atieno Odhiambo and 21 others because we were exactly 24 who were the first to sing the Kenya National Anthem.

---

1 Dr. Apollo Milton Obote *aduong' ma Uganda,* died on 10 October 2005 (my birthday). I had known Obote very well while I was a student leader at Makerere (1968/71) and had admired his Pan-Africanism and common touch.

Tom Mboya was active; he was welcoming dignitaries as they arrived. I remember the Prime Minister of Zanzibar arriving late, and Mboya was at pains to find him an appropriate seat. I believe he sat next to a man I believe was Apollo Milton Obote, though I may be wrong. But I was convinced then that I saw this young leader with a lot of hair on his head, which made him stand out among the dignitaries. When it comes to hair on the head Obote was only rivalled by Kitili Mwendwa, whom I later learnt was his friend. But I will say something on that later.

I entered Makerere in July 1968 as a BA student studying English, political Science and Philosophy. Uganda was hot with politics. In 1966, Obote had become President by abrogating the independence constitution, ending the alliance between Kabaka Yekka and the UPC and forcing the Kabaka to go to exile abroad. The UPC and Obote were the dominant features in Uganda's politics, and so was the army.

Juma Odundo, the Nyanza-born musician whose records were then very popular in Uganda as well as Kenya, made a record, which was like an anthem to the Obote fans. It was called "*UPC na Obote: Obote ameleta maendeleo Uganda.*" On the grounds of Livingstone Hall where I stayed, my friend, the late Daudi Mulabya Taliwaku, loved to sing this song while we played crocket.

When we had dances in the main hall on Saturdays, Obote frequently came as the Guest of Honour. There was always a table for him and his ministers and friends—Akena Adoko, Picho Ali, Sam Odaka—just outside the hall to the left where they drank beer, met students and talked politics. Obote also smoked heavily. Professor Ali Mazrui would pass by to say hullo to Obote, but not to dance!

The Uganda Army Band was the favourite band for us those days. And if Obote was the Guest of Honour, you were sure to see this band on stage, and they would soon be playing away '*Aduong' ma Uganda, Milton Obote; Tich mae be, Milton Obote*' (We will never surrender, Obote; Oh we will never surrender Obote!)

One of the most powerful speeches I saw Obote give at Makerere's Main Hall was when he was launching his crusade for the "Common Man's Charter", the document that was to launch Uganda into a new path of socialist development so as to keep up with Tanzania under Nyerere's "*ujamaa.*" Obote and Nyerere were then very good friends and comrades. The theme of his speech was why this change was necessary after Uganda became more or less a one-party state in the post-1966 period. In 1966, Obote argued, Uganda was pregnant with a new society, but the old feudal society prevented the birth of this new society. Force was therefore a necessary midwife for giving birth to this new society.

Although this new society had been born, it lacked revolutionaries and revolutionary ideas to lead it to maturity. The "Common Man's Charter" was there now to provide Uganda with a revolutionary ideology. And Document Number 5 would provide the electoral process through which real nationalist revolutionaries would help lead this significant process. His arguments were powerful, and Professor Mazrui later told us that Obote, like his friend Nkrumah, was a 'Leninist'. I had to read hard to learn who a Leninist was, and I added Vladimir Illych Lenin to my list of fascinating thinkers!

There was a section in the *Common Man's Charter*, which fascinated Daudi Mulabya, Joshua Mugyenyi and I. It read: "The Common Man's Charter is hereby published to guide the misguided and inform the misinformed." That is how Apollo Milton Obote was confident and sure of himself in leading Uganda. Mazrui also told us that he added the name Milton to his other first name Apollo because of his love of Milton's "Paradise Lost" while he was a student at Makerere. After being thrown out of Heaven by God as a result of disobedience, Satan remarked: "Though heaven be lost, all is not lost." This sense of defiance and determination fascinated Obote. And as a young man fed up with authoritarian colonial politics, his poetry gave him inspiration, and he also became a Milton in Ugandan and African politics.

I was elected President of the Makerere Students Guild on 10 October 1969 on my birthday. (Obote later died on 10 October 2005 as I was celebrating my birthday with family and friends in Nairobi.) In those days being President of the Guild brought you very close to the President of Uganda. But I dealt mainly with Obote's close confidantes like Sam Odaka—a charming man—Adonia Tiberondwa, Frank Kalimuzo—later to become the first Vice-Chancellor of Makerere University.

When Edward Heath decided to sell arms to the *apartheid* regime in South Africa, we decided to hold a demonstration against this. But Police Commissioner Oryema would not give us a licence to go to Kampala. We were to be confined to the campus. We thought this was obnoxious as Obote himself, a member of the Mulungushi Club, was a crusader against *apartheid*.

In the event, we tried to go to Kampala but were prevented by the police at the Makerere gate, and ugly incidents ensued as the police tear-gassed and chased us around the campus to disperse us. I issued a stern statement that if Heath sold arms to South Africa, then we would not be held responsible for what happened to British citizens in Uganda should these arms be used to oppress and kill our brothers and sisters in South Africa.

I was picked up and locked up by the Special Branch. I was later to be charged in court with "incitement", and remanded in custody at the Luzira Maximum Prison for a couple of days. When I was tried with a battery of lawyers defending me, the student body flocked to court and sheer political pressure made me released on condition that I kept peace for one year!

I have never understood why Obote allowed this to happen. But I never felt bitter about the incident. If anything, the President had been grossly misinformed about our intentions to demonstrate.

At the inauguration of Makerere University — again in October 1970 — I was carrying the University mace as the President of the Guild and Obote was immediately behind me. The mace was the symbol of his authority as the Chancellor. All around us were security people as Nyerere, Kenyatta and Kaunda walked ahead of us. As the President of the Guild, I felt proud to be walking among my colleagues who were *real* presidents!

Obote was very nervous. Nyerere was very relaxed and was whistling all through the walk from the Makerere Main Hall to the celebration grounds in the Freedom Square. Kenyatta was calm and collected and Kaunda seemed to me to have a halo of serene wisdom around his face.

I heard Obote shout some nervous orders to one of his security details to cover up better. He was speaking in Lang'i which, with my Luo I could decipher. Later on, as Idi Amin arrived at the celebrations without being included in the programme, I realised why the President was so nervous. Something was going seriously wrong in the Ugandan Government.

When Obote was overthrown in January 1971, I had ceased being President of the Guild and James Oporia Ekwaro had taken over. We were very upset and, under the leadership of Ekwaro, we wanted to demonstrate to reject the army takeover and show solidarity with Obote. But Vice-Chancellor Kalimuzo advised us not to do so. This was now a military government, and their reaction to a demonstration would be different from a civilian regime. We did not go ahead with the demonstration. But what shocked us was when Kalimuzo told us that "Obote also made serious mistakes so the army take-over was not surprising."

When I was teaching at the University of Nairobi in late seventies, I got to know Kitili Mwendwa very well through the organisation he was heading, United Nations Association of Kenya (UNAK) with people like Jael Mbogo, Mark Mwithaga and Fritz de Souza. My brother-in-law, G.Z. Owiti-Odera was UNAK's treasurer, and he introduced me to Kitili.

233

It was then that I learnt, through Kitili, how close the two were. Kitili had many of Obote's qualities: stubborn, determined, a consummate politician and a man of letters. More than that, he had a lot of hair on his head!

The two men with a lot of hair on their heads are now gone. One, unfortunately, went much earlier and at a tender age. The other has left us much later at an advanced age but having not fulfilled all his dreams. But, as Milton would say: though the earth be lost, all is not lost for Apollo Milton Obote, *Aduong' ma* Uganda.

24

If I Die: Father John Anthony Kaiser

Speech delivered at the book launch of If I Die, *organised by Cana
Publishing, at the Serena Hotel, Nairobi, 22 August 2003*[1]

As we celebrate the life of Father John Anthony Kaiser by launching a book that
records what he did in the struggle for justice, freedom and truth in Kenya, we
also note that we live in turbulent but exciting times. We live at a time when
theatrics may be elevated to the level of profound drama. We live at a time
when the loud shouts of those who engage in histrionic hyperboles to make
rather mundane points may be taken as profound wisdom when put on the
sensational headlines of our newspapers.

We live at a time when wise counsel, quietly delivered, may not reach the ears
of the silent majority as the vocal minority, fills the airwaves in the assertion of
their personal interests asserted in the name of the majority.

At a time like this, we need the resurrection of a man like Father John Anthony
Kaiser.

Father Kaiser was a man who toiled and never asked for any reward.

Father Kaiser was a man who gave but never expected any reward.

Father Kaiser was a man who spoke but never gave up even when he was
not listened to.

Father Kaiser did all he did knowing full well that, as a Mill Hill missionary,
he was doing the will of Him in whom he lived, and moved, and had his being.
He says, very humbly, that if he left anything undone which he ought to have
done in his struggles to save lives at the Maela refugee camp and to defend

---

1   My friend David Waweru of Cana Publishing invited me to launch the book, *If I Die*, the autobiography
    of Father Kaiser published posthumously. My late brother Dr. Aggrey Nyong'o had, as the Chief of
    Pathology at Nairobi Hospital, been central to the inquest into Kaiser's death. He too passed away in a
    mysterious road accident in Nairobi on 14 May 2002.

the rights of the people there, then it is only God who will forgive him. "I trust in the mercy of our Saviour who can forgive my laziness and cowardice, and whose forgiveness is available to all."

Why was Father Kaiser eliminated by "the Powers that Be" and why was his murder covered up by these same powers? The answer is very simple. If you read pages 85 to 98, the Chapter entitled "A Case for Justice", you will find out why Father Kaiser *had to die*. He stepped on toes that were big in Kenya and big internationally. There was no way that the FBI would have told the truth regarding Kaiser's death when the Big Toes were able to kick the butts of the FBI agents here and abroad.

Consider the following statements, with their forthrightness and no mincing of words:

Page 91: "The Moi Government, the President himself included, has been behind the evictions of the Bantu and Luo people from the Rift Valley since 1986. This policy has gone unchallenged for long by the donor community, especially Britain and the USA, because it fits into their overall policy for Africa, which is to reduce the human population."

Pages 91-92: "But at the end of the Gulf War, President Bush gave President Moi US$94 million as a strings-free gift in gratitude for the use of Mombasa harbour for American nuclear warships. I think this is unconstitutional by American law. And how many Americans and British know the amount paid to Kenya by their governments to train and maintain a military presence here? It is not only in Kenya where we have unchecked supreme executives who exceed their legal mandates."[2]

Let the reader judge for himself or herself who, therefore, would have been interested first, in eliminating Father Kaiser, and then in covering up the grisly murder.

My brother, the late Professor Aggrey Nyong'o, was the Chief of Pathology at Nairobi Hospital. Aggrey was a well-known scientist in the field of pathology and microbiology in the world. He also served as a pathologist in the post-mortem of Father Kaiser and was involved in the inquiry by the FBI as well as the Kenyan authorities. He was a man of very few words but we used to exchange notes in our various professions.

---

2   John Kaiser, *If I Die* (Nairobi: Cana Publishing, 2003).

I remember he remarked, several times, that he was extremely upset by the shoddy work that the FBI did and the deliberate efforts to cover up the murder of Father Kaiser. Aggrey himself perished in a rather mysterious road accident on Ngong Road in May 2002. His driver, who sustained injuries and survived, was later charged with dangerous driving causing fatal injuries and imprisoned. While we were busy making arrangements to appeal his conviction, he too died in prison.

Let the listener understand.

But we do not stand here to mourn Father Kaiser.

Neither do we stand here to mourn Professor Aggrey Nyong'o.

We stand here to celebrate the lives of those who fight and die for the truth so that their lives can be a ransom for many, as indeed Christ Jesus lived and died so that we may all be saved from eternal damnation.

If I die, I want an epitaph to be written in my final resting place, as it is in the case of John Anthony Kaiser,

Here rests a man whose life was a celebration of bounty love for humankind; his word kindled the flame of truth in all people of goodwill and ashamed the devil of the greedy and power hungry.[3]

If I die, I want an epitaph to be written in my final resting place, as it is in the case of John Anthony Kaiser, and like Paul said before King Agrippa:

"I was not afraid of the Heavenly Vision".[4]

---

3   Ibid.
4   Acts 26: 19

25

Michael Christopher Kijana Wamalwa (1944-2003)

An Appreciation of His Life

This appreciation was published in the Sunday Nation, *7 September 2003*

Michael Christopher Kijana Wamalwa: I write this appreciation in memory of you as a friend, a loving husband of Yvonne and a man who cared deeply for his family. I want to talk about you simply and truthfully, with nothing exaggerated. If you listen to me I am sure you will believe what I am saying that there were some small personal things that you enjoyed in life.

You used to crack jokes that you would have enjoyed if other people were smart enough to crack them before you did. There were some sweet moments we spent together as two family friends during the last three years which never hit the headlines of the newspapers, but which were more important to you in life than the taxing public life.

I want to tell those who have come here today to say good-bye to you not to cry and gnash their teeth in agony, but to celebrate and be grateful for the life of the man who loved his family and did so much for this country – especially during the last three years.

Yvonne also asked me to tell you all, children of God, that Michael was a human being like us all, with his weaknesses and frailty and his rare moments of courage and heroism. He used the best qualities not simply to massage his ego, but to help build his country; and that is why we are all gathered here today to celebrate his life. Like all of us he was mortal; and like all of us he lived as if life would never come to an end.

Yvonne told me to remind you that Michael was the father of their daughter Chichi: the little girl he so much loved and who will miss him so terribly. In her innocence, Chichi is lucky. Unlike the mother, Chichi does not realise that Michael is gone. Told of her father's death, she replied in a happy and innocent tone: "Mummy, I will meet him to-morrow in heaven."

Let us all be honest with ourselves: nobody in this world will miss Michael than his old mother, his wife Yvonne and his little daughter Chichi who was just beginning to know him. Yvonne Wambia Wamalwa asked me to ask you all — fellow mourners — to pray especially for these three members of the Wamalwa family and to ask God's grace that they may find solace on this earth with the departure of their loved one. Let peace reign in their hearts; let God's grace take care of their trials and tribulations.

I do not quite remember when I first met and knew Michael. But I remember very clearly our first political encounter that was at the Bukhungu Stadium in Kakamega at the FORD rally in February 1992. Michael had not — by that time — been at the centre of the FORD movement. Since he knew me as the Executive Director of FORD, he came and sat next to me at the dais and requested me if he could speak. I went and talked to Jaramogi Oginga Odinga and asked him if Michael could be allowed to speak. The late Jaramogi was quick to respond: he requested me to bring Michael forward to him and he personally introduced Michael to the crowd. A long political journey with these two working together started with that simple introduction.

Michael and I became political buddies from then on; not terribly very close, but respectfully appreciative of each other. Our closeness developed during the last three years, especially with my wife Dorothy and his wife Yvonne bringing us together more often at the family level and as neighbours in New Runda estate.

At family meals that we occasionally had together with friends, Michael always amazed me with his knowledge of famous films, classical music and literature. I remember one night on 14 June 2001 at a dinner in our house, when he and the Argentina Ambassador — Jose Luis Casal — made Graciela Casal, Yvonne, Dorothy, Leandro and Esther Arellano (the then Mexican Ambassador and his wife), Carlos Faustino Stern and myself completely irrelevant in a conversation they were having on the greatest actors in the world's most famous movies during the last ten years! In his Oxford English Michael pronounced the names of the actors as if he had memorised them for the Cambridge Higher School Certificate literature examination!

That was the vintage Michael.

Michael Christopher Kijana Wamalwa, as you take your last journey to your last resting place in Kitale, I want to thank you for two things you did to me. First, it is you who proposed me to chair the National Alliance Party of Kenya negotiating team with the Rainbow Alliance. With my friend Joab Henry Onyango Omino heading the Rainbow team, we never disappointed you. We shall forever be grateful to you and your colleagues in the Summit, and all leaders of what came to be known as the National Rainbow Coalition, for the opportunity you gave us to serve Kenya and make NARC a reality. Let us build NARC as a strong party in the service of Kenya and in your eternal memory.

Second, just before the Nanyuki meeting of the NARC Parliamentary Group, you asked me to work with you on the speech that you were going to deliver at the opening of the meeting on behalf of H.E. the President. Yvonne requested me a few nights ago not to forget to celebrate the discussions we had together and how we crafted the speech together. You promised Yvonne that you would deliver that speech word for word and with the right expressions and pauses it deserved. Mike you did just that at Mount Kenya Safari Club. We were all there. NARC Members of Parliament were so happy for you and for Kenya. You brought us all back to our senses.

I thank you Michael. May God be with you till we meet again.

26

Thomas R. Odhiambo and the Problems of Development in Post-independence Africa

A Tribute

Speech given at the first T.R. Odhiambo Memorial at the Intercontinental Hotel, Nairobi, 6 May 2004

The Professor and I

I cannot really remember when I first met Professor Thomas Reysley Odhiambo, TRO—or TR—as he was always called by those who knew him closely. All I remember of my earliest contact with him is that, as a high school student at the Alliance High School in the sixties, it was a name we often heard of from among the Kenyan leading academics. The others were Simeon Ominde, the geographer and educationist, Ali Alamin Mazrui, the political scientist who lectured at Makerere in those days, Mohammed Hyder of the University College, Nairobi, Dr. Porter, then Principal of the University College, Nairobi, Bethwell Allan Ogot, the historian who also taught at Nairobi after his earlier *sejour* at Makerere, Ahmed Mohiddin, who paired with both Tom Mboya and Mazrui on discussions on African socialism, and many others.

I graduated from Makerere in April 1971 with a BA in Political Science and Philosophy, and was immediately recruited by Prof. John Joseph Okumu, then Chairman of the Department of Government, University of Nairobi, as a Special Lecturer. I spent half a year at the University of Nairobi before proceeding to the University of Chicago, in October that year, to do my doctorate as a Rockefeller Fellow in the staff development plan of the Department of Government.

It was during this short stay at the University of Nairobi that I came to know that TRO was struggling to found the International Centre for Insect Physiology

241

and Ecology (ICIPE) from a small office at the Chiromo campus of the University. Rumours in those days had it that the university authorities did not think much of what TRO was doing, and soon he would have to severe links with the University if he was to pursue this rather adventurous and outlandish idea.

I left the University that October and never really got back in earnest until 1977 when I had completed both my MA and PhD at the University of Chicago and took up full-time lectureship in the Department of Government, University of Nairobi. By this time, ICIPE had become an idea to reckon with and an institution of international repute whose founder director was none other than TRO. The person who introduced me to what ICIPE was doing was the late Joel Meshack Ojal who, on the grounds of All Saints Cathedral one Saturday afternoon, while both of us were attending a wedding there, told me that he was very excited in his new career at ICIPE. When I asked him what he was doing, he told me he was helping TRO impregnate tsetse flies. The only difference between the tsetse flies they impregnate and the two people who were marrying that day, is that the tsetse flies are impregnated not to have children while the man "catching a wife that afternoon" was surely doing it with the intention of impregnating his wife so as to have a child.

My discipline, Political Science, is definitely very far removed from entomology or insect physiology. But Mzee Ojal made me very curious about ICIPE, what they were doing in Lambwe Valley with the tsetse fly and what ICIPE was all about. My life in the Department of Government was, however, very intense and I never really got time to get to know TRO more and what was happening in ICIPE beyond what Mzee Ojal told me. In those days, we lectured and waged struggles against political oppression as well. Every now and again the police came in, picked us up, locked us for interrogation and even detained some of us. I left the university for an early sabbatical in December of 1981 for Mexico just in time to escape the dragnet that swept most radical lecturers into detention after the attempted coup of 1982.

It was not until December of 1986 that it was possible for me to come back to Kenya and begin preparing to work and live in my motherland. And TRO had a lot to do with my return. It is now fitting to describe our journey together.

Sometime in 1985, while I was lecturing at Addis Ababa University, TRO and I met at a conference in Dakar organised by the United Nations University, the Third World Forum and the Council for the Development of Social Science Research in Africa (CODESRIA). The conference was on "Africa and the New International Economic Order", and the discussions were wide and varied, with Samir Amin elaborating on his "self-centred development theory" and

Thandika Mkandawire talking on the "predicaments of African agricultural systems faced by failed industrialisation projects". What model of economic growth would help Africa conquer economic backwardness and poverty?

TRO never said anything during these discussions, but he took voluminous notes. Halfway through the conference, he invited me out for dinner. For the first time in our lives, we had a long chat, and I felt that he was genuinely out to try and know me while also trying to grasp the issues that these social scientists were grappling with.

A tribute to TRO

It is not often that a cabinet minister who holds the portfolio of economic planning and national development gets asked to deliver the inaugural lecture in a series that is designed to memorialise a scientist of such great achievements and international reputation like the late Professor Thomas Risley Odhiambo. I am therefore greatly honoured to have been asked by the African Academy of Sciences to deliver the first memorial lecture in his honour tonight for a number of reasons.

First and foremost, Professor Odhiambo's life is living testimony to the fact that with the brightest ideas that the human brain can produce and a spirited personal determination, we can achieve what we dream and what we desire. In these days when there is so much pessimism about the political and social prospects for Africa, it is necessary to always bear in perspective the sterling legacy that an African scientist like TRO left to the world. He demonstrated that Africa and Africans can conquer the seemingly insurmountable, that we can prevail in the conditions of adversity.

This is why tonight I have chosen to focus on the contribution that TRO made to the resolution of Africa's development problems in theory, in practice and by personal example. For although it is understandable that most people associate his name with world class achievements in the scientific discipline of entomology and with the founding of the International Centre for Insect Physiology and Ecology (ICIPE), TR was a polymath, a true Renaissance man, whose contribution to knowledge extended from entomology to the application of science in African development, and to research and development as a tool for industrialisation in Africa. All of these are now issues of concern to most governments in Africa, and their international development partners. But his intellectual interests went further still. TR was profoundly concerned with philosophy and indigenous African spirituality, as well as the philosophy of

243

science and technology, discovery and invention, and reform in education and the appropriate methodology of teaching science to pre-adolescent youth.

Second, I had the chance and the honour to work under Professor Odhiambo as he and his colleagues laid the foundations of the African Academy of Sciences, the institution that is our host tonight. In all his years, TRO worked hard to ensure that distinguished African scientists, like their counterparts elsewhere in the world, had their place in the sun. In devoting so much energy to the founding of the AAS, his motivation again was to bring the enterprise of science to the centre of African development. For the more Africa honoured her scientists, the greater would be their motivation to achieve. And the greater their achievements were, the more solutions to our social and economic problems they would generate. African peoples would be the better for this.

In the quest for economic growth and development in Africa today, nearly all the experts in the field agree on the role for effective national institutions as the foundation of any meaningful economic progress. Above all else, we now recognise the role of effective public organisations play in facilitating market-based transactions that lead to growth. We have come to this conclusion through a tortuous path that once emphasised the need for savings, national development plans, development aid, and external technical assistance.

TRO was a man ahead of this time, in this and many other aspects. He not only talked about public institutions, he built them and the AAS is testimony to that.

Thirdly, I am pleased to be here tonight because this lecture will begin yet another annual series lectures that honour Kenyan men and women who have gone before us, and whose national and international achievements deserve to be memorialised as a way of keeping alive the noble aims for which they dedicate their professional lives. Nations live on ideas and the ideals that their citizens honour and consider not only worth preserving, but also fighting for. We must desist from acting like the contribution of great people to Africa ceases immediately we inter their mortal remains. Like the abolitionist John Brown, their bodies may lie in the grave, but their spirit marches on. It is our duty that the march continues in perpetuity. We had had the Annual T.J. Mboya Memorial Lecture since 1969, which I consider a perfect example of the tradition I am championing here. I am sure that under the auspices of the AAS, the TRO Memorial Lecture will be an annual event in our national calendar that Kenyans, Africans, the global scientific community, and the citizens of the world, will look forward to from here on. This is why I feel humbled to have been asked to set the ball rolling in that monumental bust necessary enterprise.

Entomology and economic development

I need not report to you that Africa south of the Sahara now contains the highest number of the poor — defined as those who survive on less that one US dollar a day compared to any other region of the word. The figures are staggering because given Africa's total population we are talking about some 300 million people. Even more saddening, about a half of that number are experiencing malnutrition and hunger. Africa has 13 per cent of the world's population but it accounts for only one percent of the goods and services that the world enjoys. If you add to this the scourge of the HIV/AIDS pandemic, it is clear that we are in the threshold of one of the greatest tragedies in human history. And we must ask what science can do to reverse this tragedy.

If there was one thing we will never forget about TRO's academic lectures, it was his emphasis on the roles of insects — both harmful and benevolent — in that task of agricultural productivity and enhanced food security in Africa. Add:

- Insects consume 40 per cent of post-harvest food intended for human consumption in Africa. What do we do about this? Remember agriculture is the largest sector of African national economies — other than oil producers (a few states notably Nigeria, Gabon, Angola, Congo-Brazzaville) who are few. And even they are now looking for ways to promote agricultural development. African economic development is — in the short run — that of agriculture, followed by industrialisation. Management of insect pests is at the core of that strategy.

- Insects make large sections of the continent inhabitable to humans. Land shortage in Africa has been blamed for political strife, and also for poor productivity in agriculture. Subdivision of small family parcels that are further subdivided from one generation to another may serve subsistence peasant household needs — peasants self-exploit by putting more labour hours on the land. (This is not unique to Kenya. Chayanov made the classic study on the peasant household economies in imperial Russia at the turn of the nineteenth century and reported similar observations). But this does not help economic take-off and production of surpluses from agriculture. Africa needs more land to be brought into productivity. Eliminating pests that stand in the way (e.g. tsetse fly) is one solution.

- Eliminating insects that increase our national disease burdens in Africa. Malaria and the anopheles mosquito are at the very top. The reason

245

behind the high rates of infant mortality in Africa is still malaria! Malaria, HIV/AIDS, and TB are now the leading killers of adults in Africa. Disease burden measures the amount of human investment lost in this manner, and the poor quality of labour due to illness. And it is one of the leading explanations of poor growth and poverty in Africa today. So the search for a solution lies as much in science as it does on government policy.

Building new institutions as the key to African development

I have already mentioned the difficult economic conditions that our region is going through at the moment. If we are to utilise science and technology to resolve Africa's development problems, as I believe we must, then we must build a scientific community of our own, with a wide range of institutions to back it, be they in our universities, independent research centres, professional institutions, or the private sector. Our scientists in all these institutions must also be adequately remunerated. Funds for research and development in Africa must rise, preferably to one per cent of the GDP, which is the norm in the OECD states and the newly industrialising countries in the world today. Higher spending on research and development is one of the soundest investments a developing country can make. At a time when many external commentators on African development, economists and other scholars are pointing out the need for building institutional capacity to manage African development, it is worth bearing in mind TRO's legacy as an institution builder.

Africa came to independence in the 1960s with a very sparse scientific community. Then:

- Universities and research institutions were established in the 1970s and 1980s. Even at their best, African countries have not produced the number of scientists to meet the task I have outlined. South Africa, the most industrialised country in Africa, has 350 scientific researchers per million people. In the developing countries the figure is twice or thrice that. In Kenya, however, we have only 35 researchers in science and technology per million as compared to 40 in Nigeria, and 30 in Zimbabwe.

- In the 1980s, as the economic crisis in Africa set in the universities and scientific research institutions that had been founded in the 1960s began to suffer rapid deterioration. The purchasing power of African researchers declined in some cases by as much as 75 per cent. Africa as a result suffered the brain drain.

246

- According to a recent UNESCO survey 92 per cent of the scientists working in sub-Saharan Africa said they were dissatisfied with their salaries and working conditions. In South Africa the figure however is 42 per cent.

In my introductory remarks, I spoke about TRO's incredible ability to found world class institutions designed to outlive him, and to deal with the most urgent economic and social problems facing Africa. ICIPE was just one of those. But TRO also had a passionate desire to leave the scientific community of Africa in a better condition than he found it. In the quest of doing so he helped found a series of institutions that are now part of the scientific landscape in Africa. He was the:

- Founding Dean of the Faculty of Agriculture at the University of Nairobi in 1970-71.

- Founding Director of ICIPE, 1970-1994.

- Founder Director of Randforum (Research and Development Forum for Science-Led Development in Africa).

- Founding President of African Academy of Sciences (AAS).

- Founder and Vice-President, Third World Academy of Sciences.

- Founding Chairman, Foundation for the Promotion of Children's Science Publications in Africa (CHISCI).

Conclusion

I began this lecture with my personal initiation into academic work at the University of Nairobi and on how the work of TRO affected my own at that stage, and much later when our paths crossed at the African Academy of Sciences. As I look back I find that the five years I spent with TRO at the African Academy of Sciences were perhaps the most productive years of my life.

TRO taught me perseverance, persistence and optimism grounded on realism and unflinching hard work. He also taught me to be a champion who never looks backwards and rarely weighs his soul down with unnecessary regrets. As the famous saying goes, champions are not supernatural; they just fight one more second when everyone else quits. Sometimes one more second of effort fives you the victory. TRO was such a champion.

27

Bishop Alexander Kipsang Muge[1]

Speech given at the Memorial Service for the late Bishop Alexander Muge
in Eldoret on 12 August 2004, at the invitation of Mrs. Herma Muge and
her family

This anniversary of the passing away of the late Bishop Alexander Kipsang' Muge comes at a time when we need the late Bishop most. This is a time when major decisions on governance and social progress are facing this nation, and men and women of principle and commitment to the nation are in great need. Bishop Muge was such a man.

I do remember that during his time he, together with the late Bishop Henry Okullu, steered this nation towards the path of righteousness when it was neither easy nor fashionable to do so. For that they suffered and answered with their lives. Today, it is much easier to stand on the platform and shout in defence of democracy. Even the oppressors of yesterday are today's democrats. Bishop Muge and Bishop Okullu were pioneers of the democratic struggle at a time when such pioneers were few and far between.

At a time like this, we should remember that our journey is still long. We are still far from liberating our people. We are still far from giving our people the kind of life Muge wanted them to have: A life of dignity and self-respect; a life full of genuine love and mutual social responsibility.

I do hope that the family of the late Bishop will be taken care of, respected and given the opportunity to live a life Muge himself would have given them.

We thank God for a life well lived and a journey completed with dignity and self-respect.

---

1   Bishop Muge died in a strange "road accident" on 14 August 1990 while driving to Eldoret back from Busia where he had gone to preach in defiance of a verbal "prohibition order" that Peter Okondo, one of Moi's ministers, had issued against him. The Rev. Dr. Timothy Njoya later coined a term for such eliminations by saying "Muge was *road accidented*".

28

Ramogi Achieng' Oneko
A Tribute

First published in New Path *a forum for African intellectual thought,*
Vol.2 No.3 June 2007

When he passed away at his lakeside home in Kunya Village in Rarieda in Nyanza Province, Kenyans mourned him as the last of the Kapenguria Six; the little town of Kapenguria gained notoriety in Kenya's struggle for independence when it became the scene for the trial of Jomo Kenyatta, Achieng' Oneko, Paul Ngei, Kung'u Karumba, Bildad Kaggia and Fred Kubai. These nationalists were christened the Kapenguria Six.

In what was essentially a kangaroo court, the six were found guilty of having been involved in organising the Mau Mau rebellion against the colonial order and were put into detention following their arrest on October 20 1952. This date, celebrated since independence as Kenyatta Day, should appropriately be celebrated as the National Heroes Day or, more specifically, as the day of the Kapenguria Six.

Jomo Kenyatta never accepted, either at the trial or later on in life, that he was involved in the Mau Mau. What he conceded to and had no apology for was that he had always championed the freedom of the African people from colonial oppression, and in this he had freely associated with other Kapenguria colleagues in organising the first nationalist political party in Kenya, the Kenya African Union (KAU). Kenyatta's association with Oneko can therefore be rightly traced to their work in KAU in which Oneko featured as a prolific ideologue, political organizer and superb tactician.

Born in 1920 to peasant farmers and later baptised as Richard, Oneko attended Maseno School under the missionaries and was taught by the legendary Carey

249

Francis and the fiery Kenyan nationalist Jaramogi Oginga Odinga. He was a good athlete who always excelled in the short distance races. He was eloquent in speech and attracted friends and admirers with ease. His elegant gait and love for smart dressing earned him the nick name "Nyakech" which means "antelope", an animal the Luo people admire for its gracefulness and charm.

My father, the late Canon Hezbon Shimei Nyong'o, was only two years older than him when they attended Maseno School together and lived in the same dormitory. This generation of Luo intelligentsia, led by Jaramogi and Oneko, founded the Luo Thrift and Trading Corporation (LUTATCO) as a co-operative and business entity to pool resources together for business ventures and trading. They built office blocks in Kisumu, established a supermarket in Maseno — Maseno Stores — ran flour mills in various market places in Nyanza, built houses and real estates under the direction of Mzee Ong'er and published newspapers which Oneko edited — *Ramogi* and *Nyanza Times*. It was around this time that Oneko dropped his name Richard and took Ramogi; the initial "R" remained the same.

Oneko introduced Kenyatta to Jaramogi while the latter was on a visit to Kisumu a few months before they were arrested for involvement in the Mau Mau. Once the two were detained, Odinga took it upon himself to continue the struggle for Kenya's freedom and to demand for their release.

The first election of African members to the Legislative Council in 1957 was therefore held with the Kapenguria Six still under detention although the Mau Mau as a rebellion had virtually been defeated. Jaramogi, however, rallied African nationalists, and African Members of the LegCo — organised as the African Elected Members Organisation (AEMO) — to champion the release of the detainees as a priority in the agenda for independence. In this Jaramogi was ably supported by Thomas Joseph Mboya and C.M.G. Argwings-Kodhek, who had also acted as the lawyer of many of the Mau Mau detainees and their families.

When Oneko was finally released together with Kenyatta in 1961, he was already more than a household name in the Kenyan political landscape. He immediately assumed his responsibilities as Kenyatta's private secretary planning the logistics of the nationalist campaigns and running in the inside lane when Kenyatta took over the leadership of the Kenya African National Union (KANU) that year. In the so-called "Kenyatta Election" of 1963, Oneko captured the Nakuru Town seat on a KANU ticket, trouncing his nearest rival by thousands of votes.

When Kenya gained independence on 12 December 1963, Achieng' Oneko was in Kenyatta's first cabinet of some powerful eighteen ministers. He was Minister for Information and Tourism. He performed his duties with excellence and commitment to national goals. He initiated, nurtured and established the Kenya News Agency (KNA) which has remained the backbone for news gathering in government to date. Many of the people trained through the KNA went ahead to join the private sector media houses and to build them to what they are today.

Post-independence politics led to differences between Oneko and Kenyatta that somehow became irreconcilable. Oneko strongly believed in championing the interests of the poor, particularly with regard to access to land. Like his political comrades Jaramogi Oginga and Bildad Kaggia, he was an uncompromising Fabian socialist who could not put his total faith in the market as the "deliverer of development to the common man". At that point in time African socialism as was expounded by Nyerere in "Ujamaa: The Basis of African Socialism" was in vogue. Oginga Odinga and Achieng' Oneko were perhaps the strongest Nyerereists on the north-western side of the Kilimanjaro.

As Kenyatta's Vice President, Odinga had too strong of a popular base to be ignored by the old man in any political dispensation within KANU. Combined with Mboya's support in the trade union movement and the growing middle class, Kenyatta and his ethnic associates found themselves out of depth in controlling KANU. The first scheme in1965-66 was to marginalise Odinga with Mboya's help. This succeeded at the famous Limuru Conference in 1966 which saw Odinga, Oneko and other left wingers move out of KANU to form the Kenya People's Union (KPU) whose manifesto, "The Wananchi Declaration" was written as an alternative to Mboya's "African Socialism and Its Application to Planning in Kenya" published in 1965 by the Kenya Government.

Achieng' Oneko's resignation speech from Kenyatta's government remains to this day a solid example of words of integrity, well thought out and succinctly summarising the crisis of moral authority that African nationalists faced at that point in time with regard to the aspirations of the masses. Oneko stated that he was painfully leaving a government he had helped to put together, but one he had to leave because of its departure from the principles that were supposed to be its foundation. He could no longer justify to himself why he flew a flag as a minister, symbolising the independence of Kenyan Africans, while he himself was still literally in chains.

The years in the KPU were both exciting as well as frustrating. Exciting in the sense that the majority of the people supported the ideas expressed by the KPU leadership. Frustrating because the Kenyatta government made it difficult for the KPU to operate as the authoritarian state grew vicious by the day. I joined the KPU Youth League while in high school in 1966. Poised to win the local government elections in 1968, Tom Mboya manipulated the process thereby disqualifying all KPU candidates except Mrs. Grace Onyango in Kisumu Town. Soon after that the political entourage behind Kenyatta began plotting to get rid of Mboya.

Achieng' Oneko became the intermediary between Tom Mboya and Jaramogi Oginga Odinga. Given the plot against Mboya it became necessary for the two to come together. Both Mwalimu Julius Nyerere of Tanzania and Milton Obote of Uganda felt this rapproachement was vital, and several messages were exchanged through intermediaries to speed up this process soon after the sudden death of Kenya's Foreign Affairs Minister in early 1969. I was at that point in time a student at Makerere University in Kampala, and a student leader on the campus. I was also active in KPU politics and got to know the goings on in the party.

When the news of Mboya's assassination on that fateful Saturday morning of 5 July 1969 reached Oneko, it is said that he almost fainted. The history of Kenya was never to be the same again; generations of Kenyans have been adversely affected by that event. It is quite possible that Kenya would have followed in the footsteps of Singapore had that bullet not been fired at one o'clock on Government Road that day.

By the end of that year, Kenyatta had proscribed the Kenya People's Union, detained all its leaders and turned Kenya into a one-party state. The British Government, styling itself as the flag bearers of democracy and the US government, never reluctant to proclaim its support for freedom everywhere did not say anything against Kenyatta. Oneko ended up spending another six years in detention under a government he had fought to establish by spending eight years in detention under the colonialists.

Ramogi Achieng' Oneko was released from detention in 1976 when I was about to finish my graduate school work at the University of Chicago. When I came back to Nairobi in 1977 to teach at the University of Nairobi, I visited him at his modest house in Woodley Estate and we had some porridge together. He was as lively and as cheerful as ever. He had no trace of bitterness in him. He laughed mirthfully. We immediately started plotting on how we could still play an active role in Kenyan politics.

Some time after that we put together a group of academics with his son Ongong'a to discuss this matter further at the Woodley residence one Saturday afternoon. The question was: in the likely event that Kenyatta passes away, what would be the best alliance the pro-Odinga forces should make so as to be in government under KANU? We came out with several scenarios but agreed that all had to be kept secret else the secret police would make mince meat of us before we put anything in practice. Unfortunately one big mouth left the place to boast immediately in a public bar how Oneko had been consulting him on some political project. We buried the scheme before it was even born!

With Kenyatta's death in August 1978 and the ensuing politics under Moi and Njonjo, Oneko became very cautious. Some time in 1980, Hezekiah Ougo resigned his Bondo Parliamentary seat so that Jaramogi would take it over. This was with the understanding that Jaramogi would team up with Moi so as to help give some political counter weight to the Gikuyu bourgeoisie. We were at that point in time also raising funds for the building of the Ramogi Institute for Advanced Technology (RIAT). Oneko was the chairman of the Nairobi committee.

I noticed one Friday morning that the *Weekly Review* had carried a rather unflattering article abound Odinga, and warned Oneko that we should shield Odinga from journalists that weekend. Odinga was due to be travelling to Mombasa that evening and I pleaded with Oneko to accompany him so that Oneko would ensure that his public utterances and interactions did not fall into the trap I saw being laid by the *Weekly Review*. Oneko declined arguing that Moi's system was more preoccupied with the "Muthemba Trial" than what was going on in our camp. Muthemba, a relative of Charles Njonjo, had then been accused of plotting to overthrow Moi's government.

Odinga's journey to the coast proved fatal. In a public address he accused Kenyatta of having been a land grabber and promised the coast people that he would join Moi's government to help the president fight this vice. The next day the forces in this government, including Moi himself; came out in a chorus to denounce Jaramogi. The Bondo seat disappeared from both Ougo and Odinga; the land grabbers had joined ranks; forgot about Nuthemba and once more threw Oneko and Odinga into the political limbo. When I met Oneko in the wake of these events, all he could tell me was *"A Luta Continua!"*

In 1989 we started plotting seriously to restore democracy to Kenya with Paul Muite and Joe Ager. Raila Amolo Odinga was then still in detention. Following the collapse of the Berlin Wall we felt the global scene was changing fast and very soon we would have more friends to support our stand within and outside Kenya. Bishop Henry Okullu and I started working within the Church. We communicated with Jaramogi as well. Very soon we brought in Oneko, then Luke Obok and Munyua Waiyaki. Okullu had introduced me to Paul Muite, and I introduced Muite to my friend Joe Ager. We decided to form a team to start working on an opposition political party which we eventually called the National Democratic Party (NDP), the forerunner of the Forum for the Restoration of Democracy (FORD).

I noticed during our struggle to organise the NDP that Oneko was no longer as fiery as he used to be. He was becoming more cautious, more circumspect in doing things. This was quite understandable. For a man who had spent 14 years of his life in detention a time comes when you want to say that life needs to be lived a bit at a time, and that those who come after us must also continue with the struggle: *A Luta Continua.*

With the passing on of Oneko *(Nyakech, Mbalawandu)* a generation of profiles in courage in Kenyan politics is gone. The only unfortunate thing is that Oneko did not live long enough to witness the final transition to democracy in Kenya. This, I dare say, is a legacy we have to pass on to Oneko's family as a cherished memory of one who fought wisely and enduringly that we may be free from colonial oppression as well as post-colonial authoritarianism. He built for the future.

Index